THE NUN AND THE PRIEST: LOVE, CELIBACY AND PASSION

A Memoir
Evelyn McLean Brady

*To Joan —
Thank you for sharing in my story. ♡ Evelyn*

NFB Publishing
Buffalo, New York

NFB
NFB Publishing/Amelia Press
119 Dorchester Road
Buffalo, New York 14213

For more information visit Nfbpublishing.com

When I die I want your hands on my eyes...
to pass their freshness over me one more time
to feel the smoothness that changed my destiny.
—Pablo Neruda

HAIKU
A mother blue spruce
felt our love rise through her trunk.
Memorykeeper.
—Sister Emily

Dedication

I offer this writing in gratitude to:
my mother Patricia
and my father Eric
who gave me life
and to life itself
that gave me
my story
and to
my sister
Marnie
and
beloved
Hugh
and
the new
love stories of
Eric ~ Matthew ~ Marnie
Benjamin ~ Madeline ~ Ramon ~ Greyson ~ Maeve

INTRODUCTION

For almost 50 years, a priest's love letters tied with a frayed, black-velvet ribbon and my journals packed in the small, convent trunk marked 1965-1970 waited to see if I would ever read them again. This memoir is my answer. *THE NUN AND THE PRIEST* tells the story of a revered and beloved priest and a young, aspiring novice who fall in love and find themselves caught in the web of the Church's intractable rule of celibacy. Their love story is inseparable from their spiritual journeys and the love they have for the people in their lives and ministries. It is also a story of a mother and daughter and the daughter's search for her true self.

In the telling, I have tried to stay true to the language and theology found in the era that the letters and journals were written. For example, even though I am light years away from this understanding today, I refer to God as masculine. When I was a novice, moreover, Father Brady was my spiritual director and, although his theology was forward thinking and often perennial, his scholarship, spiritual insights, and language were situated in the context of 1960s Church, as this story reflects.

I entered the convent at a time when the Church was updating the life style and practices of religious communities. My training as a postulant and novice is a glimpse into the medieval practices to which we were subjected and the healthy freedom that came with the reforms of the Second Vatican Council (1962-1965). Some names of the Sisters have been changed.

THE NUN AND THE PRIEST takes place in a whirlwind of changes. The United States was imploding with protests against the tragedy of the Vietnam War. The country's psyche was also permeated with the confusion and grief that led up to the 1964 Civil Rights Act and the backlash and blatant racism that followed its passage. Of even greater significance to my story is the Second Vatican Council which introduced historic, some would say revolutionary, changes to bring about *aggiornamento*, meaning renewal, that was intended to reform almost every aspect of the Catholic Church.

Father Brady and I also experienced tumultuous, personal challenges we could not have anticipated, but which brought us insight and growth, and, sometimes, regret. Out of this cauldron of changes emerged a love story about a nun and a priest who experienced human love under the dictates of celibacy and the force of human passion.

Spring passes and one remembers one's innocence.
Summer passes and one remembers one's exuberance.
Autumn passes and one remembers one's reverence.
Winter passes and one remembers one's perseverance.

—Yoko Ono

Contents

1965-1967

THE FIRST SEASON

"Spring passes and one remembers one's innocence."

Chapter 1

DECISION MAKING

"Don't let someone keep putting out the flame God keeps re-lighting;
we all have a purpose. As a wing to a bird. As wind finds destiny over the sea."
—*Anthony Liccione*

"ANYONE WHO WOULD RATHER dance than eat should not enter a convent!" I laugh thinking about my sister Jan's comment as I drive along the rural roads from our family home in Hornell, New York, to go to Rochester, where I will ask admittance into the Sisters of Mercy. With my convertible's top down and the radio volume up, I sing out loud with Buddy Holly, "Yes, that'll be the day, when you say good-bye/That'll be the day when you make me cry/You say you're gonna leave, you know it's a lie ..." Most people would say that the words "You say you're gonna leave, you know it's a lie ..." refer to me. Who could blame them? I am not exactly the nun type.

I have always been two people: one who will shove aside anything and everything to be at a party and the other who is pulled to the beauty of silence and contemplation. People had witnessed my double life since I was a kid. My friend Kit summed up her feelings about my convent plans: "You'd dance better in a dress than a habit."

But the nuns in school often told us that religious life was the highest calling: to be at one with God and to live for others. That is my desire.

To follow the highest calling. To be at one with God. To give my life for others. I am not escaping anything. I am becoming a Sister to be my best self—and I hope I can figure out how I can still dance. Today is June 28, 1965, six days before July Fourth, my twenty-fourth birthday.

When I turn into the Motherhouse's horseshoe-shaped driveway at 1437 Blossom Road in Rochester, however, a trepidation overcomes me. My legs are shaking, and, on this hot, humid day, my arms are covered with goose bumps as I hesitantly walk up the steps of the large stone porch. As I approach the door, pulling my shoulders back, I move my finger toward the convent doorbell. Suddenly my finger stops before pushing the white buzzer. It begins to trace the metal circle frame around the bell, as if it wants to get to know it better, as if it wants to understand why I should push it. Thoughts admonish me. *You are here. Just push the bell.* Suddenly, as if my finger hears me, I push with full force.

Who would have ever imagined that ringing a convent doorbell that July afternoon with my heart full of love for Jesus and my great desire to give up my life for those in need, would lead me to the love of my life: the man of my dreams, a human man, a holy man, a forbidden man. A Roman Catholic priest vowed to celibacy, the same vow this very priest would help me prepare for.

A small, thin Sister whose age is indiscernible anwers the door. She smiles briefly and says, "Mother is expecting you." Without saying another word, the Sister, with her head bent down and tilted a little to the left, quickly walks me to a formal parlor. The convent halls smell strange—a little like pungent incense mixed with the odor of Pine-Sol. I wait in the large parlor with its oriental rugs, tapestry-upholstered couch, wing-back chairs and Duncan Phyfe tables. The windows in the front of the room are open and a soft breeze makes the sheer curtains waft back and forth like they are angels. I can hear the twittering birds, probably gossiping about who just arrived. I imagine their wings covering their beaks so that they won't laugh when they hear my name. They stop their chriping when they see who now enters the parlor.

In her floor-length, black wool habit and her veil pinned to a starched wimple, Mother Bride, *Brigid* in Gaelic, the head of the Mercy Order, floats into the room, almost as if she is on hidden ice skates. Maybe she is. The highly-waxed floors are that shiny. I am surprised at her small stature but not with her reassuring presence.

"Welcome, dear, dear Evelyn. I am very happy to finally meet you," Mother says with a genuine warmth. She hugs me to her cheek.

I feel my eyes smile at her as I respond, "I'm glad to meet you, too, Mother."

Prominently on the wall, facing the two wing-back chairs where Mother Bride and I sit, hangs a crucifix with Christ crowned with long thorns pushing into His bloodied skull and with cruel nails through His bleeding hands and feet. I glance away from the sorrowful Christ, as I usually do. Jesus' suffering always seems too much for me to bear and fills me with guilt, even helplessness that He endured so much because of our sins, mine definitely among them. I quickly redirect my attention to Mother Bride. She and I had corresponded by letter several times over the years and talked on the phone on three or four occasions. She knows I am not here to explore religious life; I want to request entrance. She seems to think it is a given.

"I am so happy you will be coming to join us. The Sisters are in a 'tailspin' right now responding to the Vatican II's document on renewal of religious life, *Perfectae Caritatis*. It means perfect charity, something we Mercy Sisters hold as our ideal. This is an exciting time to enter a religious life. You are older and mature, a perfect candidate to implement many of the changes needed to update our way of life."

I do not see myself in the perfect or mature category, but I am glad she thinks so. Before I leave, Mother tells me she has one request. She wants me to meet Father Hugh Brady, her spiritual director and close friend. Father had just been reassigned from the seminary to St. Ann, my parish in Hornell, a small town nestled in the foothills of the Allegheny Mountains in southern New York State. She adds that she has implicit trust in Father's judgment. "Father Brady is a very holy priest, my dear. With Father, everything is about love." When I return home, I make an appointment right away. I am impatient to become a bride of Christ. I greatly desire a life where everything is about love.

The morning of my meeting at St. Ann's with Father Brady, not wanting to look as if I am already in the convent, I wear my favorite mid-calf, rose-colored, straight skirt that has a slight flare at the bottom and a short-sleeved, white-eyelet blouse with a gold cross around my neck. I use my older sister's mascara; she buys the good stuff that actually makes eye lashes look longer. I check that my page-boy hair is brushed carefully even though I like the way I have to flick it back when it falls across my right eye.

The rectory secretary escorts me to a sparse office with its soft leather chair for the priest behind the large mahogany desk and two straight-backed upholstered chairs in front of it. The room smells like a musty attic and the color of the walls is a nondescript soupy green-grey. It's humid and I decide to open a window. It won't budge.

"Let me help you. That window sticks," says a voice behind me.

When Father puts his arms over me in order to push up the window, I can't get out of the way quickly enough. We both laugh nervously as we skirt around each other. I make my way to one of the chairs in front of the desk; instead of taking the priest's chair behind the desk, Father sits next to me.

When I can finally look at him, I am taken aback. With thick, wavy

black hair, chiseled face bones and square jaw with a dimple in his chin—
and a perfectly proportioned body of almost six feet—Father Brady is
very handsome. Yet, the gentleness in his eyes and kindness in his voice
exude a calmness that comforts and brings me assurance.

"Well, at least that breeze feels good," Father says with a smile and
not one bit embarrassed about our *window dance*. "I have been looking
forward to meeting you. Mother Bride told me of your plans to enter the
community. But how are you going to give up that snazzy convertible in
the parking lot?"

"I can't bring Skycar to the convent?"

"Just doesn't seem to fit the vow of poverty," he says with a twinkle in
his eye.

"It does if you are making the car payments!" I exclaim.

Father laughs, crossing his legs as he comfortably leans back in his
chair with a casual ease. There is something confident about him, something urbane. Something very attractive. Sitting primly upright with my
hands clasped at my waist just like a proper Catholic girl—which is hardly
the case—I feel at home. As we banter back and forth, I am relaxed with
myself and with Father, as if we were old friends who hadn't seen each
other for a while. It is a feeling of relief, having heard how "holy" he is.

"Welcome to Hornell, Father. Thanks for meeting with me. Hornell's
pretty different from the seminary. What did you do at St. Bernard?"

"I was the spiritual director to the seminarians."

"Wow, it must have been hard to leave them."

"Well," he pauses, "my theology is not exactly working for the Bishop."

I am not sure what his "theology" is, but these are tumultuous times
in the Church. I think he must be what is called the "new breed," meaning Catholics who want to return to the radical and challenging Gospel
message of Jesus rather than rely on doctrine and rules. Father is probably

a Vatican II Catholic, what I want to be.

"I was worried about adjusting to a parish again," Father continues. "But the parishioners have been very kind. I will miss the seminarians, some swell guys. I know God has sent me to Hornell for a reason. There will be lots to do in this vineyard."

"Hornell's a regular Peyton Place," I joke.

"Hadn't heard. Guess my work is cut out for me," he responds with a healthy laugh.

Father Brady seems as down to earth as anyone I'd ever met. I have a favorite uncle, Clint, who has a calm and centered temperament, too, and Father reminds me of him. As we continue talking, Father asks why I'd waited so long to answer God's call. At that time, most girls entered the convent right after high school. I explain that after high school, my mother questioned my decision and insisted I go to college first and then I needed to teach to pay off college loans. Having been stationed in Corning, he is interested in my teaching job at Painted Post, which is a village west of Corning and not far from Hornell.

"Painted Post? How did that go?"

"I loved it, but the classes weren't just typical teen-agers. There were returning veterans."

"Veterans?"

"Yes. Back from Vietnam. At first, one or another of the vets would come up to my desk to supposedly ask me a question and suddenly I would feel his arm around me! Most of the guys were my age or a little older. I had to draw a chalk line on the floor around my desk that no one could cross. They called it the *DMZ*."

Leaning back laughing and clapping his hands, Father says, "Now, that is rich!"

As this easy chatting continues, strange feelings suddenly take over my body. At first, I notice my stomach has a soft, warm glow that gradually radiates through me and anchors me in perfect contentment. Then, a humming vibration, like a singing bee hive, feelings foreign and pleasurable. I smell the honeysuckle through the open window and hear children in the alleyway jumping rope and singing, "In comes the doctor, in comes the nurse, in comes the lady with the big fat purse." I experience a oneness with everything, a place of awareness I did not know existed but is eerily familiar. My world has changed. And I am sitting across from a Catholic priest who is part of it all.

As heat crawls up to the back of my neck and across my shoulders, I am suddenly embarrassed to be sitting here. My crossed legs become heavy and my fingertips turn cold. Palpable currents move between Father and me. I do not know if I should allow myself to feel this enveloping and pleasurable energy between us; nor do I know if our banter keeps Father from observing my unsettledness. I am surprised he does not appear to be affected. The palpable chemistry gets stronger the longer we are together.

When cold prickles appear on my arm, I decide I have to leave the office to get hold of myself. I ask Father if he would mind if I make some tea. "Of course," he responds and starts to get up. I tell him I can get it myself as I am familiar with the kitchen. In high school, I counted the Sunday collections right in this office.

"Would you like some tea?" I ask.

"Not a caffeine drinker," he replies.

"Guess that's why you seem so peaceful," I smile.

Father smiles back at me, but I worry that he will question my sudden departure. I am sure my unacceptable emotions are obvious, and I feel the redness rising in my face. At the same time, Father seems either unaware of what is happening to me, and maybe to him, or maybe he's in complete control of himself.

In the strong morning sun streaming through the side kitchen window, I lean back against the counter. I inhale and exhale deep breaths and feel a strong urge to stay in the warmth and protection of the kitchen, but I force myself to shake out of this strange state and search for black tea in the well-stocked pantry. I put water in a small, white-enamel pan, strike a wooden match and turn on the stove's gas and light it. I often made tea when I worked at the rectory, so I am comfortable here. Gratefully, the water takes its own good time to boil. When ready, I pour the boiling water over a Red Rose tea bag and let the flavors steep and change color from caramel to strong mahogany. I add a little milk from the glass milk jug in the refrigerator.

I have experienced similar emotions when attracted to other men, but this is completely different. It's sudden. Like a lightning strike or a sudden shower of stars. The feelings are physical but beyond physical. Feelings of something right. Something true. Like a dream that seizes you and holds you in a strange hypnotic world of warmth and security and you don't ever want to wake up.

But these are feelings about a priest. I revere priests. A priest is another Christ, a man with a special calling set apart from us. A man who belongs only to God. I know my emotions are unacceptable. As I sip the tea, I hold the hot liquid in my mouth before it slowly slides down, warming my throat and my stomach. I close my eyes and will the heat to travel to every cell of my body, to burn away my feelings. I concentrate only on the tea's taste and warmth. I try not to feel anything. I become calmer. I wake up.

When I return to the office, Father stands, smiles, and without a trace of suspicion, kindly says, "I hope you found everything." As he pulls back the chair for me to sit down, I hold on to my hot teacup for dear life. Then Father sits, leans forward, placing his elbows on top of his knees and holds his cheeks in his cupped hands. His eyes spill tenderness all over me. I put the teacup down.

Chapter 2

How I Came to This

"It is in your moments of decision that your destiny is shaped."
—Tony Robbins

THIS GOING-IN-THE-CONVENT THING would have been so much easier if I had entered right after high school, which was what I'd wanted to do. My widowed mother vehemently objected at that time, saying unequivocally that I was "definitely not convent material," and insisted that I go to college to "get this crazy idea out of your system once and for all." Mother's strict stands had a strong influence on all of her children, especially on me, not one of her easiest to raise. We did not have the financial means to pay for college, but, she argued, if I got a college education first, I would know myself better. She was right.

During my first week at Mercyhurst College in Erie, Pennsylvania, a Catholic girls' school at that time, I quickly discover that education is much more than academics. Friends are teachers, too. I kind of majored in one friend: the irrepressible Kit Reese. To the rest of us freshmen, Kit seems to be a Scandinavian goddess. But, like many of us, she is of Irish descent—with *extremely* bleached hair. Whether a goddess or not, Kit is the quintessential 'Hurst girl: tall, beautiful, friendly, and very smart. She definitely seems a little above the rest of us. So when she chooses to sit next to me at our first freshman class meeting, I find myself in a rare state: at a loss for words.

I am surprised that Kit invites me to a secret party where there will be "strong whiskey sours." Alcohol is strictly forbidden for Mercyhurst girls. I tell her I'd taken "The Pledge" and don't drink. Like many eighth graders at the Sacrament of Confirmation, I vowed I would not drink until I was twenty-one years old, an idea from the Irish priests' crusade for the suppression of alcohol for "The greater glory of God."

"We all took 'The Pledge', Evie, but now we're free," Kit emphatically responds.

"I'm going to keep it, Kit, but, *please*, I still want to go to the party."

Considering how cool her other friends are, I have no idea why Kit includes me in what become regular parties. I bring Pepsi, dance, and meet the Gannon College boys, whose requests I happily accept when they ask me out. Although I have a full social life at Mercyhurst, I also have a great desire to learn. For me the best place to study is in the library where the nun librarian keeps "certain books" locked up, novels such as *Lady Chatterley's Lover* and plays like *A Streetcar Named Desire*. God forbid we have desires.

Throughout our years in college, Kit and I become close friends. We are an unlikely couple, she a disciplined science major and a total party girl and me an English major who also studies theater and religion. But, no one makes me laugh like Kit, and we become so close we can discuss anything that comes up—except one thing. Whenever I share my plans to be a nun, Kit responds with the same words, "Evie, I will hang you upside down if you don't stop saying such nonsense."

I am often included in Kit's and her friends' high jinx. They tell me that even if I am a religious nerd, they have hopes for my "redemption." I know they don't mean redemption from sin. We live in a Victorian world and often joke that we all entered the convent when we chose Mercyhurst. A religious atmosphere, including optional daily Mass which I attended, is to infiltrate and influence our lives. This is typical of the culture of

Catholic girls' colleges in the 1960s. Unlike my friends, I am comfortable in it and want to deepen my spiritual life and strengthen my dedication to the Church—not exactly Kit's priorities.

I read every book in the library about the saints and devour anything written about the upcoming Second Vatican Council, which Pope John XXIII convened in 1962 to "open the windows" and to bring about aggiornamento, renewal of the Catholic Church's teaching and practices. The new theology is exhilarating and the Church's new spirit of openness and collegiality only strengthens my desire to serve it. Interest in religion is as natural to me as going out with my often-irreverent friends and the very adorable Gannon College boys.

Because I minor in theater, I spend a lot of time backstage on college productions and occasionally do some acting. For my junior year, I sail across the Atlantic on the *SS Mauritania* to attend University College, Dublin, where I study Irish literature and theater and feel completely at home with my outrageously humorous Irish friends.

One misty day in February, 1962, I am walking down Dublin's Duke Street when I see a large group of students outside the Bailey Pub where I am heading. They jump in front of me and raising their drinks shout, "Way to go, Yank! God bless John Glenn." John Glenn had orbited the Earth in a spaceship and I hadn't even heard! One young man, with his tri-colored university scarf wrapped haphazardly around his neck, wants to buy "the American lass a pint." I try to refuse but, before I know it, I have a Guinness in my hand. "Down it, Girl, down it!" I take one swallow and spit out the black, medicinal-smelling national beer. "Now that's a mortal sin," calls a bystander. I laugh and hand the pint back. I am anxious to see Brendan Behan, the Irish actor who is playing at the Abbey Theater and who is a regular at the Bailey and has a huge capacity to entertain—and to drink.

My year in Ireland broke open my world. For the first time, I had complete autonomy in deciding how to live my life. The confinement of my strict family home, the narrow culture of Hornell, New York, where I grew up in the conventional 1950s, and the closed environment of Mercyhurst College could no longer limit or protect me. I was opening my own windows of renewal.

I return to Mercyhurst for senior year and, just before our graduation in 1963, I tell Kit I am definitely going into the convent. On a soft May evening with the fragrance of cherry blossoms wafting through my dorm room window, Kit arrives with Colleen. They lock the door, tell me to sit on the floor with them, pull up the tab on the top of a can of Genesee beer, and pass it between them. I pray the hall monitor has a cold. The smell of beer travels.

Taking a swig, Colleen proceeds. "Evie, you are all mixed up and you don't even know it. Going to Mercyhurst *is* being in the convent. Now you need to live a real life. Come to Boston with us after graduation."

Wanting this conversation to end, I purse my lips, close my eyes and say, emphatically, "Okay, okay, okay!"

Kit and Colleen hug me. "You are going to love Boston and husbands are waiting for us there. We'll get an apartment in Cambridge!" As things turn out, Kit and Colleen find a charming turn-of-the century apartment in Cambridge—and their husbands.

The next day, as I had already intended, I call my mother to tell her I've decided to enter the convent. But, once again, my plans to become a Sister are put on hold. Mother does not have the money to pay back my college loans and says I will have to teach for "at least" two years to settle the debt. Again, I feel the air leaving the balloon of my dream. Fortunately, I find a job as a teacher of English and speech and drama at Painted Post High School outside of Corning, New York.

I take hold of these two years as a single, eligible woman. Besides teaching, I direct two successful high school plays, date the engineers at the Corning Glassworks, star as Abigail Williams in the Corning Community Theater production of "The Crucible" and, the best thing, I buy a Ford Galaxie convertible I name "Skycar." Its dark blue leather interior smells just faintly of a shoe-shine shop. When I'm behind the wheel, I feel I can drive right to the moon. I can't afford both an apartment and a car because of the college loan so I rent a single bedroom in a family's home. Skycar is worth it. My friends are sure the years of teaching will "cure" me of thinking about becoming a nun. They are wrong.

As I look back at this time, I have been trying to answer questions about when I decided to be a nun instead of the more normal choices I could have made. Was it as a young girl using my babysitting money to light candles for the souls in purgatory? Or as a confused and hurt teenager whose suffering opened her heart to the afflictions of others? Or as a college student who discovered the study of theology can be an experience of the divine? Or as a teacher in a rural high school where I carried my students' problems in my pocket and knew that literature could be medicine for their broken lives?

I can't seem to isolate this one decision from my other choices, whether known or unknown, conscious or unconscious, recognized or disguised. Sometimes I wonder if I chose to enter the convent or if the decisions over a lifetime made the choice for me. In whatever way the decision came to me, I am telling the priest that I am choosing to be a celibate as a sign of being a bride of Christ and he is telling me he will help me and I am falling in love with him.

Chapter 3

ENCOUNTER

"The first duty of love is to listen."
—Paul Tillich

AT THIS FIRST MEETING, Father is looking at me with such intensity that I think he is going to tell me the secrets of the universe. But he simply says, "Entering the convent is a huge step, Evie. Do you mind if I call you Evie?"

"My college friends call me Evie." I sense my body lean forward.

He tells me that going into the convent is like going to a foreign country. I will need maps. But because of so much time to discern God's will and so many life experiences, I will be fine and he will be happy to assist me along the way. Father says he knows many Sisters, maybe hundreds of them. They are regular people like me with their struggles and graces and everything else in between. The convent takes a little getting used to, he warns, but he also assures me I will grow to want no other way of life. A religious calling is an invitation to give my entire life to God and, by living in community, a deeper spiritual transformation can occur. We both pause in silence to take in these last words.

"When did you start thinking about being a Sister?" he asks, breaking the quiet moment.

"I can't remember when I *didn't* want to be a nun. Just got delayed."

"You will bring many experiences and that will help you and the community," Father responds enthusiastically.

"I don't know how to say this, Father, but I don't exactly see myself as the ideal candidate for religious life, as much as I believe this is exactly what God is calling me to. It will be pretty hard for me to give up friends and music––and my Skycar. Also, I am a person who can be bossy, I gossip about people, and I can be very superficial, selfish, and self-centered."

"You sound perfect so far," Father replies with a smile.

"Can't tell you how far from perfect I am," I insist. "I am terrified. I know I won't follow the rules correctly and I absolutely don't know how I will handle weekends."

"Weekends?"

"I always dance on weekends."

"What kind of dancing?"

"Mostly jitterbugging, but lots of dances. I love to slow dance and square dance."

"Well, you are just going to have to teach the Sisters to dance!"

"Bring my '45s' records? Don't think the convent has a record player. I'm serious. I didn't tell Mother Bride, but I am worried about giving up my social life."

Then in a very sober tone, Father looks directly at me. "Evie, many entering religious life think celibacy will be the most challenging vow, and it will be hard at times, but obedience, submitting your will to a superior with acceptance and love, will most likely be the most difficult."

"Probably," I respond. "I have never liked taking orders, even though I have a lot of experience. Being the seventh of eight children, I've had a lot of bosses."

He tells me he was the youngest of six for many years, the only boy until he was ten when his brother was born, so he got away with murder.

We both laugh about that. Then, focused again, Father continues. "I'd like to know more about how God brought you to this moment, right now, this summer. You seem to have the 'world on a string.' Friends and family, Skycar, teaching, dancing. Everything. Marriage must be a possibility."

"I know it's a possibility, but I believe there is something more. Can't explain it. I want to be available to people who need a Sister to give her all to them. It sounds strange but it's like there is something bigger, something that is connected to a goodness I want to share in and give. I just can't explain it."

"The Spirit speaks in these unexplainable nudges," he smiles. "That is what you are experiencing. Is your family okay with your decision?"

"My family thinks I am crazy," I reply. "My mother says I will be back in a month. Maybe I will. She pretty much sees me as superficial and doesn't understand how the convent will ever suit me. I love my mother, but if I leave the convent, you know, if it doesn't work out, it won't look good and that is what she's worried about. Appearances mean everything to her. She is sure I won't stay. But you asked, why this summer? The yearning never leaves me. I want to finally face it."

"Your yearning for God is God's yearning for you."

"It doesn't go away." Tears spill from my eyes as I say this.

"Yearnings can be painful, Evie. We often don't know why we are experiencing these emotions when they come with confusion and paradox, but I assure you, truth will emerge from the anguish." He pauses and then says, "I can see you already know this."

"So much confusion, yet the longing is always with me."

"That is why you can know with assurance it is genuine. That is how the Spirit operates."

"Yes," I answer somberly with my mouth dry and my eyes damp.

"What about your dad?" Father gently asks.

I then share the painful saga of my father. How he died of alcoholism shortly after we moved to the small town of Hornell, about a hundred miles from Buffalo. It was 1951. I was ten. In Buffalo, he had a successful World War II factory and invented some kind of ball bearing that they used in almost all of the American tanks. Made a ton of money. After the war, he renovated a large plant in Hornell because it was closer to raw materials just over the state border in Pennsylvania. He planned to make parts for cars. I remembered my dad as a pretty charming guy, and he attracted clients easily. Had an amazing mind for math. Maybe a genius. He could have the world, but he died from drinking shortly after we moved. He was in his late 40s.

I continue my story of how, after my father's death, my poor mother had to sell our beautiful house on Maple Street in Hornell because my parents had put all their money into the new factory that never got off the ground. Mother moved us into a small three-bedroom duplex on the edge of town and tried to squeeze her beautiful too-large furniture into it. She gave the oriental rugs to the convent. We were cramped, but she thought it would be easier to raise us in a small town rather than back in Buffalo with all the car pools and private schools.

She could no longer rely on my father for social status, money from the factory, or even his infrequent help raising children; nor did she have the magnanimous support she had relied on from her sisters in Buffalo. Yet, even with all this disruption, we younger kids adapted quickly to our new world of a small town. We rode our bikes into the surrounding hills, spent summer days at the Hornell pool, and went to the YMCA to learn to swim and later to attend high school dances. We could walk everywhere and we were safe. My siblings in high school were slower to adjust, but eventually their social life developed and school and family life absorbed them.

"But it was a long fall for Mother," I explain. "She knew she would have to get a job. It took a lot of courage, but she did find a low-paying job as a clerk in the Unemployment Office. She kept us together. She was in her mid-40s."

"Really difficult," Father responds, focusing so intently on what I am saying that I can almost hear him listening to me.

"I don't think I realized how difficult," I say. "Eight kids. The two oldest were in Buffalo for their careers. That left seven of us in our small home. Mother became like a sergeant. I tried to do what was right. For some reason I have never made the grade with her. I shouldn't talk about my mother because she is really very kind. But I can tell you, she has always had trouble with me."

"Hard for me to understand how your mother could ever see you as trouble."

"Not that I wanted to be, but I was. Maybe still am. It wasn't so much that I got in trouble. It was more about who I am. How I was born, I guess."

"How you were born?"

"You know, my temperament. Just who I am. Even as a child I was always wanting to do things, go out, have fun. I pretty much saw life as a world full of adventure. I absolutely love people and love to be with friends. I wasn't exactly one to toe the line."

"A creative child?"

"Some people might say so. Not my mother. I am too much like my dad."

That was the message I hated to hear all through my growing up. "Just like your father." I share with Father that my dad wasn't good to Mother and it hurt me so much to think I could be like him. Yet somehow what Mother saw in him, she saw in me.

"You were a child," Father says softly, as softly as if I still were a child.

It hurts to say it, but with my eyes looking down, I share that Mother always told me I was a "street angel and a house devil," exactly what she always told my dad he was. It wasn't true of me. I tried to be a good daughter. I might talk back or forget to finish a job or was sometimes late or something, but I would never hurt her. I love my mother. Whenever she said I was a street angel and house devil, under my breath I'd repeat, "I am an angel, an angel, an angel."

Father Brady's eyes never left me, and I did not know what was happening. It was as if the flood gates of my life opened up. I kept talking, talking about things I had never told anyone before, like that the irony about my dad was how attracted people were to him, really liked him, and our house was filled with our father's friends and customers. But my mother needed him to be a good husband and father. She worked so hard and wanted a secure family, something she was deprived of growing up. I could see how she had trouble with me being so much like him. I didn't try to be like him, but I knew I carried his sins. I look directly at Father and tell him, "I was always looking for absolution."

"Nothing to absolve." Father replies with his quiet, serious voice, and now swallowing me into his eyes.

"Thank you," I respond. "I've matured. She had to cope with all that responsibility, day in and day out. Nobody to help her. Anyway, I am free."

"Freedom is a sign of the Spirit's presence. It is only in freedom that you can make a genuine decision," Father replies in a quiet voice. "I think we should take a little break. Tea or lemonade and this time I can get it!"

"Lemonade sounds wonderful," I reply.

When Father returns and hands me the lemonade in the tall frosted glass, I taste the bitterness of the lemon mixed with the sweetness of the sugar. Just like my story. Just like me.

Chapter 4

SECRETS

"One of the deepest longings of the human soul is to be seen."
— *John O'Donohue*

AFTER HIS LAST SWALLOW of the cool lemonade and with a big, "Ahh," Father Brady says, "Oh, that hit the spot. What do you think? Shall we continue or wait until our next appointment?"

"I'm fine," I say with a certainty that surprises me. "I'd like to continue if *you* think we should." No one had ever delved into my life with such genuine love and concern, and I am comfortable, even anxious, to resume this strange and compelling conversation. I think to myself. *Is it the final confession of a dying woman or of a woman entering a convent? Is there a difference?*

"Absolutely, then, let's continue. Just wondering how you survived it all," Father asks, looking at me with eyes filled with kindness.

"Most of my siblings took my side," I begin. "We knit our lives together so tightly that one dropped stitch, any unraveling, would make us do whatever was necessary to knit ourselves back together. Lillis and Janice and I were the last three children. We became inseparable."

Father and I hardly resume talking when there is a knock at the door, and he is called away. As I sit waiting, memories I had forgotten suddenly begin to well up. I think back to my sophomore year in high school. I had decided the only thing I could do to survive my mother was create my own life, live the way I thought was normal. But going out—doing normal teen-age things—made Mother angrier and, in some ways, me stronger. She wanted me to stay home on weekends. I wouldn't. I was miserable. I'd get my work done and be out the door. Leaving brought me relief, but I was in trouble a lot during those years. I was too much for her. I was too much for myself. High school was sailing on a teen-age ship without a compass.

We all wanted to protect Mother, to take her side while we were trying to support each other. I was often confused with guilt I did not understand or loyalty I did not want. Even when Marnie knew I hadn't done anything wrong, she'd always say, "You can't do anything she might even imagine you would do."

Blanche reassured me that Mother was loyal to us. That was true. After my father's funeral, one of his sisters, Aunt Muriel who was Protestant, asked Mother if she could take me back to Buffalo and raise me. She would give me a Catholic education and, because she was a seamstress, promised I would be dressed "to the nines."

Mother did not hesitate. She said no. She would keep me with her. That was more important than anything. Now I realize what a temptation this request must have been for her. I had not been easy for her and she could have easily rationalized having one less mouth to feed. But as a little girl, she had experienced a seven-year separation from her own birth family. She couldn't do that to me. Mother had what she called "moral fiber." This was a firm decision, and I am grateful. Throughout my life, no matter what was going on, I experienced the security of identifying as a full-fledged member of my birth family, a gift not everyone is given.

Although I did not move to Aunt Muriel's, I remember how I would daydream that Aunt Muriel would come and steal me away back to Buffalo.

Just in the middle of these musings, the secretary knocks on the door again to tell me Father had a long-distance call and would be further delayed. I say, "Thank you," and fall back into reverie. As the sun spills in through the windows, memories keep tumbling into my mind, including an incident in junior high.

When I was in the seventh grade, I was invited to a pajama party. It was fun to be with girlfriends sitting around in our pajamas, drinking Pepsi and talking about who among us would make the junior cheerleading team and who had crushes on the eighth-grade boys. Sometime around midnight one of the girls dared us to go in the back yard and climb a tree with low branches. We put on our saddle shoes and turned the lights on in the dining room so we could see where the branches were. One after another, the girls climbed the tree giggling and laughing. I hadn't gotten my turn yet when the father of the friend whose home we were at came out and yelled at us and told us he was taking every one of us home. And he did. We piled into his black Chevy, and no one said a word except to give the father the address. I crept into my bed without my family even knowing I was back.

The next morning, I wished I had never gone to that party. My friend's father called our house. From the breakfast table, I remember watching Mother shake her head like she was saying no. She had anger in her eyes. I knew something must be terribly wrong.

"Were you going to meet boys in that yard? Own up to it. How could you take advantage of those parents giving you a party?"

I can still hear her words. "You've brought shame on yourself and on all of us."

No one could defend me. I was guilty and hurt the way you feel hurt but don't know why. I never spoke to my friends about our being taken home that night. Surprising to me, they did not seem that fazed about what had happened. Once, though, I heard Mary Anne joke about it. Maybe she could joke because she did not feel the sting of the slap.

I would eventually realize that Mother's rage was not about silly girls trying to climb the low branches of an apple tree at night; it was about how my behavior reflected on our family image. How it reflected on her. I was thirteen and I hurt my mother; I did not protect our reputation. It broke my heart, but it never occurred to me that I was innocent. All I knew was that I had to shield Mother from being criticized—which I did not do. I lived with guilt through the remainder of seventh grade because of this one incident.

When Father returns to the office, he apologizes saying that he is involved with the impending deaths of two people, one in Hornell and one in Rochester. But even with these heavy concerns, he quickly refocuses on me with attention that seemed to fill the universe. He sits down, again next to me, holds his hands like he is praying and takes me inside of his eyes, gently asking in almost a whisper, "So, Evie, only if you're comfortable, a question. Were you not happy growing up?"

"I actually thought I was happy as a child," I tell him. "I guess I am a person who feels happiness most of the time, but to tell you the truth, there were times when I would ride my bike through neighborhoods, look in windows, and wonder how people lived such normal lives, such happy lives. I wanted to be normal too. I knew I wasn't normal, that something was wrong with me because something was wrong with my dad. Yet, for some reason, in the middle of all of it, I always seemed to find happiness somehow or another. I was usually happy if Mother was happy. I love people who make me laugh. I love my family and my friends. I love to dance. I just always loved life. I guess I was happy!"

"Grace," Father replies as if he is talking to himself, but then he looks right at me and says, "God is with you, Ev, and with your mom and all of you, as He was with your troubled dad. You've done so well. The Paschal Mystery. God's love. You must have relied on Jesus and his Holy Mother to guide you."

I thought back on the cream-colored plastic statue of Our Lady I received with the Holy Childhood stamps I earned by giving money for the starving children in other countries. I placed the small statue on a side table in my bedroom I shared with Jan. When no one was looking, I would pray to Mary to help me be a better person, to help my Mother not have so much to do, to not be upset. I hesitantly tell Father, "I prayed."

"What about high school?" Father asks in a tone like he is afraid to ask.

I explain that Hornell doesn't have a Catholic high school so I attended Hornell High School. But my religion was still somewhat important to me. Yet, those were the hardest years in my life. I felt isolated, like I didn't belong anywhere, something many teens suffer through. The Church didn't mean as much to me, either. But there still was something that told me to rely on God. As painful as life was, I knew God was with me. None of my high school friends ever knew the weight of sadness I carried each day to school or what went on inside my home. I think people saw me as fun loving. I learned to be an actress in those four years. "I know I don't make sense," I say to my listening friend.

"Everything makes sense," Father says, making me feel like everything did actually make sense. "But through all you've experienced, you still feel God is calling you to live only for Him?" he asks.

"Believe me, I've tried to deny this." My throat aches as I try to speak. Feeling a little shaky, I continue, "I just can't seem to get rid of this urging. I honestly believe I will be my best self as a Sister. Marriage could bring me happiness, but religious life seems truer for who I am, as strange as this seems to everyone else, and sometimes to me, too." I grab a Kleenex off the desk and dab my eyes.

Father responds by telling me that what I am experiencing is called an "existential knowing," a recognition of what you must do to be your truest self. These days, he explains, it might also be called a "fundamental option," that decision which grows out of an undeniable integrity of self. He says I am making a fundamental option because of who I am. Father's explanation is very encouraging and I feel my body relax. He even states that he has no doubt my call to religious life is genuine.

"So, I pass?" I ask him between laughter and tears, worrying that my sister's mascara might not be waterproof.

"With flying colors. Our talk has truly touched me, Ev. I will hold you and your family close in my heart and prayer. I believe you are blessed with a special calling. I would like to meet with you again to talk about convent schedules and rules."

"Don't think I will be good at those," I choke out with a half laugh.

"You will grow to find religious life a genuine fulfillment of yourself."

"Yes," I respond quietly, slowly nodding my head up and down. "I believe I will."

My body now seems anchored to the chair. I don't know how to leave the warm, peaceful energy swirling around me and in me, or the palpable energy between Father and me. I feel safe, not safe from danger, but safe with the most trusted friend in the world. Father doesn't seem in any hurry to end our meeting, either. Our eyes look down at the carpet so long that it is beginning to feel uncomfortable. Father finally stands and then with a big smile tells me to enjoy Skycar. I tell him he can bet on it! I also ask him to be good to my mother when he meets her and add that how she is toward me is not how she is. I just push her buttons.

"I bless your mother, Ev. She is a brave woman who lives out of some brokenness. We are all broken in one way or another. Please don't worry. I will see you next Tuesday, after 8:00 Mass."

After saying, "Thank you, Father," I pick up my yellow cotton, summer purse, smile at Father who seems to be beaming at me, and I leave the office.

I cannot say now how long Father Brady and I talked, but I knew that I'd had the most honest and freeing conversation in my twenty-four years of life. It was the first time I had ever shared the depth of my desire to give my life to God and have it understood. I had also revealed private information about my relationship with my mother; yet, somehow, I felt a security that it was okay to be honest with this gentle man who listened with a reverence I never knew existed.

As I walk down the rectory's sidewalk, Yeats' "Is it the leaf, the blossom or the bole?" comes into my head. "Is it Father Brady, myself, or my vocation?" When I get into my car, I do not turn on the ignition. I sit back in the seat and suddenly say out loud, "Oh, my God, love at first sight is real. I am in love. I have fallen in love with a priest. A priest who is a person."

Chapter 5

ORDINARY TIMES

"Ordinary times is when God does His best work."
—Anonymous

SEVERAL WEEKS LATER ON an August morning, I am enjoying the scent of freshly cut grass as I walk across a property adjacent to our house. I see Mother standing in our yard with her hands on her hips. Staring, maybe daydreaming, she is looking into the stand of evergreens near the back fence and wears a starched-green cobbler apron over her faded blue housedress. On her feet, she has tightly tied what she calls her "nun shoes," the medium-heeled black oxfords she wears when she washes clothes, irons, or does housework. She stands almost motionless and doesn't hear me approach.

"A penny for your thoughts, Mother," I call to her.

"Oh, good morning, Evelyn. I was just thinking of you. Come help me hang this wash. Then I'd like to talk to you."

Mother had already brought up from the basement the heavy wicker basket filled with "whites." In the yard are two permanent steel clothes poles about twenty feet apart that hold four lines between them. Mother wipes the lines with a damp cloth to make sure that no flick of dirt or dust will get on the washed clothes. She then starts to hang the "unmentionables" with the wooden clothes pins on the two inside lines. I know that

I am to hang sheets on the outside lines. No one can ever know we wear underwear! When we finish, we sit on the metal grey chairs in the shade of the garage.

Catching her breath, Mother says, "What a good wash day. That breeze will dry the clothes quickly. I have four more loads, but I wanted to have a chance to talk. Before you say anything, I don't want you to think I am going to tell you not to go into the convent. You are your own woman now. I want your happiness. But, Evelyn, something is very wrong with all of this. You are not yourself."

"Why?" I ask.

"Where are your friends? They call and you don't go out. I don't see you dancing around the house. What is going on? Do you have something to tell me?" Mother inquires in an intimate tone.

"I have nothing to tell. This is a big step for me," I say clearly. "I plan to enter the convent and I want to."

"Well, you've got a strange way of showing it. You can change your mind, you know. You will probably come home anyway. You don't have to go. I am not going to tell you not to go, but this behavior isn't normal. Has Father Brady been able to help you or has he only made it more confusing?"

I stiffen. *Is she on to me?* Taking a deep breath, I quickly explain. "No, Father goes over schedules and expectations. He helps me understand community life."

"He seems like a nice man, but I can't understand why you are so out of sorts. Some trepidation is to be expected. But where is the joy?"

I can feel guilt slowly rise through my body. I feel like screaming. I do not know what I am doing, yet I do know I am making life harder for my mother. That is not how I want to leave her before my departure. On the Church's liturgical calendar, we are in Ordinary Times. But for me

nothing is ordinary. I am going in the convent and I am in love and everyone thinks something is wrong with me. I couldn't agree more. I continue
to go to daily Mass. But that is not ordinary for me, either. Father Brady
celebrates the Mass!

The first morning I attend, it is immediately evident that Father Brady
is the consummate priest, totally at one with God in the tabernacle and at
one with the people in the pews. Vatican II has already instituted signifi-
cant changes to make the liturgy of the Mass more accessible to the people, and it is evident that Father implements these changes with reverence
and respect.

The priest no longer keeps his back to parishioners as he celebrates.
Now he faces us. Latin is replaced by English. The altar railing which
separates the people from the sacred ritual has been removed, signifying
that we in the pews journey *with* the priest to the Great Mystery of the
Eucharist, not behind him. We are no longer lowly lay people; we are
fellow pilgrims.

The first time I receive Communion from Father Brady, he smiles *into*
me as he places the host in my hand (instead of placing it on my tongue
which I experienced since I was age 7 at my First Communion). Looking me straight in the eye, Father says in a low whisper, "Evie, the Body
of Christ." I stop breathing. The next few days, I watch to see if Father
addresses anyone else by name or gives his loving smile when offering
Communion. He doesn't! Each morning I anxiously wait to receive Communion—and Father's smile. At the end of the service, Father raises his
hand to bless the congregation. "Go in peace to love and serve the Lord."

I will, Father. I will go and serve the Lord, I say to myself with closed
eyes and tightly clasped hands on my chest. These times are anything but
ordinary.

When Father meets me for follow-up appointments during the next weeks, I continue to feel the same emotional stirring in my heart that I know is unacceptable and wrong. Questions plague me: *How can anyone entering the convent feel like this? Why do I think Father is a perfect match for me? How do I dare admit to myself how attracted I am to this priest?* I walk through my days as if in an altered world.

While I work at not showing the anguish and joy I am experiencing, inside of me I rail against God, questioning why He invites me to devote my life to Him and yet sends me the only person who could actually be the love of my life. I wasn't looking for the love of my life! I was looking for complete union with Jesus. I was looking to devote my life to people who need love. Only that. It is crazy. I wonder if Father experiences any of the feelings about me that I have about him. He gives me no reason to think so.

During our appointments, Father continues to focus his full attention on me, not missing a word or a sigh. It is as if he takes my words into his eyes and holds them there until I understand them in a new way. He encourages me to prepare for religious life with an open and loving heart; he advises me on how to adjust to the rigors of the convent schedules and lifestyle; he celebrates that I will grow in God's love through my commitment to religious vows. Father explains that the Church sees the vows of poverty, chastity, and obedience as a way to reach perfection and a preparation for the world to come. For him, vows are not so much a way to be perfect, or a sign of our heavenly home, but a means to be free as a human being to love and to live for others without the responsibilities of family life or the burden of materialism. To concentrate on growing in God.

I ask him if lay people can be just as blessed helping others as those called to religious life. I use my sister Lillis as an example of someone giving up everything to serve people in Africa.

"There are many kinds of service," Father tells me, "but celibacy is a gift that allows us to give everything without personal ties or obligations. We witness with our consecration to Christ alone."

I am beginning to recognize the weight of the vows and wonder if the gift of celibacy will be given to me as it has been given to this holy priest. Yet, even though he shows no interest in me other than for spiritual counseling, Father seems to really enjoy my company. We talk about how delicious the ice-cream is at the Elmhurst Dairy, new movies and the impact of Vatican II. We laugh easily over one thing or another. Whenever I am with him, my heart is swimming—or drowning. I often wonder: "Could he be flirting? Am I?"

This is a summer of contradictions. I am entering the convent but dreaming of the kind and gentle priest. I am of marrying age and I am given a shower for things needed for a celibate life. A shower for girls entering the convent is a common practice for Catholic families. Although I am choosing to give up any attention on myself, people act as if I am special. My Irish aunts, for example, suddenly see me in a whole new light, not as their wistful, daydreamer niece but as their ticket to heaven. You know, "my niece the nun." And when the FBI comes to our small town to do a background check on my sister Lillis, who has applied to the Peace Corps, the townspeople continually tell them that they have the wrong McLean girl. Lillis is serious and entering the convent. Evelyn is the likely Peace Corps candidate. Lil is none too happy about this.

I had planned to use my time during this summer of my "last hurrah" with friends from high school. But, with all the confusion I'm experiencing, my plans are dissipating. Friends say I am in the convent before I get there. I truly feel in crisis. Even if Father Brady were attracted to me, and he certainly does not indicate it, thinking about a relationship with him is futile. He's a celibate priest. My luck.

These ideas fill me with even more doubts as I get closer to the date of entering the convent and my journal is full of questions:

Will I be able to live a full and happy life as a celibate?
Can a celibate be in love? Can I find a love deeper than
desire? How can I keep Father in my life? Will I be
able to change my disposition with my family?

My disposition does not indicate change is coming soon. I cry for no reason, and I mope around the house. I do not feel like eating and am definitely not focused on preparing for the convent with the certitude my family expects.

As my symptoms of depression and restlessness increase, Mother decides to get to the bottom of it. She tells Lillis to find out if I am pregnant! After Mass one Sunday, Lil suggests we go for a ride into the hills so she can talk to me alone. I ask her what the mystery ride is about. "You," she says. I figured.

With the top down, I drive Skycar up the twisted dirt roads into the hills, only a few minutes away from our house, and pull over to the side of the road near some caves where Lillis, our younger sister Jan, and I had played as children. Clouds scud across the sky and the warm sun peeks in and out as if the clouds and sun were playing hide and seek with each other. The waxy yellow buttercups, hyacinth-blue cornflowers and daisies with long white fingers and beaming golden centers mix in the long grass along the roadside. I love wildflowers, but God's garden is not lifting my spirits on this morning.

I turn the engine off and Lil gets right to the point. "Mother is really worried about how you are acting, Ev." Then she asks outright: "Are you pregnant?"

I couldn't believe she would even ask this. I tell her. "Of course, I am not. These are not medieval times when pregnant girls are sent to convents. I am going into the convent because it is my vocation, for God's sake!"

Lil looks down. She bites her lower lip and, I know, hates being the messenger.

"All of us are confused. You are acting weird. If you are going to enter the convent, please don't turn weird. Are you sick or something?"

Tears come like a flood and I keep blowing my nose as if I have the worst cold in the world. I can hardly speak. Then I tell her with staccato-choking sounds. "I am sick. Love sick. I'm in love. With Father Brady. Don't tell anyone, Lil. I can't help it."

Looking at me as if I have lost my mind, Lillis replies in no uncertain terms, "This is the craziest thing I have ever heard you say. You can't love a priest. You just can't. My God, I think you do. How did this happen? Does he know? How does he feel?"

"He doesn't have a clue and, of course, he is not allowed to be interested in a woman."

"And you're not allowed to be interested in a priest! He's vowed to celibacy."

"It's just that I've never felt like this. About anyone. My heart is always running to him. I can't stop thinking of him. This happened out of the blue. This isn't one of my eternal crushes. Something so true and real about him. About how I feel. God knows, I am not looking for a husband, but I really think he is the only person in the world meant for me. But he's a priest and I definitely want to be a nun." More tears sting my cheeks and I feel chilled. I keep blowing my nose as if it were mid-winter and not a perfect, halcyon summer day.

"You have tipped over this time. Yes, he is a priest who is at least forty years old."

"How do you know how old he is?" I say in a short, sharp tone.

"When he introduced himself at Mass, he said he'd been a priest for fifteen years. So, twenty-five when he was ordained plus fifteen makes him around forty. Too old for you. Anyway, he's not available! Not even a wish on a star. I am *not* telling Mom that her daughter is in love with the village priest! Forget the convent."

"No, I have waited too long. I am going."

"Move to Boston with your friends," Lil pleads. "See how you feel. Meet someone who *can* marry you. Maybe it's a sign."

I sense my cheeks getting red. "It's not a sign. It's just how I am! But," I whimper, "I have no right to be. I don't want to meet anyone else. I don't even want to know Father Brady, but I am so in love with him."

"Okay. You will just have to get out of love with him. I'll tell Mother you have the convent jitters, whatever that means. I don't know if she will buy it, but you've got to be more pleasant. Nuns are supposed to be pleasant!"

I am not more pleasant. But there are some humorous times, like the day my brother-in-law Andy brings me the men's tee shirts we are required to wear under our habits. The list from the Motherhouse states: "six white, size large men's tee shirts to wear under the habit as habits are not washed daily." When I put one of the tee shirts on my 118-pound body, I can wrap it all the way around me. It comes down to my knees.

We are rolling with laughter when Andy says, "Hey, Ev, if you ever leave, could I have those tee shirts? I bought you the really good ones and they are just my size." Laughter erupts again.

Another day on which my family laughs about my convent venture is the first time Father Brady comes to our house. It is only days before I am due to leave. He presents me with a large box, all wrapped and tied with ribbons. I wonder what he could be giving me. My body tingles with delight until I realize it is a joke gift. The box holds a huge comb—my hair would soon be cut even shorter than I had it cut in preparation to go, an empty perfume bottle and, among other things, a bright, red lipstick. Everyone is having a good time, joking and commenting.

"Take the lipstick and just keep blotting it so people will think it's your natural color," Jan laughs and then adds, "But leave the blue eye shadow for me. Joe will love it."

I want to go along with all the jokes. But I also want to hide. I want Father to stay. But I want him to leave.

When Father finally does go, a song of longing that often came to me when I was growing up starts playing in my head: "Where is Love?" from the musical *Oliver*. *Where is love?/Does it fall from skies above?/Is it underneath the willow tree/That I've been dreaming of?/Will I ever know the sweet "hello"/That's meant for only me...*

I had often thought, *Will I ever know the sweet 'hello'/That's meant for only me?* Now I think I've found it. Yet I also believe I will find love in religious life. I am sure that God will be with me wherever love finds me.

These days as I read my journals, I think about destiny or God's plan or just the coincidence of meeting Father Brady. In 1951, I moved to Hornell. In 1951 Father was ordained a priest. In the summer of 1965, after many delays—were they destined—I was entering the convent from my family's home in Hornell. In the summer of 1965 Father Brady was assigned to my parish in Hornell. Is there some hidden design in the universe? Do we have a preordained fate? Coincidence? Is it the hand of God?

Chapter 6

A Postulant

*"And suddenly you know: It's time to start something new
and trust the magic of beginnings."*
—*Meister Eckhart*

At 12:30 p.m. on a hot Sunday in late August 1965, I put my small
convent trunk into my mother's black Mainline Ford. The trunk holds
pretty much all my earthly possessions for my new life. With Marnie and
Janice accompanying us, Mother drives me to the Mercy Motherhouse.
Even though my bewildered heart is strung out along the road posts, I
feel certain that this is what I am meant to do. I am wearing my favorite
three-quarter length suede jacket with a yellow rose on the lapel from my
mother's garden and underneath the jacket, a long-sleeved, scarlet sheath
dress of polyester-silk that has a tie at the waist of the same material. I
wrap the tie around my hair: a red badge of courage. I also make sure
some of the highlights on my hair are visible. My mother seems as relieved as I am that this day has come. At least she knows I'm not pregnant.

We walk up the Motherhouse's steps to the heavy double oak doors
that open to an unknown world. In the large, front marble hallway, many
Sisters greet the new candidates and families with much joy and warmth.
Soon my "band," a convent term for a group of women who enter the
community at the same time, is escorted to the front of the chapel for

Mass. The family members are asked to follow and sit behind us.

When Mass ends, we postulants (from the French *postulare*, "to ask" for those seeking admission into the convent) are led out of a door at the front of the chapel. We hear the sniffles and soft crying of our families left behind. Just about then I feel a bit of shell shock. But something keeps moving me, as if I am on a conveyor belt. I am on my way. As to where and why, I feel completely at a loss. We are escorted from the chapel to the refectory, where we are welcomed with a wonderful meal. The new postulants try to make small talk. Whenever I introduce myself as "Evelyn, but you can call me Ev or Evie," one of my band interrupts, "She means Sister Evelyn."

Sister Evelyn? Could that really be me?

Many Sisters come to our tables to say hello and offer their blessings. I feel the goodness in the air. When Mother Edward, the Mistress of Novices, with her kewpie-doll face and piercing blue eyes, introduces herself to me, she says, with a twinkle in her eye, "Oh, here is Father Brady's special friend."

I am stunned by her comment and feel the heat in my cheeks that I know will soon turn them red. I want to deflect this unexpected and, to me, worrisome comment. I smile and say, "Yes, Father Brady has been wonderful. He has so many special friends."

It is in fact true that many of the Sisters think of Father Brady as their friend and counselor. I eventually learn that he is a regular visitor at the Motherhouse and, as one Sister told me, is known for his "quiet and extravagant heart." He believes in religious life and supports the Sisters by saying Mass, hearing confessions, giving retreats, and counseling with spiritual direction. He is a special friend to the Sisters of Mercy. Yet Mother Edward's comment concerns me. Could she read into what I was feeling? Had Father Brady picked up on my feelings about him and said something to her?

This incident brings up the emotions I had struggled with all summer, and I quickly try to tamp them down. Thoughts crowd my mind. *This is the life you have chosen. Give yourself a chance. You can learn to serve the Lord and his people like these Sisters do.* I am determined to.

After dinner, we postulants are assigned to our individual "cells," each an 8 foot x 7 foot area surrounded with pale peach curtains held up with rings on rods. These cells are where we will sleep and keep our few belongings. We are told to dress in our new habits—over our size large tee shirts—and to put on the short veil of black netting that is on the bed. I am happy that four bobby pins are provided. If I lose even one bobby pin, which I did, I have to admit to this failing of not being respectful of my possessions.

Sister Norma, the Mistress of Postulants, welcomes us in a large room with long wooden tables and hard wooden chairs. This is the postulants' community room. "Mistress" is a title from another era that, as far as I am concerned, no longer works but which the Vatican II changes have not yet caught up with. Sister Norma is a slight, matter-of-fact, good woman who takes her responsibilities seriously. Because I am Irish, I expect her to give us a cup of tea. Instead she offers her welcome, the rules, the schedule, and a brief smile. I am "a stranger in a strange land."

As the days pass, I adjust to the 5:30 a.m. bell—God calling us to a new day—and the 10:00 p.m. bell for the Grand Silence. These first weeks, I feel secure in the strict routines and the feeling of goodness among the Sisters. Yet sometimes, looking around in the chapel or in the refectory, all I can see is black. Black! One night a little poem creeps into my journal and it is about crows! *"Like a hundred black crows/holding all the colors/of the spectrum/we move as one prayer/ Hidden rainbows."*

Although most postulants entered the convent right from high school, I am one of three college graduates in our band who had already begun a career. With our similar backgrounds, and the difference of almost six years in age between us and the other postulants, Carol, Terry and I immediately bond. Throughout our time together, my two friends are lifelines for me, especially Carol. She and I could not be more different. She is blunt and practical; I am hesitant and a dreamer. She takes to the rules; I question almost everything. She enjoys our superiors; I am always on my guard.

We pretty much operate as a threesome but know that if two of us want an exclusive friendship, or appear to have what is called a "particular friendship," it will not be tolerated. The term "particular friendship" means being too interested in and spending too much time with one other person.

I come to understand "particular friendship" in a real way several months after we enter, when I befriend another postulant. She is full of life and love and can make a joke out of the craziest things, especially when I have trouble with the rules. Sometimes we cannot stop laughing at the incongruity of some of the practices of religious life. Her humor helps me get through. Yet she also has a serious side and is a great reader. With not a little awe, we share the new theology that is coming out of the writings of Vatican II. I am extremely interested in everything about renewal and appreciate her knowledge and suggestions for reading. When we gather for recreation, I seek her out.

One day I get a message from Sister Norma saying she wants to speak to me. I knock on her open office door, Sister nods, which means I can enter, and I kneel down. I keep my eyes down waiting for her to start the conversation. We have to kneel in front of our superiors for any communication. Still on my knees, Sister Norma starts talking and I lift my head to face her. She says she wants to discuss the relationship I'd developed with a Sister whom I'd "chosen to befriend exclusively over other Sisters in my band to whom I should also offer friendship."

I do not know what she is talking about. I am friendly to people without even knowing it, and I do not believe I am excluding anyone. It seems to me I have made friends with everyone. Of course, some Sisters enjoy certain friends more than others; it is human nature. As far as my friend and I are concerned, we are simply two Sisters who respect and enjoy each other.

The meeting with Sister Norma feels strange to me, even wrong. But she is clear. I am to end my friendship with this Sister immediately. I am not to seek her company. I am not to speak with her. I feel an immediate pain in my chest. I am, however, well aware that obedience to my superior is my response to "God's will". I obey. Whenever my friend and I see each other, we simply look away, feeling the hurt and wondering why this is happening. I miss her. I am beginning to experience the difficulties that the vow of obedience will pose for me.

The Vatican Council's call for renewal includes a new understanding of spiritual practices for religious communities. By my third year, for example, the censure of "particular friendships" is no longer practiced. Nor are other unreasonable practices such as the Chapter of Faults. At the Chapter of Faults which is held on Saturday evening, each young Sister kneels in front of her superior with everyone else in the band present and shares a particular mistake, a shortcoming or the commission of a sin during the week. We humbly ask God and the superior for forgiveness.

There is a list of possible faults from which to choose. Or we can come up with some transgression on our own. The purpose of Chapter of Faults is to rid ourselves of ego and to embrace humility. It reminds me of being a little girl trying to think up sins to tell in Confession. Even then I knew I was a sinner. I was just not sure which transgressions were actual sins and which were simply mistakes. On Saturday evenings at the Chapter of Faults, I feel as far away from dancing as any soul can be.

Another time we young Sisters have to kneel is when we need to ask for even a simple thing, like toothpaste or a bar of soap. We go to the Mistress's office and kneel down in front of her. With our heads down, we wait for her to acknowledge us, and then, we look up and make our request. This practice feels unnatural and embarrassing to me. It's as if I am less a person when I have to kneel to relate to another person who is sitting or standing. It gives all the power in the relationship to the superior and removes any chance of friendship. Besides, it just seems inhuman.

I try to accept the training of formation. But inside I rebel. I do not know what to do with the emotions I feel. I pray that I can live through this. But I cannot accept these lifestyle practices as God's will.

"I will put up with this, but I feel like a fool," I tell Carol and Terry.

"Don't think about it," Carol says. "Just do it." If I could only be like Carol.

Over the span of the three years of what is called "formation," however, in response to the Vatican Council's recommendations for renewal of religious life, several fundamental changes are made. There is a shift from focusing on destroying our egos to upholding our personhood. Friendships are not only encouraged but celebrated. Now, several decades later, it is clear that life-long "particular friendships" between and among Sisters sustain them and, as all healthy friendships do, bring Sisters meaning and joy.

When I think now about the unnatural practices that were imposed on religious in the name of "holiness," I am struck by how close to heroic the pre-Vatican II women religious were. In many cases, they were subjected to even harsher disciplines using medieval practices and other un-forgiving conditions and rules. In some cases, this training, which could be seen as abuse, intentional or not, had harmful effects on Sisters. Adults remember how severe and unkind some Sisters were to them as children and teens and even as adults. I believe those Sisters acted harshly toward those in their charge because their communities had subjected them to self-denigration to the point of abuse as the way to "holiness". Or maybe they had experienced abuse in their family homes. These Sisters acted out their pain on others in their charge, including on me.

When I was in second grade at a Catholic school, I came back to class from lunch feeling very sick to my stomach. We sat in long rows of wooden desks. There could be as many as fifty students in one class. But somehow the Sister could see all of us. I felt dizzy and put my head down on my desk. My teacher called out to me: "Evelyn, put your head up."

I tried to pick my head up. But my stomach heaved and my eyes could hardly open. I felt feverish. Everything seemed to be swirling around. I could hear Sister's long habit swish down the aisle and her rosary beads knock on the sides of the desks of my aisle. Suddenly a wooden dowel that was used to point out certain words on the blackboard slammed on the scrolled-iron side of my desk. Tears squeaked out of my eyes.

Bravely, my friend Sheila said, "Evelyn does not feel well, Sister."

"Doesn't Evelyn have a voice?" Sister asked with anger in her voice. "If something is wrong, Evelyn can tell me."

I couldn't respond and kept my head cradled into my skinny arms because it throbbed and my stomach was churning. I wanted to ask per-mission to leave, but I didn't think I could speak. Until I said the words myself, I had to stay in the classroom. A neighbor drove me home after school. The next day I was taken to the hospital with appendicitis and peritonitis.

I share this example not to paint women religious as if there is something wrong with them. In fact, I have always known Sisters who were normal and kind. But some were not. I believe the training and the hardships of convent living in pre-Vatican days broke the spirits of some Sisters. Despite these sad and sometimes tragic encounters, most pre-Vatican II Sisters built the Kingdom with fierce generosity and courage and goodness. Today vibrant and loving women religious, thankfully freed from medieval training, are the yeast of the Gospel, the bread of the Church, the ones most likely to be found serving the poor, the imprisoned, the sick and the dying. The ones organizing fair legislation on every level of government to give voice to the voiceless. Sisters are our "gospel bearers." They live out what Jesus calls us to do.

Despite the clericalism that has isolated priests and the overwhelming horror of the tragic reality of pedophilia, the majority of Catholic priests also bear witness to the Gospel and serve out of pure hearts with compassion for their flocks, especially for those who are the least among us. These true priests ache with anguish and disbelief when they hear of their brother priests' deplorable and unconscionable sins against children and adults. Unbelievably, they also have had to endure the shocking and unpardonable cover-up of these sex offenders by too many American bishops. In my Diocese of Buffalo, New York, over many decades, bishop after bishop, including our present bishop, transferred priest sex offenders from one ministry to the next. The Church's reputation became more important than the protection of its people. We are growing in the realization that we are not only dealing with the crimes of pedophilia and cover up, but a long-standing culture of systemic abuse of power.

It may be hard for outsiders to believe anyone would remain a

Catholic after such a scandalous and heart wrenching history. Yet the vast majority of Catholic priests are innocent men of great dedication. In fact, the percentage of pedophiles among Catholic priests is similar to the percentage of pedophiles in other denominations. But the cover-up by bishops makes this repulsive story of the Catholic Church excruciatingly painful. There has been a mystique about priests, a belief that they are Christ on earth and that somehow makes them unaccountable. Initially, many people simply would not believe priests could do anything morally wrong, let alone criminal.

Yet, each time a priest or bishop or cardinal is brought to justice, the Church has a chance to admit it is a human church, a church of failings—and possible redemption. I believe the Church needs an annual international month of atonement for the sex-abuse tragedy so that all of us, as a people of God, can witness to what the abuse survivors have endured. There is a relief that the truth is out so, in some way, we can share our sorrow and our support for those abused by our leaders. As a community and in a public way we could offer communal prayers and healing to every victim living or dead. These victims are our family; individually and communally. We all need to heal our hearts that, at least in Buffalo, keep breaking.

Daniel Berrigan is one of the many priests of great worth. As part of the renewal efforts, the Motherhouse sponsors programs to update our community on Vatican II's message. Fr. Berrigan, the legendary peace activist, is our first speaker. I am mesmerized by the authority of this small, wiry Jesuit's commitment to nonviolence. He challenges us to work for justice for all people, especially the marginalized, to be peaceful in our own lives, and to open new eyes to the political forces of war. He is also realistic about the toll it takes to follow Jesus the Peacemaker.

"Commitment is like medicine," he said. "If you take too little, healing won't happen; if you take too much, you get sicker." Wisdom to keep in a postulant's journal.

Although this kind of event is rare, speakers of Father Berrigan's quality give me courage and strength to throw myself headlong into my formation as a Sister of Mercy. I need time and prayer and these experiences to figure out how to be a Sister. I also need to figure out how not to be in love. In my heart, I know I am not doing a very good job of it.

Chapter 7

ADJUSTMENTS

Vocation ... comes from listening. I must listen to my life
and try to understand what it is truly about—
quite apart from what I would like it to be ..."
—*Parker Palmer*

I AM TRYING HARD to listen to my life as I adjust to convent living, to understand this new way of being. I want to be happy, to be fulfilled, to be part of a community dedicated to serving God's people. I want to live out who I am created to be.

I felt at home during the first weeks' comforting rhythm of prayer and recreation and classes on religious life. But now that the school year has started, things are changing. My schedule is like a vise. Not a minute is wasted in the postulant's life. We hike through our days with purpose on our journey to God, but the path becomes a blur for me. Although I am worried I will lose my way, I keep walking, running when necessary. I long for a rest stop. Except for recreation, when we are encouraged to sew or knit or write letters, I realize regular community life does not include down time. No one has the work ethic of women religious.

I have heard that when people experience a disaster, their ability to adapt to totally new and unfamiliar circumstances is remarkable. Although I am not in a disaster—even though my friends might not agree with me—I am learning how quickly, how seemingly effortlessly, human beings adjust to a new culture. I live with twenty-five normal and healthy young women who have come from a secular life style with the freedom of going anywhere they wanted, eating their particular foods and dressing in their own style and now we are adapting to the convent's prescribed rules and culture—as if we have always been here.

I am amazed at how quickly I too fall in step with a life so entirely different from the way I had spontaneously lived my life before the convent. When I start to question why I am really here, it helps that I keep focused on my reason for entering a religious community in the first place: to be consecrated to Jesus and to give my life for others. Although I do not know how deep these mysterious waters are, or how far I can swim, I have a strong desire to embrace my vocation with openness and enthusiasm.

Yet, because of the strict rules and schedule for postulants combined with my heavy teaching responsibilities, I am beginning to fear convent life might be too difficult for me. Already assigned to teach four English Regents classes, which culminate in high-stakes tests for juniors, I am also given an Advanced Placement English class. The Advanced Placement seniors read one or two books a month. That means that I have to read both the books and literary criticisms on them, formulate lesson plans and mimeograph reading guides which must be corrected weekly. In addition, there is a weekly essay for each of the over one hundred students as well as the juniors' college applications that I am asked to correct. The only blessing of the demanding schedule is that I do not entertain any romantic thoughts. I am too exhausted.

The postulants follow a sacrosanct schedule: up at 5:30 a.m.; meditation from 6:00-7:00; Mass from 7:00-7:45; breakfast after Mass; arrival at school by 8:10; after school mandatory recreation, prayers, dinner; after dinner, recreation and an hour to prepare for school, prayers and bed. There is very little time for my heavy teaching responsibilities. And some of the rules do not help. I am frustrated that, because postulants cannot be seen there, I am not allowed to walk through the front hallway of the Motherhouse, which is a shortcut to the high school. When I ask for permission to do so, Sister Norma says, "That is the rule for postulants, Sister. You must never walk through the front hall. You are a postulant. Don't ask to be something you are not. This is all part of humility." I am 24 years old and I can't walk through a hallway to be on time for my classes.

So, I start each day anxious and out of breath, all because of a false way to keep me humble. Doesn't the community know I already feel humbled? Every school day, after I take a stairway to the basement, follow a long corridor, and run breathlessly up the stairs to the high school, I call out to my students waiting for me to unlock the classroom, "Okay, girls, I am coming!"

Another great frustration is that I have to go to recreation with the other postulants after school. This is time I desperately need to prepare my classes. I gather all the courage I have to ask Sister Norma if I could please use this time to prepare classes.

"Why do you think you are an exception, Sister Evelyn? Everyone has to fulfill our way of life. That is what living in community means. Recreation is a time we can enjoy each other. Many have much greater responsibilities than you, and they find time for recreation. You must learn that you are not an exception."

"Thank you, Sister Norma," I respond as I get up off my knees when she nods. Her response fills me with anger and I walk down the stairs and out of the Motherhouse without permission. I wait outside in tears until I hear the bell.

Even though I have a little over an hour after dinner for my school work, it seems I just get started when the bell rings to go to chapel to chant Compline, the beautiful evening prayer of the *Divine Office,* which people all over the world pray.

Yet, I love evening Compline which becomes the bookend at the end of my day, my protection, my feeling of safety. As I chant, I let the psalms sink deep inside me and I hold them in the sweetness of sleep and hope their words penetrate my spirit.

> *Save us, Lord, while we are awake; protect us while we*
> *sleep; that we may keep watch with Christ and rest with*
> *him in peace. Let us pray. Lord our God, restore us again*
> *by the repose of sleep after the fatigue of our daily work so*
> *that, continually renewed by your help, we may serve you*
> *in body and soul.*

I eventually figure out a way to find time for my class preparations after lights out. I sleep a few hours, get up around midnight, and go into the bath area where there is a tinted glass-enclosed bathtub with a light. I climb into the bathtub and put a towel behind my back for comfort. When I have enough material ready to somehow get through the next day of classes, I go back to bed.

Getting up by 5:30 a.m. is difficult. In the chapel, I sleep through most morning meditations. I am beginning to lose weight, am anxious about my classes and, in general, drag myself from one responsibility to the next. I also remind myself that this is the life I have chosen and I do love teaching the fresh-faced, beautiful girls at Mercy High. Determined to persevere with as much kindness and dedication as I can, I simply trudge along. No one seems to notice how hard this is. *I am giving my life to God*, I remind myself. *Our Lord gives us nothing we can't handle.* At least I hope so.

One evening on the way to Compline, Sister Norma stops me to say that Father Brady will visit me for spiritual direction the following Wednesday at 3:30 p.m. This news travels joyfully through me, and I feel a sudden lightness. Yet it also adds to my anxiety. My spirits are down from lack of sleep and the demands of teaching. Father has not seen how I look with my short hair, black dress and make-up-less face that now looks drawn and pale. My heavy black stockings and oxfords don't help, either. Because I am so tired, I had given little thought to my appearance. But now I am embarrassed that I will appear in what I am suddenly thinking of as prison garb. I am also concerned about how I will relate to Father in my new identity. I think back to my rose-colored summer skirt with a longing which I know is not acceptable.

When Wednesday comes and I walk into the parlor, the same formal room where Mother Bride originally met me, Father stands and gives me his great warm and shining smile as if he were meeting a long-lost friend. Lost for sure.

"Sister Evelyn! How are you?" he calls enthusiastically.

I stand in the doorway a minute and, in a flat tone and with a slight smile, I answer, "Okay, Father. How are you?"

"Great, busier than ever, but loving the colors of the trees," he responds as he greets me with his hands folded like he is praying and not letting on that he must be thinking, "What the heck happened to her?"

"The ride from Hornell was glorious," he says enthusiastically as he waits for me to sit down. "I could have driven off the road with the colors."

"I know what you mean. I love this time of year," I respond with a flash of happiness. We are sitting in the big wing chairs with the huge crucifix looking down on us.

Smiling, I say to him, "Thanks for coming."

Father quickly reports, "I saw your mom at the Altar and Rosary Society this week. I told her I was visiting you. She asked me to send her love. I will call her when I get back." He knows I would be worried about how my mother is.

"Thanks. Please tell her I send my love, too. Let her know I am fine. How does she seem?"

"I don't think she is convinced about you being here."

"I'm sure of that. But does she seem okay?" I ask anxiously. "I'll see her next month on postulants' visiting day."

"Seems fine. Don't worry. She will adjust. She's a good woman. How is convent life? How are the Sisters treating you?"

"Fine. Good. I am adjusting slowly but surely."

"It's a huge adjustment, Evie." Father changes to a serious tone which seems to indicate that he recognizes that things may not be working out for me. "Especially when you are older. Is there anything I can do for you? Are you okay?"

"I'm fine, really. Just a little tired from the early mornings."

"Early nights, too," he responds with a sound of relief in his voice. "That should help." If he only knew.

"Ev, we only have an hour. Are there any questions?" he asks. I sense his genuine concern. "Do you want to talk about anything?"

"No questions I can think of," I answer, trying to figure out if I should tell him how exhausted I am. How Sister Norma hurt me. How teaching seventeen-year-olds and coming home to the convent and living with teen-agers the same age is driving me crazy. I decide not to. I simply ask, "But would you mind if I took notes in my journal?"

"Not at all. A journal can be a spiritual map." Father responds gently. "If you're sure there are no questions, I would like to begin. So little time, but let's go over some basic components of spirituality as a start."

"I'd like that. What's first?" I ask as I put the date, October 20, 1965, on the top of the page of my journal and a note: *Road map to God.* I am becoming a cartographer of the spiritual life.

Chapter 8

SPIRITUAL MAPS

"Map-making has never been a precise art ..."
—*Terry Pratchett*

MOVING UP IN HIS chair and folding his hands on his knees, Father looks at me with his smile that makes my heart open and says, "This is all you will ever have to know. God loves you completely, entirely, totally. He is fully in you, fully in all of us, in everything He creates. He is the creator and the creation. That includes his creation of you. Together you and God are co-creators of life. Just as a Mother and Father are always in their child, you are inseparable from the action of the divine within you, Ev. That is number one, but so much more to say about this later on." He speaks emphatically.

"And number two?" I ask as I scribble as fast as I can.

"For me, number two is our obligation to find and accept ourselves as the persons God created us to be. To simply be yourself. Not worry about how anyone else is. Your God-created self, Evie. The more you are your true self, the more you reflect the God within you. Just be who you are and share yourself with everyone."

As Father is speaking, I am thinking, *My true self? I hardly feel I have a self. I am a robot, a teaching machine, a soulless worker. Mine is a false self who smiles and says "yes" and wants to understand her decision to be here. Who has no idea if she has a true or false self.*

With my pen gripped tightly in my hands, I simply ask, "And number three?"

"We can find God through our spiritual practices, through prayers and liturgies, our reading and the sacraments. But Jesus comes in the fullness in our daily lives, in the lives we are living right now. Because God comes through the people and events, He is always right where you are. No separation. He loves you there."

"I think I understand but could you explain some more?" I say.

As I am turning the page of my journal trying to capture every word, I am suddenly aware of Father Brady in a whole new way. He is a spiritual teacher guiding me to a deeper relationship with myself and therefore, with God. Not guiding me to a relationship with himself, which I had looked for, dreamed of, and imagined the previous summer. I don't question his formal approach at this first session of spiritual direction. I am much too tired to question much of anything.

Father answers deliberately. "Maybe how you prepare your classes or treat the students. How you bring God—goodness—to them and how they manifest the divine back to you. Or maybe having fun with the other postulants or doing the dishes. Wherever you are or whatever you are doing, God operates within you. There is no separation of our human life from divine life. God is not only found in prayer. God is totally, fully, completely in your particular life and spiritual practices."

"Like what spiritual practices?"

Father smiles at me. "Not going to let me get away with that one, are you? Well, I am not talking about formal prayers, which are important. I am talking about how we live."

He uses the example of patience, saying that I can read about and pray to be a more patient person, but that it is in my classroom or with the Sisters that the spiritual practice of patience will be honed. I have to practice patience with myself first. Not only in my prayer life, but in all of daily life. I should first be "patiently" patient with myself and then with others. I have to put energy into this practice. Work at it. He calls it gospel "praxis" or the practice of Jesus' teachings in my own life. He tells me that God will be manifest through signs and people and the events of life. What is going on even right now. If that is the case, I figure God must not know about sleep.

When Father says our hour is up, I feel a sudden, sharp pang of loneliness. I desperately want him to stay for even five more minutes. I hadn't yet felt at home in the convent but am now experiencing a great peace and security in Father's presence. He suggests we pray before he leaves. Blood drains out of me.

"In the name of the Father and of the Son and of the Holy Ghost. Amen. Dear Jesus and your heavenly Mother Mary and all the holy saints, hold Sister Evelyn in your loving care, lead her into the beauty of her vocation, and keep her with peace in her days and nights. Let her discover and live out of her true self, the self You created her to be. Let her continue to reflect your love and your goodness to everyone she meets."

Father ends saying, "God bless you." Then he stops for a moment and says, "No, I mean, *let* God bless you." My eyes squint with a questioning look.

"We all say 'God bless you,' but God is always blessing us. The grace of His presence is always here. I want to say to you, "*Let* God bless you. Keep your heart open."

After that, at least to me, Father Brady always says, "*Let* God bless you." I am trying to do just that.

During the hour, I am surprised how the atmosphere of the convent, my habit, Father's priest outfit and his focused intention to lead me into spiritual life affect my emotions. I love being with Father Brady. But this meeting is different from the summer. My emotions aren't on high alert.

It's true I am feeling deep fatigue from so little sleep, teaching all day, and returning to the convent to fulfill obligations for religious life. Yet I sense a change in Father Brady. Or maybe it is a change in me. Or the bewilderment of adjusting to convent life. But this fall, romance moves to the back burner and somehow that is a relief.

Outside the Motherhouse's windows on Blossom Road, the autumn lawns strewn with rust-colored maple leaves surrender themselves to the snow that eventually melts into spring grasses. I begin to thaw out, too. Although my feelings for Father come back with the spring buds, I am also adjusting more easily to religious life and am determined to appreciate and live my special calling. On the third Wednesday of each month, Father seems just as determined to help me. I also have become convinced that no special relationship with Father is possible. To keep me focused on my decision to give myself only to God, I rely on the many years, almost a lifetime, of thinking I was called to be here.

At our subsequent meetings, Father encourages me to reflect on ways I can find personal happiness. My self-fulfillment is a sign of personal growth, joy, the presence of God. Discovering what my interests and strengths are and what brings me personal satisfaction are not selfish pursuits but the way I discover how my gifts and talents will serve God's people. Honoring our desires, our inclinations, our preferences is essential if we are to grow in spiritual life. "We should follow our desires for God is in them," Father says. I wish he had not said that!

This view is not what I am hearing in the convent classes where we are taught that giving up what we want will lead us to "holiness." "Be less to be more" is a constant teaching. One day, however, a visiting lecturer, the great Thomas Merton scholar, Father William Shannon, tells the story of how God's grace works. He sounds like Father Brady. The story makes God's love real.

There was a young waitress from a poor and broken family, who worked in a diner where a handsome young lawyer came every day for lunch. The two struck up a friendship and bantered back and forth about their opposing football teams. More than once the young man asked the waitress to go out on a date with him. She refused; he persisted. Finally, she accepted and they started dating regularly, then courting, and eventually married. To others, they seemed to be mismatched, he being so well educated and from such a stable and wealthy family. But he saw the beauty in the waitress and fell in love with her. They grew in their love for each other and brought their love to others.

"That is how God operates," Father Shannon tells our postulant class. "That is what grace is. God's presence, God's endless pursuit. God's seeing us as we are, not our circumstances."

I begin to understand God in this way, and Father Brady's teaching supports it. Convent rules, even prayers, are not the only way to holiness. I begin to question the outdated rules and customs even more.

"We are meant to be happy," Father Brady tells me one Wednesday in late winter. I have never thought that happiness, or what many call joy, is essential to spirituality. I'm Irish. I thought you had to suffer—and the more the better.

Father points out, "Happiness, contentment, feeling peaceful are indications of the Spirit's presence. Suffering is not to be sought after like an imposed asceticism. Learn from any suffering that comes, Evie, be patient with it, and grow in it. It will be an agent to develop more compassion. But don't seek it out. That was what the Church used to teach. We've grown up. Living brings enough suffering if love is our priority. We don't have to seek pain or impose it on ourselves or others. We need to be loving."

Father encourages me to continue to use my journal as an examination of my vocation and a reflection of where I want to change but, more importantly, where I can build on my strengths. At almost every session, he talks about accepting myself, which includes my limitations. He tells me that Nietzsche said that one of the best days in his life was the day he "re-baptized" all his negative qualities as his best qualities. Years later, when I hear the lyrics in Leonard Cohen's "Anthem," they remind me of Nietzsche's words and Father's belief about the gifts of our limitations. *Ring the bells that still can ring/ Forget your perfect offering/There is a crack in everything/That's how the light gets in.*

Father, who by now knows so much about me, seems to accept me with all of my cracks and fissures and seems to see them as not bad but as just a part of who I am. He even enjoys my foibles and missteps and laughs at my many blunders in religious life. I slowly start to laugh at them, too.

From my journal *May 17, 1966:*

> *It is easier and easier to be completely open about myself with Father Brady. Just like last summer. What causes this openness? Will I always have him to put up a mirror to me and not drop it so I would see only the cracks when I tell him who I really am? He amazes me with his acceptance. Where did this guy come from???*

There is a laser focus on me at these meetings. We talk with an objectivity that makes it seem as if we are talking about someone else. I am more and more secure on this journey into myself, which for Father Brady, is God life. Yet even as my spirit deepens, the demanding schedule makes me question my decision to be a woman religious. February 1966 journal:

> *Can I find energy to live the life of a religious? I think Mother might be right about this.*

Yet I am also growing to appreciate why so many Sisters cherish Father Brady's friendship. We are all benefitting from his commitment to the spiritual path with his open and "extravagant" heart and his scholarly study of theology. But I have to admit I am jealous whenever I hear he is at the Motherhouse visiting other Sisters. I am not allowed to say hello to him and wonder what Father and the other Sisters share—and whether he talks and acts the same way with them as he does with me.

My jealousy is exquisitely painful and a sin. I am a sinner because of Father Brady. *How could that be?* I taunt myself. I also wonder how women can stand living in polygamist marriages. *How can I even think about marriage, polygamy or not? I am supposed to be concentrating on being a nun. How can I want religious life if I am feeling these things?* I begin to doubt I am growing spiritually. *Why can't I be simply committed to religious life like everyone else around here?*

In mid-March, I tell Father that I am concerned about not doing a good job with teaching. As I explain my schedule, my throat gets dry and my hands become moist. I can feel a red hue slowly coloring my cheeks.

Father responds in a tone of genuine concern and worry. "This is not good," he says, "Not good for you or anyone. Why didn't you tell me? I sometimes question what happened to your sparkle, but no one says this first year is a picnic. I had no idea that you were going through so much with teaching. I'll let Mother Bride or someone else know, that is, if you don't want to."

"No. I'm okay. I have one semester down and only four months left. I would appreciate if you do not tell anyone. Honestly, there is no one who is free to take any of my classes. Besides, I know the students so well by now. I can get through the semester. It just came out of my mouth. I didn't even mean to tell you."

"I am asking you to tell the community. You could get sick or worse. Please tell someone."

"I'll see," is all I can manage to say.

A few months later, Father Brady as well as others notice my weight loss. Unfortunately, he mentions this to my mother, who now is allowed to visit every month but has not realized how many pounds I have lost. At her next visit, she tells me that I have to see a doctor and that she does not think my constitution is strong enough for religious life. Mother asks me directly to please consider coming home. She assures me my brother will find me another convertible. She knows my temptations.

I agree to the doctor's visit and again explain to her my desire to have complete unity with the Holy Spirit as a Sister so I can dedicate my life to those who have no one to help and love them. I explain that it is the schedule that has caused my weight loss, not my vocation. She believes me. I am also beginning to sense she is proud to have a daughter who is a nun. She is most concerned, nevertheless, about my health.

Even with Father Brady's help, however, I often feel so far away from my dream of being at one with God. I feel inadequate in my apostolate of teaching and lacking in my life as a postulant, especially when I see many others in my band living with a joy I do not experience. All of it brings up lifelong insecurities. I carry all these internal messages with me to the convent, and it may be the reason I somehow believe my postulant year is not successful, though I don't think anyone else notices my struggles.

I understand why. Since early childhood, I'd been an expert in covering up my emotions and generally appearing happy. I give no reason for anyone to think otherwise. Even my friends Carol and Terry, who often tell me I look tired, have no idea of the confusion and insecurity I am experiencing. Of course, there are many times when I am very happy during postulant year because, fortunately, that is my natural disposition and I sometimes do have fun with the postulants. Yet underneath my easy demeanor, I believe I am not making it.

Despite these personal challenges, I eventually gain some weight and feel somewhat better with the doctor's prescription and a special diet. I try to keep my focus on spiritual formation despite the fact that feelings about Father Brady creep in, filling me with guilt and confusion as well as the sweet and painful attraction that I seem subconsciously to nurture. I recognize that I am living in two worlds at the same time, longing for union with both Christ and Father Brady. Yet even in my confusion, I continue to strive to make my dream of becoming a woman religious a reality. Something is moving me forward. I think it is the desire of being the best person possible, to be totally for God, to be the person I was born to be.

1967-1968

THE SECOND SEASON

"Summer passes and one remembers one's exuberance."

Chapter 9

A CANONICAL NOVICE

*"The ordinary activities I find most compatible with contemplation
are walking, baking bread, and doing laundry."*
—*Kathleen Norris*

WHEN MY POSTULANT YEAR ends, I become a Canonical Novice, and
Mother Bride gives me the religious name "Sister Mary Emily." Canonical
Novices spend this year training in the ways of the contemplative life.
Even though we are an "active" order with ministries in the world, prayer
and contemplation will always be the foundation of our lives. I now wear
a "modern" habit, which is similar to a regular long black dress which has
a pleated bodice with a white rolled collar and white veil, a sign of my
Canonical status. When I hear that some hair is allowed to show on the
forehead, I can hardly contain myself with such good luck. My high forehead goes on forever and I would be self-conscious without any bangs. I
may pull a little more hair out than the superiors envisioned but I need
to! Needless to say, my Audrey Hepburn streaks are long gone. Another
good fortune for me is that only two years before, the Canonicals wore
white bridal attire for the ceremony to begin their lives as brides of Christ.
Thank God I do not have to look like a bride when I am not one. Those
Canonicals' hair would then be shorn and they would wear the cumber-
some habits. Things are definitely changing. I only have to don a white

veil that comes to my shoulders; my dress (habit) is actually fashioned for a human body. I am in the makings to be a modern nun.

After the Mass to commence Canonical Year, a reception is held for families and friends. Father Brady concelebrates the Mass and then visits with my family and me. There is a photo of Father, tall and handsome in his black priest suit, and me in my new white veil and habit smiling in the sunshine, our arms and hands close to our sides.

It might seem strange that I continue on this road to be a Sister after the challenges of the first year in the convent and the persistent feelings I have about a man, priest or not. Nothing is keeping me in the convent; almost three quarters of the young women in my band left by the end of the first year. I can also leave, but I want to give myself every chance to explore what, on some level, still seems right for me: a life consecrated to Jesus and people in need. Yet I also have these human emotions that are not acceptable for a celibate life. Fortunately, I have always had the patience to live with unsettled emotions. And I am grateful I do not have to wear those medieval habits!

Growing up, I had only seen Sisters in their traditional habits: long, ankle-length, billowing, black wool skirts with large rosary beads attached to wide leather belts and long, black veils held by a coif and stiff headdress of starched, white material that kept their faces in a kind of circular vise. A large, inflexible, white bib called a "gamp" covered their chests. Their rosary beads often rattled with clicks when the Sisters walked.

When I was little, the Sisters looked so tightly bound in this medieval dress that I wondered how they ever went to the bathroom—or if they had feet. I am grateful Vatican II recommends that women communities update habits to "be suited to circumstances of time and place and to the needs of the ministry." When we are told of the new regulation, I am bursting to shout, "Thank God! Thank God! Thank God!" (Really, I should be thanking those enlightened Vatican II Council participants—and probably the few women attendees, and I do mean "few".)

The recommendations for a new attire cause much tension among the Sisters in my community, as they do in most orders. Imagine elderly Sisters who entered the convent in the time period when wearing floor-length dresses was the fashion of their day; now, forty or fifty years later, they are asked to wear what they consider short skirts. The new habits are hardly short; they are about calf length. There are younger Sisters who say they want to continue to wear the traditional habit as a sign of celibacy and service. Without the habit, how could we witness to the eschatological reality that this life is only a waiting room for eternal life?

The tension is resolved by allowing the Sisters who want to wear the traditional habit to continue to do so and the others, including my band, to wear a simple, black dress-like habit. Who would believe it was designed by Irish fashion icon Sybil Connelly? Today, most Sisters wear lay clothing. Some orders still wear uniform habits, as we have all seen in the photos of Mother Teresa's Missionaries of Charity who are dressed in white habits with bright blue inlaid stripes. Whatever I am wearing, I am a little scared of the life of a Canonical nun.

Canonical Year, a year set apart from "the world," focuses on spiritual development and requires living in silence and in contemplation. Mother Edward is the Mistress of Novices, and although I find her much more *laissez faire* than Sister Norma, we are still subjected to the same medieval disciplines. It seems I am on my knees with my eyes cast down waiting for her to acknowledge me for the simplest requests even more often than I had been as a postulant. "Custody of the eyes," which means keeping my eyes focused only on myself, not even glancing at anyone, becomes second nature.

I throw myself wholeheartedly into this time, participating in classes about religious life, engaging in spiritual practices, and helping with the work needed to run the Motherhouse. The work assignments are known as "charges."

This is the first time I have ever lived with silence. I am sure there are many people who would bet their last dollar that this practice would be impossible for me. Yet I feel at home in the rhythm of comfort and peace that quiet brings. I am also beginning to realize that silence is not so much about the absence of sound as it is about the undisturbed peace in my heart. Except for the shuffling of feet and the whispers of necessary (and sometimes unnecessary) communication, I live swaddled in the silence of the days. Its companionship fills me with contentment.

With the new routines and lifestyle, I sense I am changing. My world as a Canonical novice is focused and dictated by and dedicated to a way of life I seem ready for. Everything is planned and decided for the Canonicals. I now choose not to question the customs or rules. I do not have to make decisions. I do not live with the pressures of teaching. I slowly begin to surrender to God who is shaping me and loving me through my religious community and the spiritual practices.

Within the limitations imposed in this year, my creative energies spontaneously emerge. I find myself writing poems and prayers, which I sometimes decorate using the few available art supplies. It is a form of play, splashing water colors, exploring word arrangements, combining my simple sketches with poems or favorite quotations. This time gives me the opportunity to create in the external world what I am experiencing internally. I discover that when the obligations of "the world" are lifted from us, there is a sense of relief, a freedom to "rest" in life, to be playful! We give ourselves permission to respond by making art or other outlets we cannot explore with the pressures of working in the outside world. I recognize in myself a new, lighter spirit that stays with me. I write as much as possible in my journal. I create handmade books of poetry illustrated with my simple art. I devour books on spirituality. I meditate. I chant. I start to gain weight. I believe Jesus' words, "Look, I make all things new."

One of my most memorable experiences of Canonical Year's spiritual formation, however, is not the formal religious training but my assignment to the bakery. The bakery is a small, narrow room off the large kitchen with four industrial-size ovens and a long, stainless-steel table in the middle of the floor with just enough room for one person to stand on each side. Two single light bulbs dangling from the ceiling and two small windows provide blessed little light or air.

Here presides the captain of the bakery's ship: Sister Phillip, the tiniest adult I have ever met whose wrinkled face looks as if one map is overlaid by another. Or maybe a dried-out apple would describe her beautiful countenance more accurately. Her crooked, swollen, arthritic fingers work fast and carefully as she kneads the dough day in and day out. When the flour rises and scatters through the air, filling the bakery like incense, Sister Philip always says, "The bread of life." In the evening when we attend Exposition of the Eucharist with real incense, the priest pronounces, "This is the bread of life." I do not think God separates the two. Nor do I.

At eighty years old Sister Philip's primary role is as the baker for the 100 to 150 Sisters who live here. But I think her most important contribution is her example of a loving woman religious in the training of young Sisters. I suspect our superiors would never consider Sister Philip a spiritual director. But, for me, she is.

I actually love to bake. But I make some unforgettable mistakes. One day I put baking soda instead of powdered sugar in the brownies. The community said those brownies were the most delicious they'd ever eaten. "Not that too-sweet taste." The next day, with her crinkly smile and twinkly eyes, Sister Philip greets me. "Sister Emily, today, let's use sugar in the brownies. I think the Sisters are just being charitable." She slaps her knee and starts laughing so hard she is bending over, not afraid of showing her human side and definitely not judging me.

It is Sister Philip's acceptance and joy that I treasure. The first time I unconsciously break "the silence" of Canonical Year is when I slip into ordinary conversation as we work side by side rolling out dough for pie crusts. When I apologize, Sister responds, "Say anything you want, Sister Emily. God is in your words." She is the kind of nun I want to emulate.

 Christmas comes and I am feeling much healthier. I am growing into the life of the community and feel content, although I still deal with underlying feelings about Father Brady. However, I realize they are futile and let them go a little more easily. I am beginning to live in one world.

The second semester finds me out of the bakery and into the laundry. I miss Sister Phillip. But I am learning how to wash linens and clothing for almost 150 Sisters five hours a day, five days a week. This assignment teaches me that doing laundry, that doing any kind of domestic work, provides an opportunity to be in the present moment. I focus on sorting the clothes, folding the laundered pieces with care and putting each item in its proper bin to deliver to the Sisters. Completing my tasks without distractions is a way to express externally the order I attend to interiorly. Doing laundry is a way to love. I am finding God where I am.

I am also growing in being myself in solitude and quiet. I have a holy card that I keep on the shelf in the laundry that says, "Be still and know I am your God." Each day I can feel the quiet press down through my head, enter the atoms of my skin and become my body. I experience God without hearing a sound and respond with some poetry in my journal. *Let silence come/ fall through empty space/ of tangled branches/ where birds lift wings/ to welcome quiet/ … Let silence come/ blow its mute horns/ in soundless praise.*

Blessedly, meetings with Father Brady continue throughout Canonical Year. During one appointment, he returns to his favorite theme: "All you have to do to be one with God is to accept yourself just as you are. If you are just you, you will know perfection."

I laugh and say, "Oh, sure."

"It's about being poor in spirit, Ev, I mean Sister Emily."

"'Please, Evie's good, Father. It makes me feel like myself. But I have never understood 'poverty of spirit.'"

"It's a profound concept," he replies with so much love in his eyes that I have to adjust myself in the chair. Intent on giving me every insight, he continues earnestly.

"The Beatitudes are the core of the Gospel. 'Blessed are the poor of Spirit for they shall know God' is about being loving in our limitations. Knowing we can't wait for perfection to love. The way we love in our imperfections is our perfection. Self-acceptance of our weaknesses is the beginning of self-transformation, the furnace making gold out of ore. Our limitations may be the most sacred part of us. Through them we know God. He awaits in our frailty."

Father then quotes Thomas Merton: "'A tree is holy simply by being a tree.' It's easy," he says with a warm smile. "You just have to be yourself."

He asks me if I understand what he is saying. I tell him it reminds me of a poem I had taught the seniors, "Last Night I Was Dreaming" by Antonio Machado. I recite:

> *And the golden bees*
> *were making white combs*
> *and sweet honey*
> *from my old failures.*

"Yes," he responds enthusiastically, "sweet honey from our old failures is exactly what happens. Jesus waits for us in our failures, in our sorrows, our slip-ups. He loves us there; that is how heart-change happens; that is *metanoia*. We must accept others in their 'un-mended' spirits as we ourselves love in our frayed garments. Acceptance may sound like capitulation, but it is the opposite. Acceptance is openness. Not to change others, but so our own hearts can change and be more Godlike." He smiles as I recite the last stanza of the poem to him: *I dreamt/ that it was God I had/ here inside my heart.*

Still smiling, Father nods in agreement. I share with him that I had read that when a Japanese artist makes a mistake with a painting, he or she integrates the mistake into the whole and often realizes what was thought an error becomes an important asset to the work.

"I think you've got it, Sister Emily," Father tells me in his soft, raspy voice. "And I know God is inside your heart. I know He is. I always see His love there."

Sometimes Father even seems impressed with Sister Emily's little steps into the life of the Spirit. I've found the perfect friend to help me discover how my life can reflect God life.

Yet I always wrestle with Father's constant message that I need to accept myself, my incomplete, frayed self, and especially to accept my mistakes which often sear my spirit. Growing up I had heard that I had to improve, correct, change, mature, be better, try harder, etc. Making mistakes was not "acceptable". Even Father's catchy phrases "If you lay an egg, stand back and admire it." or "If you've got a lemon, make lemonade." don't make a difference. Father is just getting too human. Too close to me.

From my journal. 1967:

> *I think that Father's teasing me about not accepting*
> *myself is really a way to flirt, teasing about what only we*

know about me with an intimacy in his voice. I know that tone of voice. How can someone listen so completely to the most intimate thoughts of another and not love? Father's love is pure and spiritual, even if I project something else on it. This relationship is driving me crazy.

Even in my confusion, I continue to experience more joy and satisfaction in religious life as the second year unfolds and, ironically, Father Brady is an important reason why. He continues to come faithfully the third Wednesday of each month. The only thing that changes for me is that he becomes more handsome and even more dedicated to my spiritual development. I wonder what he thinks when my entire being brightens when I see him. I can't hide it. I probably am projecting but sometimes I think he becomes full of light seeing me, too. Maybe all the Sisters respond to him this way. Like he is the sun.

Chapter 10

Teacher and Student

"We cannot hold a torch to light another's path without brightening our own."
—*Ben Sweetland*

THERE ARE SESSIONS WITH Father when, instead of writing in my journal, I want to talk about my life, or I should say, complain. Things like how some Sisters equate polishing the screws on the chapel's kneelers with holiness. Or how other Sisters gossip and how I do, too. There is definitely some whispering in Canonical Year. We are in such a closed community that gossip seems unavoidable, except for the truly holy Sisters, and I have not yet met them. I also share how hurt I am that some Sisters are simply mean.

I tell Father about my using a community car to go to a doctor's appointment. As I was backing out of a space in the parking ramp, I did not see a low concrete pillar behind me and dented the fender. I dreaded kneeling down to report the accident to the superior in charge of cars, and I was shocked and hurt by her response. "How could you be so careless? These cars are expensive and now I have to file an insurance claim. You are irresponsible, Sister Emily."

I was crushed. I also knew I would have to kneel to tell Mother Edward the same news. She simply said, "It seems even our more mature Sisters don't appreciate community property." With a stronger tone, she dismisses me, saying, "Wake up, Sister Emily." I bit my tongue.

Most Sisters show kindness; still there are Sisters I avoid, even if Father says "life itself" is where God is waiting. I certainly do not find God in certain Sisters; at times, I do not find Him in myself either.

Every once in a while during spiritual direction, I talk to Father about how slowly our order is implementing the Vatican Council's suggestions for renewal. Many rules we Sisters live under leave us infantile and dependent and do not promote a positive sense of ourselves. When a culture is narrow and insular, neuroses breed and thrive. Because I try hard during Canonical Year to totally surrender to my formation through the structures and rules, I let my defenses down. My own emotional immaturities surface, and I am losing confidence in doing even small things correctly.

One day I am alone in the large kitchen. A burner on one of the industrial stoves suddenly starts shooting out flames. I am scared that something will catch fire. Having been told that Canonicals are not allowed under any circumstances to go near these stoves, I hesitate for a moment. A professed Sister happens to come in at that moment and shouts at me, "Why aren't you turning off that burner?"

I cannot tell her I am not allowed to be near the stoves. I feel like a fool. I am twenty-five years old and relying on externals and rules more than on myself. I appear to have confidence, but the truth is that an insecurity is taking over the natural confidence I was born with.

As I look back, this natural confidence initially showed when I was in first grade. I am standing with all my classmates for Parents' Day at St. John the Baptist School in Kenmore, New York. It is time for our class to recite our class poem and suddenly everyone becomes too afraid to speak. My classmates look as if they have just seen a ghost. I am worried that we might lose our turn, so, when I hear "Grade One", I step out of the front line and not only belt out the poem loudly and clearly but with inflection and hand gestures. I kind of act out the meaning of the poem like I had been doing in front of a mirror at home. I am in my glory. People clap and yell, "Good job!" Sister Cecilia is none too happy. We'd been told to keep our arms at our sides. My parents couldn't applaud me; they weren't in the audience.

In high school, I was the first female to run for student council president in Hornell. The town became divided. "This is a boy's role," many said. I ran anyway. My friends and I developed an amazing campaign. I lost by two votes. These were actions that came out of a natural self-confidence. Now, however, being so controlled in the narrow world of the Canonical novice, my confidence, natural or not, is wearing away, as well as my initiative, self-reliance, and ordinary judgment.

Things are complicated. On the one hand, our training encourages us to give up our egos, desires, and personal likes and let the rule be our path to God. And Mother Edward's mantras are: "A harder life hones holiness" and "Be less to be more." On the other hand, Father Brady continually encourages me to be myself, discover what personally fulfills me and gives me joy, and certainly not to worry about mistakes.

He says he prays that my days will be "constant moments of grace." With the very peace and joy so evident in him, he declares, "Hold on to grace, Ev. Look for what brings you peace and joy. Run toward it." In addition to these teachings, I write in my journal:

> *Shocking statement from Fr. B. Living a community life is asceticism in itself. No need to look for suffering elsewhere. Imposed suffering is not of God. Discipline for ourselves is healthy, but not imposed suffering. Maybe he really understands how hard community life can sometimes be.*

Like me, Father Brady has complaints about the slowness of renewal in the Rochester Diocese, particularly the lack of implementation of the

Vatican Documents. His prayer, he says, is that the American bishops will wake up to do the very things they approved at the Vatican Council. He believes that if Rochester's Bishop Fulton Sheen were to use his charismatic speaking gifts to educate the Catholic population about the content and wisdom of the Council Documents, the whole country would understand the special graces, the new freedom, and the deeper life in Christ the Second Vatican Council offers.

"The Council does not want to destroy our sacred traditions," Father explains carefully to me. "But now the Church is more collegial, more inclusive and open to each person's gifts. That is why I am committed to the Cursillo. It is bursting with lay leaders for the Church; their formation is anchored in spiritual and communal values. This is the moment when the laity has the chance to grow up, Evie. No longer just as attendees, but to actually be the Church."

Bishop Sheen never becomes the national preacher and teacher of "the good news of Vatican II." Nor does the Church promote any other media person for this important step for understanding renewal. Most people in the pews do not comprehend what *aggiornamento* or renewal means, and those in the hierarchy who are not open to the changes sleep well because they know they are not promoting Vatican II. However, priests like Father Brady, and many other Catholics, work tirelessly to educate people about their new role in the new Church and they experience the blessings that come from renewal.

These days, fifty years after the Council, I run into some people who blame the pedophilia scandal on Vatican II or what is formally known as the Second Vatican Council. One man told me, "Vatican II was so permissive that it allowed this pedophilia thing to happen." When I said there are documented cases of pedophilia and cover up, well before the 1960s, he said that that is a conspiracy theory and that "Vatican II ruined my

Church." These people think the Council is the cause for the lower numbers in the pews and the lack of funding for institutions. They are part of the great divide between Catholics who do not see a need to re-examine the Church's rules and doctrines and those who want to "read the signs of the times," and make the Church more relevant to the needs of all people and closer to the message of the gospels.

This divide is not only in the US but throughout the Catholic world. It saddens me that many Catholics have not yet understood that Pope John XXIII's courageous invitation to participate is a way of saying that *they*, the people in the church, *are the Church*. If our leaders fostered a Vatican II Church, I don't think we would now be a Church of scandal because transparency and lay participation are central to the *Second Vatican Documents*. But back to my story…

All through Canonical Year, Father Brady has been encouraging me to be attuned to the promptings of the Holy Spirit. It occurs to me that I need to understand how I will know whether certain feelings are from the Spirit or from my own self-centered ego. When Father arrives one afternoon in late May, just as my year of contemplative formation is ending, I am anxious to talk about it. He suggests we walk outside for our meeting.

"Can I?" I ask.

"Of course. I will tell the Sister at reception we are taking a walk. A pretty normal thing, don't you think?"

"Don't ask me!" I answer, and we both laugh.

Outside, a wind lifts my white veil slightly from my shoulders. I spontaneously reach out my arms toward the warm sun and say, "Finally!"

"Finally is right," Father agrees with a smile as he too looks up through the waiting world of spring trees. Winter is over.

We head toward some benches, and Father insists that he take the bench facing the sun so that it will not shine in my eyes. When he sits, he slings his left arm over the back of the weathered boards and crosses his legs in his confident, comfortable way. He looks like a movie star. I turn my head toward the slants of sun spilling through the branches and see the buds in their green gloves, ready to open their leaves.

"Look," I say without thinking, "the trees are pregnant with green."

"Yes, new life awaits," responds Father with the same enthusiasm.

I open my journal and write, *Wed. May 23, 1967.*

Leaning toward me, clasping his hands on his knees, Father zeroes in on his role as spiritual director. "Evie, how are you feeling? I mean now that you are completing Canonical Year."

"I think I am afraid to leave the cocoon."

"Of course, but you never leave it because the topography of your soul is within you. Where the Spirit dwells."

"I hope this never changes. I've learned so much. I feel very lucky to spend a whole year devoted to discovering the Spirit and myself. I do have a question, though—but first, I have been wanting to ask you, will spiritual direction continue next year when I am a junior novice?"

"Look at Mother Bride. How many years she has been professed and still seeks spiritual direction. I have a spiritual director, too. We never stop growing, Ev. The Spirit is vast and endless."

"I am just asking if you will still meet with me. I don't want you to give up on me. I am not exactly an easy case."

"You are my easiest case. You are a natural. The only way I would give you up is if there were a lily in my hand."

"Okay, thanks," I whisper and then laugh, saying, "I hope no lilies soon."

"Me, too," he says as he smiles back at me. "What is your question?"

"Well, what I am wondering is, if I feel drawn to do something or to say something, how do I know if the urge is my ego or from God's Spirit?"

"You hear God's voice."

"How?" I ask.

"Sometimes you need that pause. Maybe a minute or more, or sometimes days, weeks, as long as it takes, to discern where this urge is from. Listen in silence. Listening to your interior self will become second nature. Practice. Wait for the Spirit to nudge you. The waiting is the most important thing you can do."

Father becomes quiet for a while. He then suddenly stands up and says, "Need to stretch my legs," and he begins to walk around. He finally stands at the back of his bench, breathes in the freshness of the spring air and leans forward with his hands holding on to the bench's weathered boards. He again waits for a while before he speaks. Slowly he begins to explain that being aware of the Spirit's presence is necessary for making important decisions. He tells me I need to feel grounded and patient and be in touch with the deepest place in myself before making any big choice. I should share with Jesus my dilemma and "rest in God."

He advises me to engage with all the different sides of the quandary, and when there is pain, experience the pain. "Don't run away from what you are feeling. It is a spiritual discipline to feel what we feel and live with it until we can get through it. This is essential." He warns me that even if I think I know the resolution, I should not act right away because that might be my ego taking one more chance to interfere. I will eventually notice a leaning one way more than the other. Peace comes with the right decision.

Father calls his direction "spiritual". Yet so often I find it simply practical for knowing how to live, whether a person explores spirituality or not. He has told me many times that life itself is where God is found; living a spiritual life is living life with openness. For him, there is no separation.

For me, the underlying question about living is: Will I ever be free to give my life entirely to God if I still have very real and persistent feelings of human love for Father Brady? As long as I do not see him, I am able to live in the world of religious life more than in the world of longing for an impossible love. But I also know that my life in the convent, which I honor and respect, protects me from acting on the feelings I have for my spiritual director, feelings that I worry will not go away and, at the same time, worry that they will.

Chapter 11

A Junior Novice

"Do you think the calling is the ending, and not, also, the beginning?"
—*Mary Oliver*

THE FOLLOWING SUMMER OF 1967, with the presentation of the black veil, I begin my third year of formation. I am a junior novice. This year, I will prepare for the "temporary" vows of poverty, chastity and obedience to be taken in July. After five more years, I will take permanent vows.

The vows are my chance to give myself entirely to God. All through the classes about the vows, their significance weighs heavily on me. I am changing in my thoughts about vows and everything else related to a life consecrated to Jesus. Early in my Juniorate Year, I seem to frequently ask myself if the life of a religious woman is what I really want. Whether being a Sister is who I truly am meant to be.

After the exhaustion of Postulant Year and the seclusion of the Canonical Year, I seem to be waking up. I know now the unique circumstances in my first two years are not reliable ways to judge whether I am meant for religious life. This year I am living a regular life in the community as a Junior Novice, and religious life is becoming clearer. Like the professed Sisters, I wear a black veil and am identified more as a member of the community. There is much about religious life that I still am drawn to, and one does not spend a lifetime thinking about something and then give it up easily. Yet my feelings about my vocation are unsettling. I am not sure if this is what I truly want and need. I open myself to find out. I seek silence whenever I can and, as Father Brady told me to do, "feel what I feel."

In September, I am given the same teaching schedule I had as a postulant. But, because I tell Sister Marietta that I am apprehensive about not having enough time to prepare my classes, teaching turns out to be much more manageable. In her role as my Junior Novice Mistress, Sister Marietta immediately sets in place several exemptions from the junior novice schedule and responsibilities. Each school day, I have more free time to work on my classes. And on weekends, I am excused from certain "charges" or duties so that I can correct papers and read. I sleep through the night. I am happy to be more relaxed with students in classes and after school. I am enjoying teaching again.

Today, walking through the front hallway on my way back from the high school—I am now allowed to—I notice Mother Bride coming in from the outside.

"Sister Emily," she calls to me and takes my hands when I go over to her. In her sweet brogue, she asks, "How are you, dear Sister?"

"Fine, Mother. School is going much better. I love my classes and feel very well prepared each day."

Looking quizzically at me, she asks, "But, Sister Emily, is there anything you might need to help your teaching?"

"No, I don't think so," I reply, trying to think what she might mean. Then I remember something and say, "Well, there is one thing, now that you ask, but it's farfetched anyway."

Mother presses me. "What? We must provide our teachers with as many resources as they need to be effective. Tell me what you are thinking."

"Well, one thing that sometimes is difficult is when students compare themes or characters in our literature to themes or characters they are seeing in the movies. Right now the seniors are talking about a movie called *The Graduate* with Dustin Hoffman. I don't really know much about it."

"Exactly. I personally never heard about this movie," Mother says. "But you must go to see *The Graduate*. I will direct Sister Marietta to check the movie schedule and be sure you have a car. This is the kind of updating we should be open to."

I didn't know what to say other than, "Thank you!"

The following Saturday, a bald-headed man looks with skepticism when he sells me a single ticket to *The Graduate*. Maybe he thinks I am just dressed up like a nun. I take a seat near the middle of the theater about halfway down, which is where I always used to like to sit, and take out my pen and notebook. I notice that people coming in and looking for a seat seem to avoid my row.

After the movie starts, and the scene comes on in which Mrs. Robinson seduces the graduate, I begin to worry what other people in the theater are thinking about a nun in her habit sitting among them during the seduction scene. In the dark, I concentrate on writing down some characters in the movie that might parallel some characters in class readings. Suddenly I realize people might think I am taking notes on the seduction scene! I stop writing.

I end up never telling my students that I had seen *The Graduate*. When they mention something from the movie, I simply don't comment. When I happen to see Mother Bride after that excursion to the movies, she often asks, "Any movie you should see?"

I always answer, "None, right now. Thank you, Mother."

Even with this support for me, as the months of autumn go by, I detect an uneasiness growing within me, and I sense an almost daily question of whether or not I can live the rest of my life in a community of women. Institutional living is difficult. Even though there are over a hundred women in the Motherhouse, I often feel lonely, and it seems the more Sisters there are, the lonelier I become. Also, as impossible as it is to have the kind of relationship with Father Brady that I dream about, I now know what it is like to love a man with my whole heart and soul. In the absence of human expressions of this love, I am even lonelier. I begin to wish for other things as well: sleeping in late when I am tired, having a couch on which to put up my feet, walking along a beach, making tea in a tea pot—simple things, silly things. Like the switch on railroad tracks, my mind is going back and forth between what I should do and what I want to do.

At the same time I grow in gratitude to the loving women in the community who work so valiantly to bring Christ's love to the world. What could be a higher calling? It inspires me to share with them at the Eucharist, when we meditate, pray and, especially, chant "The Divine Office." I appreciate lessons on spirituality and discussions about the Church. I feel the affection of my band and admire the professed Sisters' selfless work in soup kitchens, classrooms, hospitals, and inner-city ministry. It all makes me feel that I, too, am in some way a part of caring for the poor and that my heartfelt prayers will support the Sisters' ministries. This strengthens the remnants of my vocation.

But the feeling that I do not belong here surfaces more frequently. I am painfully aware that leaving the community means the possibility of never seeing Father Brady again, or at least not in such a special way. Certainly, we would not have this unique context for getting to know each other. The ache of thinking about not having Father in my life keeps me from sharing the feelings of not belonging with him.

Even with these ongoing doubts about my vocation, I finish the first semester of my Juniorate in good health and with a sense of satisfaction. Still trying to weigh every option about my future, I try to live as Christ-centered a life as possible. I give my all to my students and, as much as I can, to the community. I strive to live the life of a consecrated and dedicated woman religious so that eventually I will be certain of my ultimate decision. Routine gets me through these confusing days; its predictability is a lifeline.

Although I do not know what choice I will make, consistent meditation gives me the opportunity to discover and explore genuine feelings, to hear God's voice, to feel centered. I find meditation to be my most natural prayer form, and I take as many opportunities as possible to hear God's heart beat within my own heart.

One late afternoon on Sunday, January 8, 1968, while I am meditating in the chapel, a professed Sister taps me on my shoulder and whispers that I am to go to Mother Edward's office right away. I feel a shiver of concern. What could be so important that meditation time would be interrupted? Mother Edward is filling in for Sister Marietta, who is away. Because some of the archaic rules have begun to change by this time, I do not have to kneel when I arrive at Mother's office. I hesitantly ask, "You wanted to see me?"

Mother tells me that Father Brady called and asked for an appointment with me that night. An appointment at night is most unusual. With a wry smile, Mother goes on to say that Father did not tell her what he wanted to speak to me about, only that it was very important. "It was so serious," she adds, "that you are to phone him directly."

Filled with concern that something has happened to one of my family members, and especially worried that my sister Lillis might be ill—or worse—in carrying out her Peace Corp assignments in Tanganyika (now called Tanzania), I call Father. He hears the concern in my voice.

"I am so sorry to worry you," he says in an intimate tone, or maybe what I hoped was meant that way. "No, there is nothing wrong in your family. They are fine. But I need to talk to you about something very important. I hope I can see you tonight. Is 7:00 all right?"

"Of course. I have permission from Mother Edward."

My head is spinning. Seeing Father at night. Just seeing Father. I hang up the phone and feel a strong urge to dance.

Chapter 12

AN EVENING VISITOR

"If you keep a green branch in your heart, a singing bird will come."
-*The Documents of the Second Vatican Council*

WHEN I ARRIVE AT the parlor that evening, I notice through the partially open door that Father Brady's ruddy, handsome face is flushed from the cold. Trying to ignore the happiness that suddenly overtakes me, I enter the room. Father stands and says hello with a look in his eyes that seems to suggest that I should know what this is about.

As I close the door behind me, Father walks toward me. He shocks me by gently taking hold of both my hands, which feel so small in his. Without saying a word, he leads me to a chair only three feet away from his. I realize immediately that he has changed the arrangement of the chairs, and my first thought is that we were told never to move furniture, especially in the parlor. I will be in trouble, but when I realize Father is still holding my hands, I forget the chairs. I can feel the warm pressure of his perfect fingers as we sit down across from each other. He slowly releases my hands, and I am suddenly filled with dread. Something is different. Father somehow doesn't seem himself this evening. I wait for the bad news.

He starts talking slowly. "Evie, I have been dealing with a situation for a few years. I just came from a week-long retreat and shared this problem with the retreat master. It has to do with you. The priest advised that I should tell you."

I gulp a breath that seems to catch on a fish hook in my throat and hold it tight so I can feel this pain instead of what he is about to say. He is going to tell me he knows how I feel about him and that it is not acceptable.

"I'll just say it, Ev. I love you. I mean, I am in love with you. I have been for so long. Please. Don't be upset. I have prayed and struggled to get rid ..."

Birds fly across my heart. Emotions so tightly bottled up, spill out. I interrupt, almost bursting. "But I have been in love with you since the first time we met."

Disbelief crosses Father's face. His eyes blink. Then a slow smile as he leans forward and gently takes my hands again and presses them into his lips. Our eyes fix on each other. We are out of human time or space.

Medieval troubadours spoke of love as "... the seizure that comes from the meeting of the eyes." We are seized. Frozen. Yet the unmistakable tenderness in his eyes, a look on the edge of pain, acknowledges what we are given and cannot keep.

And yet, my body is overtaken with complete contentment. I know now: Love exists for both of us. How long we stay this way, I cannot guess.

With a whisper Father breaks the silence. "I can't believe it. That you love me. I secretly hoped that you had feelings for me. Sometimes I felt them but thought I was projecting." He moves up closer in his chair, holds my hands more tightly and says, "I've always been afraid of you. You are everything I would ever have hoped for, if I were not a priest."

"You are everything I have ever hoped for, too. But you *are* a priest." I speak so seriously it feels as if the words come from some place that is not in me. I then say without knowing these words will come out: "This cannot work."

His head drops, his eyes tear and he speaks so softly I have to move closer to hear him. "I never expected this would be reciprocal. I was sure you were going to tell me to grow up, tell me to leave." Looking right at me, he asks, "You love me? Oh, my God, you love me. Please don't be sorry about any of this. You will know how much love for you I have. How unchanging it is. But this not work? What do you mean?"

"You are a priest. I'm supposed to be a Sister."

"But, Evie, this can work! Listen to me. When I asked the retreat master how I could love a woman and be a priest, he told me God does not put love in boxes. Humans do and that includes the Church. I told him about the Third Way and he had heard some seminarians talk about it, but he didn't know anyone who experienced it. Then he said that, if I were the priest he thought I was, I should consider the Third Way and share all of this with you. He thought the Third Way could be a possibility for me—for us. He told me love is God's presence and that cannot be ignored. I think so, too."

"The Third Way?" I ask, sounding confused.

"There are some priests and brothers and nuns and probably lay people who are sharing their deep human love and soul friendship with each other in a special way. The Third Way lets those consecrated to Christ experience human love for each other as celibates. They are faithful to their vows of chastity and support each other in their ministries through a very special friendship, a special love."

I listen and become very quiet. Maybe the Third Way is possible. Maybe we do have a chance. After all, we are imbued with the idealism of the 1960s, the Age of Aquarius, the Decade of Change. Even with race riots and the war in Vietnam breaking our hearts, dreams of re-making the world well up in all corners of the religious and secular worlds. Pope John XXIII shepherded the people of God as a grandfather and President John Kennedy inspired us with brilliant and charismatic ideals. We have leaders who witness to love.

Song lyrics of the '60s are often in my head: "There's a place for us, somewhere a place for us ..." "To dream the impossible dream" "... climb every mountain, ford every stream, follow every byway 'till you find your dream." Secular folk songs tell us, "The order is fading ... The times they are a' changin." And the new folk masses replace formal organ music and Latin hymns with strumming guitars proclaiming messages in English that are relevant to our lives: "They will know we are Christians by our love."

Father and I are fully alive. Vatican II Christians. Flower children dressed in black. A new world is waiting for us. We will live out the Third Way. As we share our hopes and dreams for our vocations in the new Vatican II Church, time passes in the parlor without notice. We feel giddy with the wonder of being in love. We will be like St. Francis and St. Clare, celibates but supportive of each other's ministries. Or the new Abelard and Heloise, he the scholar and I his student.

We talk with excitement about how the Third Way will allow us to pursue our love and friendship and remain committed to our religious vocations. Jesus will see us through. For us, anything is possible. As pioneers of the Third Way, we will give up the intimacy, the pleasures, the security of a married couple in order to devote ourselves to the people we will serve by bringing hope and love to them. After all, God has called us first to Himself. I already am changing my mind about leaving the convent.

During our time together, we have both unconsciously edged up closer to each other in our chairs. Our knees are slightly touching. We are close enough to kiss. I breathe in his fragrance. But it is getting late.

Quietly, Father says, "Come with me."

He escorts me out of the parlor across the marble entrance hall to the chapel. As we start to sit in the back pew, we hear a rustling outside the door. Father quickly takes my hand and leads me to the confessional—the priest's side. We are standing so close together inside this small space that Father leans over, put his arm around me, and gently, lovingly kisses me. The most perfect kiss in the history of kisses.

I am shocked. Thrilled. Father Brady has kissed my lips, the most tender and beautiful experience of my life. But we again hear sounds, now in the chapel. When I am nervous, I sometimes start to laugh. As hard as I try to stop it, laughter slips from my lips. That makes Father laugh. We attempt to muffle our voices by putting our hands over each other's mouth. Then we hear the sound of the doorknob turning on the confessional door. A Sister I have never seen before stands in the doorway. She looks at us standing in the dark with our arms around each other and, without a word, quickly shuts the door. We hear the chapel door close.

I feel so scared I can't catch my breath. I tell Father he has to leave right away. He, on the other hand, does not seem at all disturbed by our visitor to the confessional. At this point we are standing in the back of the chapel. He says he needs to tell me something important and asks me to stay just another minute. As worried as I am that the Sister or someone else will come in, Father's confidence emboldens me. I stay.

That's when Father drops a bombshell. He says he wants to tell me two things. The first one is easy: "Please call me Hugh." He then explains that he has thought a lot about the second request and says that Mother Bride will have to know about us. Because they have a very close relationship, he cannot go behind her back or deceive her about someone in her community. I do not understand.

Then Hugh looks right at me. "Evie, Mother Bride and I trust each other, but you are under her jurisdiction. I am not. Please make an appointment to talk to her. She needs to know about our love. I hope she will give us her blessing. Explain the Third Way and, when I see her, I will talk more about it."

In a breathy, stage-whisper voice, I say with certainty, "Give us her blessing? Are you kidding? And why me? I'm a lowly novice. I can't tell her about us. She's the Mother General. What would that mean about my vocation? I take vows in a few months."

"She's one of the most loving and wise women I know. She's open to life and the Spirit. Don't be afraid. Tell her about the Third Way."

"But she is my Major Superior! I have to go through my Mistress of Novices to make an appointment with her. What will I tell Sister Marietta?"

"I know Marietta. She won't ask a thing. Please do this for me."

I am still spinning from the kiss and trying to absorb our newly proclaimed love for each other. I can hardly think about sharing this with the Mother General! I tell Hugh I cannot do it. He asks me to think about it. Astonishingly, we kiss again. Right in the chapel. As incongruous as the setting is, his second kiss is deeper and I never want to leave the chapel—for the wrong reason!

But Hugh lets go of the embrace and opens the chapel door for me. He kisses me quickly on the cheek and starts to walk across the marble hallway toward the heavy oak front doors. He puts on his hat and coat and turns toward me for a moment. He places his right hand on his heart. I do the same.

He calls in a low voice across the marble, "Good-night, my Love," and opens the door to go out into the howling cold night.

Holding the words "My Love" in my heart, and with the greatest happiness I have ever known, I make my way slowly—I float—through the dark halls back to my cell. I feel giddy. "Father Brady loves me. Father Brady loves me!" I hug the words to myself. My body suddenly fills with the whole universe, galaxies of moons, planets and suns, all swirling both inside and outside of me. I am my own firmament of light.

As I lie in bed that night, however, many conflicting emotions rush through my body, and I have to calm myself down. I start to pray, to thank God, to offer all that happened to His mercy and to beg Him to keep me out of trouble. I worry about what the Sister who opened the door to the confessional will say and to whom she will say it. Her reporting on us could ruin everything, including my vocation, as tenuous as it is. I can hardly sleep with the competing feelings of knowing Hugh's love for me and at the same time fearing that, because of our indiscretion in the chapel, I will be asked to leave the community. Suddenly my vocation seems so precious. I do not want to lose what I have so sincerely tried to live. I toss and turn all night.

The next morning, Mother Edward stops me. Sounding suspicious, she says, "Sister Emily, I hope your meeting with Father was satisfactory."

Worried sick that the Sister who had found us in the confessional has already said something to her and that this is just leading up to it, I say, "Oh, yes, Mother, it was."

"Is there a particular problem?" Mother asks.

"Father has a situation," I lie, "which I was able to help him with." Then again, maybe it isn't a lie. Father definitely has a situation.

"Oh, so our novices are now advising their spiritual directors," she responds in a sarcastic tone as she walks away.

I do not care what her tone is because she has not brought up the confessional! I eventually find out the name of the Sister who'd opened the confessional door and where she is stationed. She never says anything. I fall in love with her, too.

Two days later a letter arrives from Hugh. He'd written it after returning to his sister's house in Rochester that Sunday night. It is dated January 8, 1968: 10 PM. It starts out almost as a prayer:

> *"What shall I render to the Lord for all he has given to
> me?   You don't know what happiness you have given me
> already by loving me. ... I just didn't see myself as the
> object of all of this. To discover that you, with all that
> you are, love me is so much like discovering that God
> loves me, as I once discovered. I said I was not afraid,
> but now I am ... (yet) I am absolutely convinced this is
> from God ... a gift not looked for. This also will change
> my life. I am certain of it. Suddenly my love for you has
> burst forth. I desire with all my heart to return it—to
> jump off a cliff for you."*

Then he shares the pain he feels knowing we cannot be together. *"My God how this hurts."*

Later in the four-page, double-sided neatly written letter, he alludes to the Third Way.

> *"I believe He (God) knows what He is doing. I thank him
> for the deep joy he is allowing me.... Let us both give
> ourselves and our love in his care and in his service."*

The romantic tone changes toward the end of his epistle. He gives me his phone number and writes, *"Call me."*

Call him? Does the man not remember I am a novice? But I am thrilled that the emotions he expressed Sunday night are now in writing where I can return to them and let them slowly seep into me and become a part of me. Something comes to me the day his letter arrives, something confirming that our way of loving is possible. We are predestined to love through the Third Way, the priest and the virgin. A new marriage.

I do not know that Father's tiny, neat script will come to me on five to eight double-sided pages every week from then on. Love letters in the convent.

Chapter 13

SNOW TALK

"I dreamed the snow was you ..."
—*Reginald Shepard*

UNEXPECTEDLY, HUGH SHOWS UP three days later. It is after school and I am taking a walk outside around the Motherhouse. When he asks for me, Sister Marietta tells him where he can find me.

Fingering the beads as I say the Rosary—with my own meditation method—I am distracted when I hear a familiar voice calling, "Sister Emily, Sister Emily." My heart quickens as I turn around.

"Oh, my gosh," I say right out loud. Although my legs feel heavy, and I seem to be moving through quicksand, I start walking toward Hugh as fast as I can. When I finally reach him, I ask, "Are you here?"

He looks down at himself, smiles, and replies, "Last time I checked!"

We both laugh. "I mean, what are you doing?"

"I've come to take a walk with the prettiest girl in the world."

"Oh, brother. That will be the day," I respond seriously.

"Today's the day, Ev. You are so beautiful." The way he says it, it actually feels true. "Let's walk over to Ellison Park," he suggests.

"I don't think I can go to the park, but I will ask permission," I awkwardly respond.

"I'm sure it will be okay."

"I don't think so."

"Don't worry. I've got connections," he jokes, trying to reassure me.

"Well, I don't!"

"Sister Marietta won't mind, Ev," he insists. "She knows I am with you."

"Okay. But if I get in trouble, I am blaming it on Father Brady."

Laughing again, he retorts, "Good idea."

The day is one of those rare times in winter when it is comfortable, even enjoyable, to be outside. The white winter sky has turned blue and layer upon layer of lace-like snowflakes anoint our heads as they spread an ermine coat across the ground. We walk in a snow globe.

Ellison Park is deserted. Hugh takes my hand as we walk across the snow-covered ground toward a stand of evergreens. Like incense rising through the cathedral of branches, the scent of pine is everywhere.

Finally, I break the silence that has engulfed us and ask Hugh how he is doing with all of this. He tells me that he is realizing how big our situation is, and he frankly admits he doesn't know if he can handle it. He says he is afraid of his strong feelings for me. But, at the same time, he says he is so happy and so full of love that nothing else seems to matter.

"It is like a force greater than me is moving through me … moving through us," he explains.

"No matter how life unfolds, whether this is bigger than us or not, I will always love you," I tell him. "I cannot possibly do anything else." The lacy snowflakes break on my nose and cheeks as I continue. "I am convinced that we can stay true to our vocations, serve God—and love each other. We will be the sacrament of the Third Way."

We stop walking for a moment and look up at a majestic blue spruce standing in front of us. As a low wind swishes the tree's needled skirt across the ground, Hugh turns toward me and stares at my face for so long and with such intensity, it feels like he is memorizing me. We silently gaze at each other for a long time. Then putting his arms around me, he draws me closer and kisses me. Kisses me as if he means it. He apologizes, asks me if I am offended. I say I am not, pull him to me and kiss him back with all the love I hold. In amazement, feeling the branches of the evergreen embracing us, we embrace not only each other but a world beyond ourselves. I will never forget this moment.

Shaking his head as he struggles to speak, Hugh releases my arms and talks so quietly I have to strain to hear him. "I don't understand, Ev. I have preached about love, tried to be a loving person, supported others in their love. Love is our purpose. What Jesus came to teach us. But our love, yours and mine, it makes no sense. As true as I know it is, I can explain love no longer."

"Love is," I say gently.

With a slight smile, nodding his head up and down, he responds, "Yes. Love is. I will not look for an explanation."

As we slowly walk back toward the path, dusting up the snow with our feet, we desperately want to hold each other's hand but are now out of the trees where others could see us.

"Ev, it's so amazing. I feel you've always been inside of me. Like I've always known you. Nothing is new and everything is. Honestly, I feel you in my breath."

Years later I read the poet Rumi who says, "Lovers don't find each other. They're in each other all along." It was what Hugh was saying to me in his own poetic way that snowy day: "You are in me and I didn't even know it."

"When did you know?" I ask. "I mean about being in love with me."

He laughs. "I knew I loved you when you said you were most worried about not dancing when you entered the convent. I have counseled young women who aspired to be Sisters for many years. That was a first. I thought it was great," he says turning toward me with a smile. "But when did I know I had fallen in love with you? It was a long, slow fall. The more I knew you, the more I couldn't stop thinking of you. The more I was thinking of you, the more I wanted to be with you. Sometimes our Wednesday meetings seemed to never come. I tried to ignore these feelings. Didn't work. During some of our sessions I thought I would burst."

"You should win an academy award," I retort. "A master at hiding your feelings."

"It started in your postulant year and got harder and harder. I desired you, body and soul. But I knew I could only relate to your beautiful soul. I zeroed in on you, taught you everything I could, tried to share my own experience, anything that would help you grow. I gave my whole soul life to you, Ev. I could give you nothing else."

"Is that why you are so intense about teaching me about the spiritual life?" I ask. "Hardly ever asking about anything personal?"

"If I deviated, if I asked you what you were personally feeling, I didn't think I could trust myself not to cross the line. Like we're doing now. Otherwise, I would have only wanted to dwell on you, just you."

"If you hadn't been so disciplined, I couldn't have handled it, either," I respond softly.

"The one day I almost slipped was last spring when we went for a walk. Do you remember? At the end of your Canonical Year when we went outside and were so happy that spring had finally come? I was crazy in love with you, Ev. If I didn't focus on spiritual direction, I would have eaten you up! I remember I just had to get up and walk around to control my feelings. It was all so strange and confusing. And wonderful. When I drove away from the Motherhouse that day, I felt like weeping. I knew I was tethered to my vows ... And in some miraculous way, to you."

"One thing I really do want to know, Hugh," I say with all sincerity. "Do we flirt?"

He looks down and takes time before he answers. "Yes. How could we not? I couldn't help myself."

I smile. "Me neither. The devil made you do it!"

Hugh laughs. "No, you made me do it!"

My body becomes even more attracted to Hugh. I wait for what feels like a long time to settle my strong feelings before I speak of something I had been thinking about since Sunday night.

"Hugh, I am trying to grapple with everything, too." Pausing, I stop walking and look directly at him. "The question I keep asking is, why me? There are so many who are more accomplished, more beautiful, more spiritual, more pure and good. You know everything about me. I've told you every fault and sin, my past and present. You can change your mind. I would understand more than anyone."

Hugh moves closer to me and forgets where we are. He takes my hands. "Oh, Evie, Evie, Evie, I love you. I don't care about any shortcomings. I have enough to cope with in my own life. It's you. Just you. Your heart. The sunlight you bring when you walk into a room. All I know is my love for God is my love for you. My love for you is my love for God. Love bears no separation. I have never met anyone who could be more perfect for me. You are the only person I have ever truly desired or ever will."

"I hear your words, my darling. But I am afraid I will wake up. I am afraid it will stop snowing." I say with a seriousness that surprises me.

By now, the silent, sinking sun is throwing silhouettes of tree trunks and branches across the breast of the white snow. It is time to go. As we turn onto Blossom Road toward the Motherhouse, we know our visit to the park has deepened our feelings. Walking more quickly now, Hugh becomes lost in thought, and I wonder what he is thinking about.

"A penny for your thoughts," I whisper near his ear.

He turns his head toward me and says that he is thinking about Mother Bride. He asks me again if I will please consider talking to her about what is happening between us. He holds a fierce loyalty and love for her and does not want to keep such a major happening from her. He is convinced Mother Bride has to be told. He tells me that we both would be deceiving her if we did not tell her about us.

"How we feel about each other won't change. We know this. We don't want her to find out later. Like I said Sunday, you are under her jurisdiction. Please tell her, Ev. I promise she will be loving toward you."

With great reluctance, I agree to make an appointment with Mother Bride. And, imagining how a Mother General might very well respond to a novice who is in love with her spiritual director, I figure I might as well pack up my trunk. But I am bewitched by Hugh and know I will do it.

When I return to the convent, my cheeks red and my spirit full of so much happiness, I am exploding to shout, "I am in love." Of course, I cannot. The Sisters I live with would be scandalized, even my close friends, just as I would have been if it were someone else. I have such deep respect for these Sisters, who live their vows with faithfulness. I would never offend them. I keep the time of magical snow to myself.

That evening I pray mightily that Father Brady and I will have the courage to live the Third Way. More courage than we'd had in the afternoon. I wrestle with two strong feelings: the wonder of the snow and the guilt about celibacy. Yet I cannot stop thinking of the gift of the blue spruce. I quickly write a haiku for her.

A mother blue spruce

felt our love rise through her trunk.

Memorykeeper.

The next morning, when I make an appointment with Mother Bride, she sends word that she will see me at 3:30 in her office. When I read the note, my body tenses with shivers and my warm, enthusiastic feelings for Father Brady begin to dwindle. Throughout the day, I keep breathing shallowly. My head holds a long stabbing pain, and I am having a hard time concentrating on classes. I am plain scared. Fortunately, seventeen-year-old girls need attention and school keeps me distracted to get through the day. Yet 3:30 looms large. This meeting will determine the rest of my life.

Mother Bride is the beloved leader and anchor of the Rochester Sisters of Mercy. Her 4'11" height belies the dynamic spirit within this powerhouse of a woman. She'd come to the United Sates from Ireland over thirty years before and, after working in the business world, decided to enter the Sisters of Mercy. Although happy in her many years of ministry, Mother reluctantly accepted the leadership of the community, first as Mistress of Novices and then as Mother General.

During this time of renewal of religious life, she is a recognized leader not only within our congregation but also throughout the diocese. We all feel our community is capable of great possibilities under the leadership of our beloved champion. She is disciplined and organized, but also has those soft, irresistible Irish eyes that pour out love and acceptance on everyone.

When I arrive at her office, Mother greets me warmly and, with the hint of a brogue, asks me to sit down. She points to a chair and sits across from me. I am glad I do not have to kneel. I do not know how to start.

Gently she asks, "Are you unhappy, Sister Emily?"

I respond, "Just the opposite. I am very happy, Mother. But my happiness is the problem I have come to talk about. My happiness comes not only from offering my life to Christ…" My throat tightens; I can't speak. Tears spring from my eyes and I am afraid I won't be able to breathe.

Mother touches my knee and gets up to bring me some Kleenex and water. We wait. Hesitantly, trying to get the words out, I continue in clipped phrases. "My happiness. I am in love. With Father Brady. He has fallen… in love… with me. I am very sorry. To tell you of all people. I do not know how." I stop for a moment. "How to explain it. Father insisted I tell you. He could never…" Painful tears start spilling down my cheeks. "Deceive you." I sob between short, shallow breaths. Gaining some composure, I blurt out, "We still desire to be consecrated. I mean to Jesus." I grab more Kleenex to blot my face.

With her hands folded on her lap, Mother nods her head and then looks down, almost as if she were praying, but she does not respond. I sit dazed, gulping in short painful breaths as I stare at a spot on the worn beige carpet. I am wondering if she is thinking how she will ask me to leave the Order. My hands are nervously pulling apart the Kleenex on my lap; I wish I hadn't come. It is an eternity of waiting.

Finally, Mother looks at me and says, in the kindest of voices, "Sister, there is no question in my mind. If Father Brady loves you, this love comes from God. If Father were in love with me, I would follow that love. Our God is love. I believe yours and Father's love for each other is of God."

Mother's response stuns me. I think I am not hearing correctly. Tears fall down my cheeks. Again, she gives me time and suggests I take some water. She asks me how long we have felt this way.

"I knew I was in love with Father the summer before I entered. Probably the first time I met him. I have been in turmoil since… you know, about my vocation." In a low, cracked voice, I continue, "I am not exactly sure when Father knew. But last week he told me he was in love with me, too."

I struggle to find the right words. "Knowing that Father feels the same way has made my feelings come back so strongly. I mean about him. I will probably get sick again. I believe my feelings for Father contributed to my getting sick during postulant year. I know this isn't right, Mother."

"Oh, Sister, you have suffered. I never realized how much you were going through. You always seem so cheerful and outgoing. I thought everything was fine with you. But love sickness is a real sickness, my dear, and didn't we go through it with my friend Mary in Ireland. She was in love with someone who chose another. Mary came down with a fever and could not get out of bed. The body is the soul's megaphone, Sister Emily.

"You mustn't feel guilty. These are human emotions and human emotions are from God. How He made us. Father is a beautiful priest. And he will remain so and you will be an instrument of his dedication. You and Father will live out your vocations and must follow this love. This is God's will; I truly believe it is. Pray to Our Lady to guide you. I will, too."

"Mother, there is another thing. Father told me about something called the Third Way. It might have come out of the Council. How two consecrated people could have a special love for each other and how their love would strengthen them in their missions to serve God's people even as celibates."

"Yes, the Third Way." Laughing, Mother says, "Since Vatican II, there are labels for everything. Exactly what St. Francis and St. Clare followed without knowing its name! I am sure many Sisters and priests have become soul friends and bring each other great strength and joy as they live out their beautiful vow of virginity. We call it *"anam cara"* in Ireland. Soul friends. This love is possible, Sister. The Spirit is greater than all of us, and He blows where He will."

I say a weak "Thank you," as tears again roll down my parched cheeks. I am still gulping my breaths.

Then, almost abruptly, Mother Bride's tone changes. "But, Sister, I must warn you. You are young and pretty. And Father is a man of great feeling. You both must be strong and keep dedicated to your beautiful vocations. The Spirit will help you overcome the desires of the flesh. Yours must be a celibate love. Celibacy is the sign of our consecration to God alone. I completely encourage you and Father to love each other and follow this friendship from God. But beware of temptation. You must be dedicated to the sacredness of your virginity and Father's. Father Brady is a gift to our community and, I believe, to the Church. Your love will support his priesthood and his love will support your vocation. But, always be on guard. 'The spirit is willing but the flesh is weak.' You must pray to be faithful to your vows."

"Oh, Mother, I wish this were not another thing you have to worry about."

"Worry about?"

"Our being in love," I say shyly.

"My dear, love does not keep me up at night. The lack of love does."

I smile at her.

"You may come to my office to use my phone to call Father whenever you need to. Or if you ever want to talk to me. You must not be afraid of love, Sister. Love is God's presence."

Mother Bride then rises and puts her hands on my head, kisses the top of my veil and says, "I have faith in you, Sister Emily. I believe in Father Brady. I am honored you shared God's gift with me. Now, my dear, go or you will be late for chapel."

1968-1969

THE THIRD SEASON

Autumn passes and one remembers one's reverence.

Chapter 14

Living in Mystery

"You shall lovingly accept the humanity entrusted to you!
You shall be obedient to your destiny."
—Johannes Metz

As I leave Mother Bride's office, I feel a million pieces of a puzzle
fall into place. Did I just hear the Mother General of my order tell me
to embrace the gift of human love given to Hugh and me? Would it be
possible for our love to bloom within the confines of religious life and the
strictures of the priesthood?

Believing that the Third Way is possible, I envision Hugh and me on
fire for Christ through our devotion to God's people and yet dependent
upon the love that I am sure will grow between us. I see us in our old age,
best friends, secretly in love over all those years. I feel ten feet tall. My life
cannot be better. There is a way to follow human love and Christ's love.
There is a way to love Hugh. I am sure now that Hugh's love has come
from God. I also now know that this is a confirmation of my vocation and
this knowledge assuages my doubts about leaving the convent.

Considering that I am still a novice, I do not expect to have any more
contact with Mother Bride. But two days later, as I kneel in the pew at
morning Mass, something startling happens. Mother Bride is always
the first to go up the aisle for Communion. That morning, as Mother is

passing, she gives a note to the novice at the end of my pew. It says, "For Sister Mary Emily." My poor friend is so unnerved, she drops it, picks it up, and hands the folded piece of paper down to me through four or five other novices, who also look surprised. Right there in the chapel I open the note that says:

> *Let us love one another, for love comes from God. Everyone who loves has been born of God and knows God. Whoever does not love does not know God, because God is love.*

I quickly put the note in my pocket and bite my lower lip. I can also feel a warmth come over my body—and a redness come up through my neck and into my face. After Mass, when my friends inquire why Mother Bride, whom we rarely see, gave me the note. I tell them that it is just a message. "Nothing serious," I say assuringly.

In a tone of anger, Sister Elaine asks me directly, "If you are leaving, Emily, you better tell us now. We can't take any more 'MIAs.'"

"I am not leaving. And if I ever do, I promise to tell you and you better tell me if you ever want to leave, too. This note is just about something that came up."

They seem to buy it and start complaining about friends, postulants or novices who had left our community without saying goodbye. This is the custom of the community, not to let anyone say ahead of time that they will be leaving. We had no chance to get used to the idea that one of our friends would not be with us. We were given no explanation. They just went missing. The unexpected loss of these friends leaves big holes in our hearts. Like unfinished business. It is a custom that has to change.

This is the first of several notes Mother sends to me. Every once in a while, she passes a note at Communion time. Or, in those first few months of second semester, I discover an envelope addressed in her

handwriting waiting on my classroom desk. All the notes are signed
"SMB—Sister Mary Bride—and each is a passage about God and love.
Among them:

> ~ *I give you a new commandment, that you love one*
> *another. Just as I have loved you, you also must love one*
> *another.*

> ~ *Love one another as I have loved you.*

> ~ *No love, no friendship, can ever cross the path of our*
> *destiny without leaving some mark upon it forever.*

> ~ *All things work together for those who love God.*

> ~ *Love is patient and kind. Love is not jealous or boastful*
> *or proud or rude. It does not demand its own way. It is not*
> *irritable, and it keeps no record of being wronged. It does*
> *not rejoice about injustice but rejoices whenever the truth*
> *wins out. Love never gives up, never loses faith, is always*
> *hopeful, and endures through every circumstance.*

Between Mother Bride's messages and the letters from Hugh, I am
strengthened in our love and our desire to grow in the Third Way. Yet I
cannot forget the time in the park. I write about it to Hugh to tell him that
I want to believe we can live our lives in the Third Way, but that we both
have to commit ourselves to it. I want to try. Hugh writes back that he
does, too. He believes that is what God desires. I so want to believe it will
be possible. He writes:

> *It does seem illogical, humanly speaking, not to be*
> *together frequently when you do so much for me and I*
> *apparently do so much for you. But our love is not mere-*
> *ly human. Christ is its source, and so he will give the*
> *increase without our mere human efforts to deepen it.*
> *If our love is good and from God, and I am a celibate,*
> *then the honest expression of such love must be good*
> *and desirous on God's part. I see no compromise with*
> *celibacy, but I see much suffering, much self-denial, but*
> *no frustration.*

He ends with a prayer:

> *Lord, ... You know our hearts and our love for you and*
> *each other. ... You know much better than we how im-*
> *portant self-fulfillment is for radiating your love through*
> *our lives out to the world waiting to learn love. ...*

I pray constantly to live up to these ideals. I want to try the Third Way
with all my heart. Knowing my desires, however, I am not as optimistic
as Hugh.

Meanwhile, in Hornell, my sister Jan, with her adorable baby Erica, is
preparing to leave for Germany to meet her husband Joe, who is stationed
there. Without telling me of his plans, Hugh visits her, arriving at our
house unannounced to find my two aunts and an uncle visiting from Buffalo still in their bathrobes. They are very embarrassed that a priest sees
them dressed this way. Scurrying around all aflutter, as Jan told me later,
they fluff up all the pillows in the living room "about ten times" so that he
could sit wherever he would like. They are thrilled that a priest is visiting
and talk long afterwards about a priest seeing them in their pajamas, but
they say Father Brady is "like an old shoe" who doesn't seem to mind at
all.

Somehow Hugh finds an opportunity to talk alone with Jan that morning. He had decided to tell her about us, and she listens with the compassion only Jan has. He explains that we both plan to stay in religious life. Though she does not discourage him, she says she does not understand how we can live the Third Way. Never one to mince words, Jan says, "Personally, I don't think it is possible."

She wishes us all the love she has and tells Father she hopes he will keep her updated. She also tells him how upset our mother would be if she ever knew. "Believe me, she will not believe in the third, fourth, or fifth way. To tell you the truth, I am having a hard time believing the Third Way will work, too."

A few days later, after finding an envelope from Hugh with a gift for a new suitcase she'd planned to buy, Jan leaves for Germany. She is grateful that Father Brady told her what is going on. Now another sister knows about us. It occurs to me that Lillis had never said a word to anyone about what I'd told her on our ride into the hills the summer before I entered the convent. My sisters and I are not exactly paragons about keeping secrets from each other. Now two sisters keeping my secret? This is historic.

Around the middle of February, Hugh meets with Mother Bride. She tells him that she feels our love is in God's plan to strengthen our vocations and that we should be filled with both gratitude and vigilance. Temptation is the devil's work, she warns him, but true love comes from God and will overcome all obstacles. She tells him we must be fully committed to the lives we've been called to.

"Love is grace," she says, "a gift God freely gives. We cannot do anything but accept God's gift in humility and obedience. You and Sister Emily have been given this grace." She also tells Hugh that a mark of genuine love is the communion we experience with the beloved.

I don't know how it ended up with my other letters, but I discovered a letter from Hugh to Mother Bride dated February 22, 1968. I think she must have given it to me. He writes:

> *You are so right about constant communion. Sister Emily is with me in my prayers, at the Eucharist, in a crowd, while shopping, at a restaurant, while driving, in the people I meet… she is at each baptism of infants, each instruction of engaged couples. I see her in the family life of my sisters and in the families of parishioners.* He ends by saying to his friend, *Thank you for just being there. I am grateful for your sharing your joy for us.*

Receiving weekly letters from Hugh as I do, I worry about what Sister Marietta is thinking. When she was put in charge of the third-year novices, the first thing I noticed was her exquisitely beautiful face with high cheek bones, a patrician nose and soft brown eyes that always seemed to carry a secret sorrow in them. The second thing I realized was that, although she is deeply caring and sensitive, Sister Marietta is a steely woman committed to religious life.

Hugh had met Sister Marietta several times and had an instinctive trust in her. One day when he was visiting the Motherhouse, she asked him to stop by sometime to talk. Hugh knew why she wanted to talk to him but did not ask me to intervene. The meeting did not go well. Hugh was forthright. So was Sister Marietta. She did not think the Third Way was a good idea but said that, as long as Mother Bride sanctioned our relationship, she would not interfere. She told him flat out that she did not approve. "How can Sister Emily take vows? This would not be what I would have done if I were in Mother Bride's position."

After her meeting with Hugh, Sister Marietta calls me into her office.

"Emily, I know what is going on with you and Father Brady." I do not respond. "I must admit I was shocked. I knew the number of letters you were receiving. But I assumed you had a spiritual or family problem. I would never have known about this if Father hadn't talked to me. Father Brady, of all people. What can you tell me?"

"We are in love," I say, looking her in the eye. "I don't know what else to say, except we want to stay in religious life and give ourselves as fully to our apostolates as possible."

"Yes, Father told me about the Third Way. It won't work, Emily. It's against nature. We celibates must protect ourselves from the very real possibilities of not following our vows. We can't live in temptation's path."

"But we did not look for this. It happened," I say, trying to justify myself.

"I know, but it's not too late. You can turn in a new direction that will protect your vows."

"What do you mean?"

"End this, Sister. End it. It is dangerous."

"Mother Bride has more or less blessed us," I whisper.

"I will honor Mother's direction on this. However, I disagree whole-heartedly and I will tell her. Emily, I am responsible for you taking your first vows. I am completely against fostering your relationship with Father Brady. Do you have anything else to say?"

"Only that I am sorry this hurts you. You have always been so good to me."

"I am not the one who will be hurt. You and Father are the ones."

"Thank you, Sister," I say with sincerity. A line of pain crosses the crown of my head. I had grown to love Sister Marietta.

As I am opening her office door to leave, Sister calls to me. With a gentle and loving voice, she pleads, "End it, Sister Emily. You can. I will help you."

"God is love, Sister Marietta. I believe our love comes from God."

In a defeatist tone, Sister responds, "That is exactly what Father Brady said to me. I am sorry you are both so naive."

"Thank you, Sister," I say as I leave.

After her appointment with Hugh and her talk with me, Sister Marietta's attitude toward me changes. I had been so grateful for how she treated the novices as adults and with respect. She was an excellent person for the transitions needed with Vatican II, and, because of her, my teaching life was manageable and enjoyable. We had felt comfortable around each other and she would even talk to me in confidence about some issues we novices were dealing with.

Now she is detached from me, polite and kind, but never seeks me out to ask how things are going or just to socialize. I feel bad about it but do not have the confidence to talk to her again about Hugh and me. She's made her position very clear, and I do not want to change mine. I live outside of her sunshine.

While all this is happening, I try to concentrate on both my formation in religious life and my teaching. Hugh does not make it easy. He is not just writing long letters full of love once or twice a week; he is also visiting as often as he can. Because his visits reinforce the strong attraction between us, I feel overwhelmed. I try not to give in to my strong desire to hold him and kiss him. Yet sometimes when he is ready to go, we embrace each other with such tenderness and longing that one or the other of us finally, painfully, has to let go. In between visits, I can feel his broad chest dissolve into my body. I know I have to suppress these feelings. I am filled with guilt and pray for a purer vocation and relationship with Hugh. The Third Way seems impossible for me. I am beginning to feel that Sister Marietta is right.

Surprisingly, Hugh says he would like to continue spiritual direction during the second semester of my juniorate year. I wonder if it will be strange, considering all that has happened, but I agree and arrive in the parlor on the third Wednesday of each month. Although these are scheduled visits rather than the spontaneous visits that so unnerve me, they also bring me tremendous happiness.

At the first visit for spiritual direction after our "revelation," I am flush with wonder and mystery about how Father—I mean Hugh—will relate to me.

"Hello, Father Brady," I say as I step in the parlor.

"Hello, my lovely Sister Emily," he replies with a smile that could light up a starless sky. "You look rested. I hope you are."

I look up at the crucifix and then directly at Hugh and ask outright, "Are you sure we should do this, I mean continue spiritual direction together? I mean, is this right?"

"Nothing could be more right. God is the portal of our love, Ev. The more each of us grows in His grace, the more we will grow in our love for each other and for Him and all people. That is who God is. Love. There is so much more to share. I want to share everything that I can."

We pull up our chairs so we can sit close to each other. He then takes my hands and turns them over. He kisses the tips of each of my fingers and then places a kiss on each of my palms. I am speechless.

"Your hands will be a way to be with me. Whenever you place your fingers and palms on your cheeks, I am there."

I cannot restrain myself. I get out of my chair and I take his head in my cupped hands and kiss him two, three, four times. Maybe five. Maybe six. Maybe more.

"Thank you," he whispers.

I feel shaken and ask again, "Are you sure we can do this?"

"I am sure. I want to share our paths to God."

On that occasion, except for his covering my hands with his kisses,

Hugh had an amazing ability to separate his emotions from his teaching. After that, writing in my journal during spiritual direction was often the only way I could concentrate on his words and not on him. Each third Wednesday throughout the second semester, the parlor continued to be a holy classroom.

One Wednesday, Hugh brings me a little present, a book titled *Poverty of Spirit* by Johann Baptist Metz. He believes this small red book will be very important to read in preparation for vows. I read it over and over. Sometimes a book can be a spiritual director in itself. I am mesmerized with the depth of its message and discover deeper insights into what Hugh has taught me over the years about the Beatitude "Blessed are the poor in spirit, for theirs is the Kingdom of God." He encourages me to select three to five passages from the book to reflect on in the four weeks between our meetings for direction. My February selections that we will discuss in March:

> "A human being with grace is a human being who has
> been emptied, who stands impoverished before God,
> who has nothing of which to boast."

> "You shall lovingly accept the humanity entrusted to you!
> You shall be obedient to your destiny."

> "Our self-acceptance is the basis of the Christian creed.
> Assent to God starts in our sincere assent to ourselves."

> "We become so poor that even our poverty is not our
> own; it belongs to the mystery of God … who then works
> in us."

As we consider the passages, I come to a clearer understanding that the less I possess, including spiritual consolation, the more room God has to shape me to his will. We are called to live simply and in freedom from material possessions, talents, reputation and even people. I ponder what detachment from people means for Hugh and me. I am not detached from who he is. Is this what I am asked to do? Hugh points out that we must detach from the other if this attachment does not bring life to that person. I can feel my body relax with relief from his words.

Religious life is the perfect vehicle to live out poverty of spirit, for we not only choose and vow to live a life of poverty from material goods but, also, in a deeper way, choose not to live an ego-centered life. I tell Hugh that I have come to understand this beatitude best in relation to my mother. As a widow, she was forced to relinquish many material goods and personal securities. The word widow means "empty nest." But she moved forward in her emptiness, lived her life and kept her family together.

Hugh agreed. "Your mom lives life the best she can in her poverty. God expects nothing more."

"Yes," I say softly.

As I delve ever more deeply into Jesus' teaching of poverty of spirit, I come to know the Beatitude as a touchstone, a turning place, a move toward God. It is *metanoia*. The Paschal Mystery. Kingdom life. Hugh continues to encourage me to embrace the poverty of myself and grow in my own poverty of spirit. To become perfect. "The scripture '*Be thee perfect like your heavenly Father*' in the Aramaic translation is '*Be thee compassionate*' " he tells me. "And that includes compassion for yourself, your impoverished self. No human is free from some impoverishment."

I do not have time to read books on theology, which are flying off the shelves in this post Vatican II era, so Hugh often brings articles by some of the great theologians of our time: Karl Rahner, Richard McBride, Hans Küng, Karl Barth, Ivan Illich and Pierre Teilhard de Chardin. He underlines what he considers the most important points for me to focus on. We try to squeeze in as much conversation as possible about the heady ideas that emerge out of the Council. I find the writings exciting, even thrilling. Teilhard de Chardin's words are true: "Knowledge increases mind; mind deepens Spirit."

As always, just before he leaves, Hugh prays for me with his whole heart. "For the path you are preparing for her, oh Lord." With his hand making the sign of the cross on my forehead, he says, "Let God bless you. Let God bless us."

For the first time, I take my thumb and make a cross on his forehead. "Let God bless you. Let God bless us." Without water or oil, we experience a new baptism.

When Hugh and I first revealed our love for each other, I daydreamed about our following St. Francis and St. Clare, medieval saints who lived as celibates in different religious communities but who had a special friendship and human love that supported their separate ministries. Yet knowing the human passion Hugh and I have for each other, I believe we are more like the medieval Abelard and Heloise, although not with their prominence. Abelard was a preeminent priest and heralded scholar who was held suspect by the Church because of his teaching, especially his belief in the innocence of the Jews in Christ's killing. Heloise was a highly respected abbess and his student. They became lovers whose passion brought them endless heartache. Heloise became pregnant and lived out her life behind the doors of a convent. Abelard was castrated and removed from his academic life. Only their love letters kept them holding on to each other's broken lives. Not wanting an outcome like theirs, I imagine Hugh and me someplace in between these stories.

In the 12th century, Abelard, one of the most notable theologians of his day, yet suspect by the Church because of his forward-thinking theology, became a teacher of the intellectually gifted Heloise, at the request of her uncle. Abelard and Heloise fell in love and began a torrid affair making love in the kitchens of convents and in the boudoir of the girl's uncle. They wrote hundreds of love letters. When Heloise bore a child, they were secretly married, but the theologian was castrated by henchmen of her enraged uncle. At Abelard's bidding, Heloise took religious orders. Abelard took the habit of a monk. They retreated into separate monasteries and wrote to each other of the anguish they suffered because they were forced to be apart for the rest of their days.

St. Francis and St. Clare

In the 13th century, because of their intense love of Jesus Christ, Francis and Clare were united by a deep bond of spiritual friendship. They saw very little of one another, but they each followed the sacred journey of the other. A medieval folk tale portrays their relationship.

One day Francis and Clare on a journey to Assisi, stop and knock at a house for a little bread and water. The family invited them in but make snide remarks about Francis and Clare being alone on the road.

The two saints then continue on their way through the cold winter snow. As evening comes on, Francis asks, "Lady Clare, do you understand what the people back there were hinting at?" Clare is too distressed to answer. Francis continues, "It is time for us to part. You will be in San Damiano by nightfall, and I shall go wherever God leads me."

Clare walks away without turning around. Unable to continue without some word of consolation or farewell, she enters a forest and there she waits for Francis. When she sees him come into the trees, she calls to him, "Father, when shall we two be together again?"

Francis replies, "When summer returns and the roses are in bloom."

Then a miracle occurs: All the surrounding bushes and frosted hedges are covered with roses. Clare walks to the bushes and picks a bouquet and gives it to Francis. And so, says the legend, the roses represent their unity and from then on Francis and Clare will always be tied through God's grace.

Chapter 15

OUR MINISTRIES, OURSELVES

"In love there are two things: words and bodies."
—*Joyce Carol Oates*

WHETHER MORE LIKE THAT of Francis and Clare or Abelard and Heloise, the saving grace during the second semester of my third year in the convent is that both Hugh and I throw ourselves into our ministries, Hugh's as a parish priest and director of the Diocese of Rochester Cursillo, a movement to develop lay leaders in the church, and mine as a teacher and junior novice.

As soon as I turn the calendar to February, I ask the art teacher at Mercy High School if she has any red and pink construction paper to decorate my classroom for Valentine's Day. She loads my arms with markers, colored construction paper and paper doilies. Some of the students stay after school to help me cut out hearts to decorate the classroom for what the girls are calling "lovie day".

"Sister Emily," says Cathy, who is pasting doilies around the pink paper hearts, "you're so romantic."

"I am," I respond smiling. "Love is what makes the world go 'round."

"For nuns?" another student asks.

Nancy, always my defender, answers in her "How can you be so stupid?" tone, "Nuns love Jesus and give up everything to love us."

"Every kind of love is beautiful," I pipe in.

"You think even in dating?" Sara, the quietest student in the group asks.

"Of course. 'God is love. Wherever love is, God is,'" I say, quoting the exact words "SMB" had written in the note I found on my desk this morning.

"Well, I don't think Sam is in that category," Mary Lou adds, looking chagrined by the laughter of the group. Sam is her constant crush and constant complaint. We all know about him.

"If it's love, Mary Lou, you can be sure God is present," I reply.

"Yeah, I don't think so, Sister. Boys are so immature."

"Sometimes," I say, trying to have a comforting voice.

Valentine's Day comes and our classroom walls are filled with hearts and flowers and quotations about love. The best part of the day for me is reading love poems to the students. To the swoons of seventeen-year-olds, and using all my drama training, I recite the poems as if I were living their messages. I am.

"A White Rose" - John Boyle O'Reilly
The red rose whispers of passion,
And the white rose breathes of love;
O, the red rose is a falcon,
And the white rose is a dove.
But I send you a cream-white rosebud
With a flush on its petal tips;
For the love that is purest and sweetest
Has a kiss of desire on the lips.

Neither the girls—nor I—need any explanation of the last line.

Because it captures courageous lovers who secretly meet to skate on Ghost Lake where a phantom lurks, "The Skater of Ghost Lake" by William Benet is a favorite love poem of the students. Is the ghost a phantom? Does it represent the fear that Jeremy and Cicely experience? Is their love illicit? What happens to them? Will their love overcome their fears? The students talk about Jeremy and Cicely for days. That is when I know that literature is alive for them.

Teaching English expands my own emotional and intellectual life as well and keeps me focused on something beyond myself and, on that day, my own secret Valentine. Yet I am so spent when school is over on February 14 that I wonder if I can even open the letter waiting for me when I return to the convent.

> *My dearest Valentine,*
>
> *I wish I could just live for now and love you and live with you and have no concern but ourselves ... But I do want to become fully all that God means me to be, and maybe that means paying the price. I wonder how much I am willing ...*
>
> *My darling, "Set me like a seal on your heart."*
>
> > *I love you,*
> >
> > *Hugh*

Hormones rage within me as I read this message from Hugh and think of the line, "For the love that is purest and sweetest/Has a kiss of desire on the lips." At dinner, as I sit in the tangle of all these emotions, I remind myself that I am a celibate. Sexual desires can be sublimated through the work of ministry; this is how celibates cope in a healthy and natural way. *Gandhi is a good example*, I think to myself. I am feeling as far away from Gandhi as Rochester is from New Delhi. The sacrifice of giving up marriage becomes more real than ever before. My admiration and understanding of the beauty of the Sisters I live with grows this evening when I think about their sacrifices. These are Sisters who are human and loving and willing to give up everything, including their sexual needs, in order to follow Christ and bring about His kingdom. I wish I could be like them.

But my body is experiencing an aching that feels like a serial stabbing. Fortunately, I find a few minutes after dinner to go outdoors in the freezing cold. Because I do not have a coat on, I hug myself for warmth as I stand in the covered doorway listening to the heavy rain. I pray its drumming will pound me numb. I begin to feel safe in this dark and frigid night and long to remain here. But I know someone would miss me if I don't show up for my after-dinner charge. I return to the warmth of the building.

As I am carefully putting the salt and pepper shakers in correct rows on each tray marked *Salt on left; Pepper on right,* sensations with the power of Niagara Falls begin to rise and surge through me. Tears creep out of my eyes and slide silently down my cheeks. I sit down and, with my elbows on the table, put my hands over my eyes to calm the short and immediate sharp breaths breaking the sounds of my weeping. The cheap paper napkins are falling apart as I take handfuls of them to blot my eyes and raw cheeks. I think I am having a breakdown and am grateful only one other Sister is helping in the refectory.

"Sister, are you all right?" my kind partner calls from the other end of the room. "Not feeling well?" she asks as she runs up to me. "Do you want to go to the nurse?"

"No, Sister, I am just very tired," I say with my half-choking voice.

"Go to your cell, my dear. We all have our times. I can finish up. Rest before chanting."

For once I am glad to keep custody of the eyes as I hurry back to my cell. I lie on my bed thinking how incongruous it is that my simple nun's cell holds these complex and passionate human emotions. My eyes close and I immediately fall asleep. In the morning, I am amazed and grateful that I get up rested, able to go to meditation and Mass, and enjoy a productive school day. I just wish Hugh would not say what he is feeling, even though this is exactly what I want him to say.

In the meantime, Hugh is on fire with his ministries, continually telling me our love makes him more committed to priesthood. During this time, he is exploring Pentecostalism, which he sees as another way to be open to the Spirit. He is also a priest member of the Secular Institute, a group committed to the intersection of spirituality and lay life. Their ministry is to the poor. As a Third Order Franciscan, he has taken a vow of poverty, a vow not required for the priesthood. The Cursillo is a full-time job in itself on top of his work in my hometown's parish.

Most of our pastors and assistant pastors at St. Ann were known to cultivate "connected" parishioners, eating in their homes and seeking them out. But Hugh befriends ordinary parishioners, visits their homes, teaches them how to be leaders in the parish. According to my sisters, this has created a new sense of community at St. Ann. He also ministers to Hornell's impoverished, infirm, lonely and dying, the people he says are closest to God. People call him "Father Love."

In response to the Vatican Council's "open window" to other religions, Hugh starts Hornell's first ecumenical dialogue. This is scandalous to some parishioners. We had all been taught that we were the one true religion and that those outside of the faith could never be saved. Hugh preaches about *Lumen Gentium*, meaning the "Light of the Nations," one of the most important Vatican II Documents. "Nor does Divine Providence deny ... salvation to those who, without blame, on their part, have not arrived at an explicit knowledge of God ..." Suddenly Protestants and Jews, Muslims and Hindus, even pagans, could be saved in the context of their own beliefs. Catholics are not the sun, but another planet revolving around Him. Revolutionary Father Brady says so.

St. Ann also holds organized weekly discussion groups where small faith-based communities study implications of Vatican II. Groups spring up all over town. Hugh also arranges for "Missions" where speakers come to give inspiring talks. After he attends the Better World Retreat, an international movement for renewal, Hugh brings renowned Argentinian Jesuit leader and founder, Fr. Louis Dolan, to our small-town parish to lead the retreat. Nothing is too good for those he serves.

Although he has an enormous amount of God-given energy, and is meticulous about every minute detail of his activities, Hugh is an extremely quiet man. Most people do not know how full his life is. Whenever I ask him how he does so much, he always says, "It is a small test of faith." He also says Mass each day, hears confessions, counsels parishioners, visits the sick and ministers to the dying with the Last Rites. He marries people, baptizes their children, and buries the dead. And he has me.

And "me" is having problems. As much as the Third Way looks as if it is to be our way, my feelings about it wax and wane. I admire those who live it and, although I pray to be strong, I think it will be too difficult for me. When Hugh visits, I share my fears, explaining again how I will not compromise his priesthood. He says that my protecting him from being involved physically is what gives him freedom, a freedom I do not share.

When I tell Hugh that I am contemplating ending our relationship because I do not think I can endure this kind of relationship, he always responds the same way.

"Your love for me and my love for you strengthen my priesthood—and I hope your vocation. That is the only way it can work."

I wonder if it can work for me. He always tells me how much more he can do for people because I love him. I pray constantly for guidance. He thanks me for resisting physical expression of our love that we both desire. But I am weakening. I don't trust myself. I am screaming. Hugh's love letters continue to arrive and continue to drive me crazy.

> *I gave a talk … God was speaking through me about love—but for the first time I was speaking from experience… I thought up to yesterday that to love was to give… You helped when you said it is not so much about giving. It is just what I am—why you love me as a person. I know that this is true about my love for you… I will always love you! You! as you are.*

Desperately wanting to believe that God will somehow sustain our love in religious life, I write to Hugh: *We must believe Jesus Christ will be our only source of growing in love for each other.*

This is what I also believe, he writes back.

It is during this time that Hugh tells my older sister Marnie and brother-in-law Andrew, who live in Hornell and are involved with parish life, about our situation. They are startled. They know he is a good priest who does not want to give up the priesthood. Still, they spend endless hours listening and trying to help him figure out how to handle this unacceptable dilemma of being in love with their sister.

They hope this infatuation will "blow over." When he starts expounding on the "Third Way," however, they are forthright about human emotions and tell him they don't think most people can overcome physical attraction if they are around each other. Although he disagrees, Hugh is at least able to share openly with them the roller coaster of his life of confusion, anguish, and happiness.

He drops by their home at the most unexpected times, even before dinner hour. When Marnie has a baby in her arms, a toddler crying and other little ones waiting for dinner, Hugh chips right in to help. He also keeps Marnie and Andy up into the early hours of the morning. They will have slept only a few hours when a baby or preschooler awakens them, ready to start the day. I don't know how they survive these months. Nor do I know how Hugh would have gotten through his unpredictable emotions without their friendship and support.

In the meantime, I am growing increasingly more conflicted about my vocation. I realize I need a loving life partner—without guilt or constraints. My thoughts of returning to secular life make the atmosphere of the convent more and more uncomfortable. Although I appear to participate in the life of the community, the world of the Motherhouse is becoming too big, too regimented and too institutional for my small self.

At the same time, I try to persuade myself to stay in the community. How can I be so sure of something and then go back on it? I tell myself that I am not the only person to consider. If I leave, I will disappoint not only the Sisters in the community, who count on novices to help them with their many and exhausting ministries, but also some of the girls at Mercy High School who are thinking of entering the convent and look to me as a mentor. For me, of course, the greatest loss of leaving will be not having Hugh in my life. No matter how much I think about why it is right for me to return to the life of the laity, I do not know how I can live without seeing him.

Toward the end of March, I finally find the courage to be completely frank in telling Hugh about my feelings about leaving. It is at our regular meeting for spiritual direction and I start talking first.

"There is something I have to tell you. I am having a harder time than ever living in community. I keep trying to talk myself out of feeling this way. But it's useless. I am afraid I will get sick again if I stay. Yet, I can hardly think of what that will mean if I don't see you."

Hugh listens with his whole self, the way he does, and, when I finish, he responds with a surprising calmness. He reaches over and holds both my hands. "My darling, I do not worry. God is with you, with us. You will be at peace if this is the right decision. Your decision should be independent of our feelings for each other."

"How can you be so calm?" I respond a little angrily. "Doesn't this hurt you or at least affect you? What this will mean for us?"

"I only know that if you do not do the right thing for yourself, not for me or even us, our love will suffer. God is love, Ev. God leads us both. I give over every desire I have for you. Your happiness is all I want."

Later he writes.

> *It is true. I humanly fear your choice to leave religious life and the likely prospect of your marrying. Still I have long given you to God and to his all-wise plans for you. I shall always be happy for your happiness—and I shall always love you—always! Love is a great suffering, but it must be a liberating suffering, setting free and giving new life— otherwise it isn't love at all.*

He ends by saying,

> *Looking forward to my forty-second birthday!*

I will be twenty-seven a few months later.

Knowing how I am wrestling with my decision, Hugh writes even more frequently. When he visits, he assures me that I need to be me, "the person God created you to be." Although he never says how deeply affected he is by my comments about returning to secular life, I see how wrinkles cross his brow and notice how he averts his eyes and unconsciously turns away from me in his chair, when I talk about a future without him. In words, he says he only wants what the Holy Spirit is directing me to do. But his body language says something else.

Even during this confusing time, however, Hugh's letters of love and promise keep filling my mailbox.

> *Ev, I love you with all my heart. You are God for me. You*

are my experience of God, God loving me, God being
loved by me. I love you for yourself but I just know that
in loving you I am loving God."

There are many references in Hugh's letters to our bringing or being the divine for each other. He believes that God is immanent in each person and that each person offers God life to others in unique and powerful ways—and, for us, romantic ways.

On another day, he writes:

And I want to say this, that I believe that you can make a
person of me, that your love is God's love for me, the gift
of Himself to me. God's love for me comes through you.
Yours and God's love are the same.

In the tradition of troubadour writings, God is discovered through the beloved. Hugh's love for me is his love for God. As my love grows for this beautiful man, I grow in my love for the gentle Jesus. Our love for God is our experience of love for each other. I wonder how we can ever separate ourselves from how God is loving us.

Chapter 16

TURNINGS

"We must make the choices that enable us
to fulfill the deepest capacities of our real selves."
—*Thomas Merton*

DURING HOLY WEEK, THE retreat master's words change my life. His message is clear. "In the Church hierarchy, there are specific strata: The Pope, the cardinals, the bishops, the priests and then the lay people. Women and men religious are lay persons who have chosen to dedicate their lives to God and his people through their vows of poverty, chastity and obedience."

I cannot believe what I'm hearing. If Sisters are on the same level as lay people, then lay people can be as close to God as Sisters or Brothers who follow a vocation to be celibate and vow themselves to poverty and obedience. I thought I had chosen a life "higher" than that of the laity. I thought I had to give up secular life so I could be as close to God as humanly possible. That was what I had been taught. Throughout the history of the Church, Catholic daughters have forsaken marriage to become women religious for this very reason. The nuns told us to aspire to be "holy" like the Sisters. We believed Sisters were different from the laity; they were above us and therefore, because they were at one with a divine spouse, to be revered.

Because Hugh is going away to a retreat and then to a Cursillo confer-
ence during Easter week, I have to talk to him before he leaves. I call him
that evening on Mother Bride's phone to ask him to please come to see
me before he leaves as I am really confused and upset. I tell him, "I have
something startling and upsetting to ask you about."

We meet in my classroom on Easter Monday morning. No one is in
the high school. And I hope no one notices how quickly I've completed
my charge of polishing the altar floor. Rushing to finish my assignment
early reminds me of my high school years when I was always hurrying
through my jobs at home in order to meet someone. This morning I have
the same feelings I had then: that I will somehow get caught and have to
return to do the job again.

When he arrives, Hugh looks at me out of his almond-shaped brown
eyes that have always pulled me to him and says, "Evie, I can hardly be in
the same room alone with you."

I hug him. Because he's come in from a cold Easter-week rain, his
heavy wool overcoat is drenched. When he apologizes for getting me wet,
I laugh and brush the beads of water off my habit. He throws his wet
coat over a student desk and takes both of my hands in his, which I hope
warm his cold fingers. I ask him to sit in the teacher's chair near my desk
and I sit on a student desk facing him.

"Are you okay? What happened?" he asks.

"Hugh, Sisters are lay people. Why didn't you tell me?" I ask, my body
bending toward him.

"Didn't tell you what?" he responds in a surprised tone.

My voice rises as my face heats up. "That religious are lay people. On
the same level as the laity."

Thinking from his expression that he must be asking himself why he
drove all this way for such a silly question, I still do not waver and wait

for an answer. "Of course," he says. "Sisters are part of the laity. Why does this upset you?"

"I thought religious life was above the laity. A vowed life for God is not any higher than for people in the world? Could you possibly agree that this is true?"

"Yes, but why a problem?" he responds with a perplexed look.

"I thought a vocation to religious life was a special gift to be closer to God. The nuns always told us that. This is all I have ever heard and probably from you, too. Why didn't you tell me?" My words were clipped and edged.

"I guess it never came up. I'm sorry. Every vocation—to marriage or a single life or priesthood or religious life, whatever—is a special calling if it is right for the person. We are created by God with unique gifts. Certain vocations let us use these gifts to the fullest expression of ourselves. What difference does it make? God loves us because of who we are, not because of where we land on a structure."

"You are telling me I can be a lay person and be as close to God as a priest or a nun?"

"Absolutely I am telling you that. As close to God as any bishop or cardinal. As close as the Pope, for God's sake. I know we weren't raised to think of lay people on the same level as religious. But the Council has let that little secret out. I thought you knew this in all your reading. I can tell you in the last years I am humbled with the sanctity of many lay people, including people in your family.

"The difference is that religious are without family obligations and free to spend more time on spiritual practices and opportunities to minister to the wider world. It's an amazing calling."

He emphasizes that the Church will always need celibates unencumbered with worldly distractions so that they can respond to the unique needs of the body of Christ. "Religious life is a holy calling. But lay life as a single or married person is a sacred calling, too. God does not see our goodness as the result of being on a certain rung of the hierarchical ladder. God sees the individual soul."

I am as stunned hearing this from Hugh as I was hearing it from the retreat master. I can be for others and fully live for God as a lay woman. I do not say it to Hugh, but, in these few minutes, I am sure of my decision to leave.

Because Hugh is on his way to his retreat, however, we do not have time to discuss this at length. As we hug good-bye, Hugh's eyes pool with tears. I ask him if he is all right.

He takes out his carefully folded white handkerchief, wipes his eyes behind his glasses and simply says, "No, but God is with us, Ev. Let God bless you." He kisses my forehead and leaves without closing the door.

When Hugh returns to St. Ann a few weeks later, an unexpected problem arises. The secretary at St. Ann rectory where Hugh lives has spread the rumor that "Evelyn McLean is chasing Father Brady." She knows I have phoned him there—four times. When I phone and ask for Father Brady the fifth time, thinking he has already returned, she interrupts me.

"Stop calling Father Brady!"

I am startled and hurt. I hang up. Hugh does not worry. He says this woman looks under rocks for gossip and everyone knows it. But I never again use Mother Bride's office to call Hugh at his rectory. As in many small towns, gossip is the daily sport. Since there is no proof, the rumors eventually fade away. Then one day a friend of Andy's asks him, "Hey, are Father Brady and Ev 'a thing'?"

Marnie and I are worried our mother will hear. I share my anxiety with Hugh and, because he desperately wants me to be at peace, he stops calling. He also tells me I need a break from all the anxiety over both leaving the order and our relationship. He says he knows I need time to concentrate on my own life and he will not be visiting for a while.

"You need time to figure out so many things," he says hesitantly, "and you don't need me to confuse you. I am not sure I can stay in the priesthood if you leave, and I am not sure I can ever leave it, either. I'm confused, too. Honest, you won't hear from me until you are in touch with me."

Now I have the opening. I need to break from Hugh, and I know in my heart what I must do. I can no longer hope for a relationship with him. The priesthood is sacred; he must be celibate to live his priestly life. I cannot live with compromising this. I also know in my heart that I will not remain in the convent.

Although Hugh will be having surgery in mid-June for a herniated disk in his neck, I live in limbo about his whereabouts for the next six weeks. I teach my classes, but my enthusiasm wanes. I pray, but my prayers are only words. I do my charges, but my tasks are irrelevant. In mid-May I write Hugh a letter telling him I must end our relationship. I am not completely certain of the exact wording, but in my journal I have four drafts of these sentiments:

> *My love, my breath*
>
> > *Through the past years, and especially the past months, I have basked in the fragrance of your garden where you have tended to me, loved me, and let me grow. But I know I need all the sun and rain of your life. I need all of you. I am much too weak to watch for you at the gate. My love for you would break the lock.*
> >
> > *Now let us love enough to give each other the life we are destined to lead. I beg you not to contact me; I could*

not go through this again. Nor should you. Death comes
even when we are still alive.

However, when you have surgery, if someone could
let me know if you are okay, I would be very apprecia-
tive.

One rose in your garden,
Evie

With my heavy heart, I talk with Sister Marietta to tell her I will be leaving and she tells me to make an appointment to see Mother Bride. I dread telling Mother Bride even more. I feel like a failure and somehow a fool, as if I hadn't made the grade. As if I am not who I said I was.

I drag myself to Mother Bride's office. There is a note on the door. "Sister Emily, I will be a bit late. Make yourself comfortable, SMB." As I wait, I observe Mother's piles of papers neatly organized on the desk blotter with her fountain pen placed exactly in the middle of one pile. I see her closed calendar and a photo of her niece. Also on her desk, opened with bookmarks and with underlines on the pages, are a couple of books, *We Dare to Say Our Father* by Rev. Louis Evely and *Prayers* by Michel Quoist. Evely and Quoist have a way of making poetry and prayers out of what otherwise could be heady spirituality. I am tempted to pick up one of the books as their writings always inspired me. I don't.

The bookshelf is lined with many other books: tomes on spirituality and religious life, a pristine Bible, and a dog-eared copy of the Documents of the Second Vatican Council with several bookmarks in different sections. On the cross above Mother's desk hangs a resurrection Christ with his arms outstretched to be welcomed by the Father. The Christ figure tells us that we, too, are to be free. If one had never met her, the simplicity of her office, her books, and few adornments would say who Mother Bride is and what matters to her.

When Mother arrives, I immediately notice her red and watery eyes, not from crying, but from the migraine headaches she endures. I ask her if she would like to reschedule.

"No, seeing you gives me a boost," she says with a weak voice.

"Not today, Mother. I have something that is extremely hard for me to tell you."

She does not respond as we sit down. I blurt out, "Mother, I am leaving the community. I have tried very hard. I can't do it. I will leave by the summer. This is so hard and painful to tell you."

"My dear, are you sure?" She seems incredulous and asks in a shaky voice that indicates her headache must be increasing. "Why didn't you come to me earlier? How can we make things easier? How long have you felt this way?"

"For this past year. It's not the convent, Mother. It's me. I've waited because I had to be completely sure before I told you. As much as I love the Sisters and how we care for people in need, I can't do it. The vows are too hard for me. 'Many are called but few are chosen.' I have been struggling for months, probably longer but not admitting it. I was called but not chosen."

"Are you sure?"

"Yes," I whisper so quietly that I can hardly hear myself.

"What does this mean about Father Brady? You cannot have any relationship with him if you leave," Mother states, her weak voice suddenly growing stronger.

"I will not be seeing him again. I have cut it off. There seems to be no life ahead for me here or in the world, Mother. Staying is not who I am. I wish it were. As confused and sad as I am, I am at peace."

"Peace is my only wish for you, dear Emily. Does Sister Marietta know?"

"I told her this morning."

Then, in an even stronger voice for her frail condition, Mother speaks clearly, "Sister, you can never compromise Father's priesthood."

I look straight into Mother's eyes and say, "I would never take a priest from God."

"No, no, you wouldn't, my dear. I will be praying for you. You will get through this. But I think I had best rest for now. Let me know if you need anything."

"I will pray that you will feel better soon," I choke out, trying not to cry.

Mother Bride then gives me an uncertain smile and stands. She puts her two hands around my face like a chalice and kisses the top of my veil. Without saying anything else, she walks out the door to her cell. My body sears with pain, like leeches pulling blood from my heart. I can't move. I am hurting someone who believes in me and, I have come to know, loves me.

Feelings of fear and guilt often accompany me during the weeks before I leave. I survive convent life minute to minute, and nightmares plague my sleep. They are always the same. As I doze off to sleep, I am in a small, paint-chipped blue rowboat without oars. As the boat heads into huge lead-colored waves, my arms flail in the black water trying to stop the direction of the boat. I wake up either shaking or, if the boat has cap-sized, terrified. Sometimes, a person in the nightmare I cannot identify appears on the shore staring at me. At other times the person who is on the shore and the person in the boat are both me.

I shout for help in a language I cannot understand. Other people, sometimes my principal from Painted Post, my brother Keith, often my friend Kit, appear on the shore yelling at me. But I am not sure if they are angry or calling to help me. I feel helpless. I can't understand anyone. The dreams have no backdrop, no sky. The water floats through empty space. Nothing to keep me from falling off the planet because there is no planet. Nothing to keep me safe. Each night before bed, I will myself to not have nightmares. But each night after I get into bed, I find myself in that flimsy blue dinghy.

In these days and weeks, I experience the most intense yearnings for Hugh. He does not write or call or visit. Daydreams about running into him unexpectedly bring the only relief. I hope one of the Sisters will mention his name or maybe he will say a community Mass. Neither happens. I can hardly concentrate on my teaching. The students are sensitive to me. Every once in a while, a concerned girl asks me if I am not feeling well. I always say, "No, not feeling well these days."

My decision weighs twice as much as it might otherwise. I cannot hide the anguish of leaving both Hugh and the Sisters. Keeping my word, I tell the novices in my band that I am leaving "to be the best me." Ironically, those are the very words I used to explain why I wanted to be a nun. Not knowing about Hugh, they beg me to stay. They pray. They sneak extra cookies for me from the refectory. They write a list of twelve reasons why things will not be the same without me. Number seven: Who will make brownies without sugar? They clean my cell. They leave me holy cards and write scripture quotes on decorated index cards. They joke with me as we do our charges. They hug me. They make me laugh. They make me cry. But, despite all they do and the great affection I hold for them, I prepare to depart from my now small band of novice friends.

I am scheduled to leave on July Second, a month before my band will take their first vows. In mid-May, because she is working as a dorm director at Buffalo State College, I contact my girlhood friend from Hornell, Mary Anne Griffin. I ask her if she knows of any jobs I might be able to apply for.

"I'm leaving my job as a dorm director at the end of June," she says. "Why don't you apply? I will mention you to the dean."

Mary Anne phones back to say that Dean Angela Palmieri has never hired a nun and is hesitant. College campuses are exploding with race riots and anti-war demonstrations, and the dean does not think I would be equipped to deal with the enormous challenges. Convinced by Mary Anne to at least meet me, she agrees to interview me in early June. But she tells Mary Anne: "Absolutely not in a habit."

I call my brother Keith, who lives in Rochester with his wife and three darling little girls, to ask him to buy me a dress, medium panty hose, and size 7-1/2 black heels for the interview. He valiantly shops, never his favorite thing, and completes the task. The day of the interview, not wanting anyone at the convent seeing me in secular clothes, I go out the large, heavy oak doors in my habit. I change in the ladies' room at the bus station where I am to board the Greyhound bus to Buffalo.

It feels strange to be in a short, stylish A-line dress. Even worse is that I had forgotten to tell Keith I would need a slip. I can see the outlines of my legs through the light aqua linen. After wearing the black habit, black slip, thick black stockings and black tie oxfords, and now without my tee shirt, I feel totally immodest. The interview is this afternoon so I have to go without a slip.

When Mary Anne meets my bus, she pulls me into her red Chevy. "We have to do some quick fixin', girl." She scrounges around her purse and says, "Tighten your lips" and applies red lipstick first on my top lip and then on my bottom lip. She gives me a Kleenex to blot the lipstick and taps it gently on my cheeks for rouge. In an attempt to style my short hair, she runs her comb through it but says she does not think it helps much.

"Who the heck chopped your hair?" she asks.

Feeling even worse about it, I do not answer. She spreads some blue eye shadow on my eyelids and puts mascara on my thin eye lashes. I look in her car mirror; a clown looks back at me. Mary Anne tells me not to stand in the sunshine so no one will see my legs through the light linen dress and drives me directly to the college. I feel numb.

Even though I feel like I look like an alien, the interview goes surprisingly well. Dean Palmieri asks me what role a university should play in the anti-war riots and civil rights protests. I am forthright and speak clearly about my compassion for students struggling with both causes while aware of their responsibility for the common good of the university. She is glad I've had two years of experience with Vietnam veterans returning to high school. She says that vets at the college face similar problems. Having lived through "hell in the swamps of Vietnam," and suffering from the trauma of war, these veterans are suddenly thrust among college students who are more worried about what kind of food the student union serves or whether their clothes are just the right style.

After about an hour, Dean Palmieri says she will hire me "on condition". The dean makes it clear that I am not to evangelize the students, staff, or administrators anywhere on campus. I tell her I am not about evangelizing but about supporting the campus community in any way I can. The job comes with an apartment in one of the dorms, which is a huge bonus and solves the problem of buying a car that I cannot afford. Knowing that I will live and work in the same building, I am exploding with my good luck. God is with me.

That night, Keith meets me right on time at the bus station in Rochester. When I tell him I got the job, he responds, "So should the kids not call you Sister Emily anymore?"

My throat goes dry. I can't respond. I see that Keith is sorry he asked and tell him I am sure of my decision.

"Okay," he says. "Not sure why you ever thought you were a nun, anyway."

"I guess I was wrong," I softly reply.

"Are you positive you want to leave?"

"I'm trying to save my life."

Keith stands there with his hands on his hips, looking at me as if I am still in fourth grade. He shakes his head and, as he hands me my habit, says, "I never got you. Still don't."

Feeling most people don't get me, I change into my habit in the bathroom stall. We then drive back to the Motherhouse without saying a word to each other. Hoping I have gotten all the make-up off when we arrive, I am dressed as if I am still a nun. But somehow I do not feel like a nun. I just signed on for a job with real pay. I somehow crossed a line.

Because everyone in the community seems to know about my plans, my last weeks are awkward. I live among the Sisters, but in my head and heart I am not a Sister. I go to prayers as a Sister but pray as a lay women, I hear the students call me "Sister" but I long to hear "Miss McLean," I participate in the novices' lives but know I am no longer part of them. I feel embarrassed and out of place. I obviously am not accepting myself. And I have not heard a word from the priest I now force myself to think of as "Father Brady."

Two days before my departure, Mother Bride asks me to come to her office. On her tiptoes, she greets me with a kiss on my cheek and a long hug. She wants to remind me again that, as a lay woman, my relationship with Father Brady must end completely.

"You cannot be an occasion to compromise Father's priesthood. You must sever your ties and not see him when you leave."

I assure her I will not and add that it brings a suffering more painful than anything I ever knew existed. She understands but is confident that

I will get through the pain and receive the grace to move on in my life without Father Brady.

"That is God's will," she states unequivocally.

Before I leave her office, Mother gives me a small porcelain statue of Our Lady. Then she fills my arms with things she's confiscated from the supply press: a dozen pair of white cotton underpants of various sizes, two nightgowns, three toothbrushes, a hot water bottle, two tubes of toothpaste, two bottles of shampoo, two towels, four wash cloths and four bars of soap that I know will never foam.

Lovingly, she says, "It's all I have to give you." I am grateful and touched by Mother Bride's kindness—and poverty.

The day before my departure, I receive a formal letter from Father Brady saying the surgery on a cervical disk in his neck was successful. He signs off,

> *I wish you all the blessings your heart can hold.*
> *Peace, Hugh.*

He will be recuperating at his sister Dorothy's house in Rochester. I am relieved and grateful to know he is all right.

At least one of us is.

Chapter 17

CHANGES

"It is not a garment I cast off this day, but a skin that I tear
with my own hands.
Nor is it a thought I leave behind me, but the heart made sweet with hunger
and with thirst."
—Kahlil Gibran, *The Prophet*

AFTER MORNING MASS ON July 2, 1968, I put my neatly folded habit and veil in Sister Marietta's office, place the last of the items from my cell into my trunk, stop in the chapel to ask for God's mercy, and walk across the marble floor in the front hall of the Motherhouse. Keith has offered to drive me to Buffalo and is waiting in his car outside to load my trunk. Knowing it swings open and closed between two different worlds, I push open the Motherhouse's heavy oak door. I hold God's hand.

My intense suffering over making the right decision about leaving the community of the Sisters of Mercy is over. Like a gentle brook, peace flows through me. I do not feel joyous and I do not feel sad. I feel grounded in the growth I've experienced in religious life and know in "my heart made sweet with hunger and thirst" that God accompanies me into my new life.

I am wearing the same long-sleeved scarlet, polyester-silk sheath dress with a tie at the waist that I wore when I entered. I do not need to wear the dress's red tie around my hair as a red badge of courage. I have courage. I also make good on my promise and have packaged up my size-large undershirts for Keith to give to Andy. Betty Jean, Keith's wife, has kindly sent me some sandals. I know she would have sent summer clothes if I had asked, but I didn't think about it. I guess I've had other things on my mind.

When I arrive at the apartment at Buffalo State College, I am grateful to find that Mary Anne has left some dishes and pans as well as bananas, cold cuts, milk, eggs, bread, butter, and coffee with a note: "I'll pray for you." The apartment is furnished with clunky, square, institutional-dorm furniture with rough, nubby olive green and orange upholstery. I love it. My own place. Keith wants to stay with me but has to get back to Rochester to go to work on the second shift at Kodak. He hugs me good-bye and tells me that he hopes I will be okay and that I should call him if I need anything. I tell him that I don't know what I would have done without his generous offer to bring me to Buffalo.

This is the beginning of the loneliest day of my life. I begin to experience an emptiness of spirit. I long not only for Hugh but also for my religious community and my family. Since I do not know how to use the complicated phone for directors, I can't dial out to call my mother or sisters. And literally no one is around to ask. Mother and my siblings do not know my number. The campus is deserted because of the July Fourth weekend. Fortunately, Keith promises to call Mother when he gets back to Rochester to let her know I am all right. In the middle of these desolate emotions, I feel an urgent need to hang up a Sister Corita Kent poster I'd brought from my classroom. The words "Flowers grow out of dark moments" sweep over the artist's large plumes of bold, primary colors. They brighten my spirits.

As exhaustion overcomes me, leaving my body listless, I feel a deepening sense that I belong nowhere, as if I have fallen into outer space without wings. I crawl inside the black hole of myself and, even though I do not have any casual clothes to make me comfortable, cuddle up on the couch. I fall into a half-wakeful sleep, yet as sad as I feel, I am comforted by knowing deep within my body that I have made the right choice. Yet, I wonder if I will ever be happy.

Several times during the first night, I wake confused about where I am and if I will survive in a world without a community, without love. The lyrics, "Where is love?" from "Oliver" play inside me and finally put me to sleep. My dreams do not answer the song's question.

The next morning, I take a walk around the eerily empty campus and notice the Newman Center, a Catholic Center for college students, across the street from the college on Elmwood Avenue. I check the hours for Mass and show up for the 11:00 AM liturgy in the lighter and less wrinkled option of my two dresses, my linen dress—still without a slip. Even though there are only a handful of people, I stand in the back. The homily— on this ordinary weekday—is meaningful, challenging and poetic, filling my spirit. When Mass is over, Father Jack Weimer, the celebrant and head of Catholic Campus Ministry for the college, comes up to me and asks if I am new to the Center. I hesitantly tell him I had just left the convent the day before. "Oh, please come up and join us for lunch."

That was the first day of my relationship with the enigmatic and charismatic Father Jack Weimer and the beginning of thirty-eight years of celebrating with the beloved community at Buffalo State College Newman Center. In Buffalo, Father Weimer is affectionately known as the "midwife" of the Vatican II Church. With his brilliant insights into the meaning of the Vatican II Documents, his inspiring homilies about social justice and cosmology, and his command of scripture, theology, and English literature, Father Weimer—"Call me Jack"—is a rock star to progressive Catholics. The Newman Center is a lively and hopeful sanctuary for not only Buffalo State students but also many Catholics not associated with the college, including several of Buffalo's local and national leaders. Because of Father Weimer's commitment to the social gospel and his brilliance in explaining it, Newman is a magnet pulling people all across the area out of their still pre-Vatican parishes into a vibrant Vatican II community on Elmwood Avenue.

While eating Father's homemade pasta salad for lunch, I meet the enthusiastic campus minister, Sister Frances Flanagan, who was raised at Boys Town with her uncle, Father Flanagan, of the "He ain't heavy, Father; he's my brother" fame. In her late seventies, Frances has more energy than any twenty-year-old. Sr. Marianne Ferguson, the other campus minister, stops in and also gives me a warm, welcoming hello. These two women are like angels at the gate. Throughout the summer and the next years, their friendship and presence help me in the transition back into the secular world from a world of religious life they knew well. I am grateful to still have Sisters in my life.

It does not take me long to realize how many things have changed in three short years. One day, Kathy Berst, another dorm director, says she wants to get some new "slicker sticks."

"Slicker sticks, what are they?" I ask.

Kathy shows me one, puts the glossy lipstick on and later jokes that, "Anyone who does not know what a slicker stick is must have been locked away in a convent." It can be little things that make the world change.

After lunch at Newman, I return to my apartment feeling grateful that I have made some friends. I spend the rest of the day settling in, reading, praying and, as best I can, getting ready for a visit from my aunts, who had written to me before I left the convent to say they would be coming for a visit at Buffalo State on the Fourth of July, my birthday. My aunts are like a group of nuns. They, too, should be called the "sisters of mercy".

When the phone rings early in the evening, I jump, not expecting anyone to have my number. I pick it up and hear Hugh say, "Please, just let me talk to you for a minute." My heart stops.

"How did you get my number?" I ask, almost out of breath.

"Security."

"You should be a detective."

"I will track you down anywhere."

"You are not supposed to talk to me that way."

"Are you angry?"

"Not at all."

I am so relieved and thrilled, I almost collapse at the sound of love in Hugh's voice. It is a huge relief to hear how strong he sounds after the major surgery on his neck. And, despite Mother Bride's admonition that we should not communicate, I don't know how to hang up.

"Ev, I can't sleep. I can't eat. Nothing means anything. I just have to talk to you. I have to know how you are."

"I know," I respond. "I'm the same way."

After a long time talking about everything and nothing, I dread ending the conversation. We finally decide phone calls and letters will be acceptable. He tells me he will be phoning on my birthday. That night I write for over an hour in my journal. One line: *This is unreal. This is not right. This is more wonderful than fireworks.*

Throughout my life, the Fourth of July was always a special family day with a picnic, a birthday cake for me, and fireworks at night. But on this birthday, I somehow wake up with a hollow feeling. I think if I take a walk, I will feel better. Except for the campus police whom I have not met, I am the only person on campus. The college feels like a concrete desert. Even the Newman Center is closed and I know I am only pretending to think Hugh will ever be truly in my life.

Things improve immensely at 4:00 PM when, accompanied by the campus police who say they saw a suspicious car driving around campus, my Irish aunts appear. When they realize my aunts are completely lost, the campus police give them an official escort. The security police are invited to the party, but they decline, not knowing they will be missing Aunt Irene's delectable chocolate cake and my other aunts' traditional fare of ham and cheese and rye bread sandwiches along with Red Rose tea. (Any other brand is simply not tea.) Aunt Irene even brings a teapot she later gives me as a present.

As soon as they are inside the apartment door, Aunt Irene fills one of Mary Anne's pans with water, boils it, scalds a cup for each of us, scalds the teapot, puts the tea bags into the pot with the boiled water and then sits down to let the tea simmer. "First things first," she says. Aunt Kay hands me a bag with some of my cousin Karen's summer clothes she thought I could use. Could I! I immediately put on Karen's Bermuda shorts and a sleeveless blouse. Heaven. Heaven on earth. Total relief to be out of a dress.

I am so happy to be with my mother's sisters, who'd played so big a role in my life. Even before my father died, they'd acted as if they owned us—as well as our house—and came and went whenever they pleased. At the same time, they expected us to clean their homes, till their gardens, and entertain them by singing hymns when we washed dishes or dusted their tables. "Holy God, We Praise Thy Name" was a favorite. Each of my three aunts was an important help to my mom after my father's death, driving two hours from Buffalo to Hornell laden with meals and baked goods. They came ready to roll up their sleeves and organize us and even do some cooking, which was never anyone's forte. My aunts are my family, my identity, my "little mothers," what the word "aunt" means.

After we eat birthday cake, Aunt Marie starts to take off her ruby ring and hands it to me.

"What's this?" I ask.

"It's our birthstone, yours and mine. Uncle Jess gave it to me many moons ago. Now it is for you."

My sisters and I had often admired Aunt Marie's ruby engagement ring with diamonds on each side. I just don't feel I can accept it. I have always known Aunt Marie to wear this ring next to her wedding band.

"I was going to give it to you when I died," she says. "But Uncle Jess told me, 'We should give roses to the living.' If someday you want to give it to someone else in the family with a July birthday, you can."

Aunt Marie's ruby ring! I put it on, and it fits perfectly. I have never received such a luxurious gift. This is a birthday I will never forget.

That night Hugh calls and is as thrilled as I am about the ring. He tells me he has also gotten me a birthday present. I remind him I can't accept a present from him.

"That's crossing a line we can't cross," I say.

He responds that he hopes I will accept the gift anyway, just this once, and that he wants to bring it to me. I am so desperate to see him that, as usual, I show my "invincibly strong will" and give in. Hugh tells Marnie about his plan to visit. She calls me immediately.

"You two are playing with fire. Don't let him come," she states in no uncertain terms. "He is a priest and now you are off limits."

I phone Hugh in Rochester and try to persuade him not to come. At least I uttered the words. He says he wants to give me the birthday present and is coming to Buffalo whether I will be there or not. I ask him again not to bring me a present but give in on letting him visit. In my journal, I write, *Is it possible to be this happy?* Marnie is upset about Hugh's visit and tells me that we should spend the entire time out of my apartment.

"Show him Buffalo, show him the art gallery, go out to lunch, go to the zoo, go someplace. He has a car; get some groceries. Do not be alone in your apartment. This has got to end."

"I know it has got to end. But the problem is, our love won't end."

Marnie makes it clear that I will not meet anyone else as long as Hugh is in my life. She says it is unfair to me and no different from someone getting involved with a married man. The married man can always go back to his wife. The woman would be left without a future.

"I wish it weren't so," she says gently. "I know how much you two love each other. But Father Brady is not going to leave the priesthood, and you have your whole life ahead of you. Don't tempt him!"

"Well, what about him temping me?" I say in tears. She doesn't answer.

The following Tuesday, Hugh arrives at noon at Scajaquada West, the Buffalo State College dorm where I am assigned. When I hear the knock on the door to the outside of my apartment, I open it to Hugh standing in the blazing sun with a bouquet of yellow roses and baby breath in his hand. He steps into the apartment and, suddenly, all the light seems to change.

Dressed in regular clothes, he looks very normal—casual, but gorgeous. I have never seen him without his cassock, the traditional long black robe, his vestments for Mass or his black priest suit with its small white square in the middle of the shirt's collar. I wish he had come with his priest clothing on, his invisible armor. Thinking of Marnie's specific instructions, I ask him right away if he is hungry. When he says he is, I ask if he would mind if we go out for lunch. He says he would love to take me to lunch.

I follow Marnie's plan carefully and take Hugh to the Albright-Knox Art Gallery and Delaware Park. We even shop for my groceries. Because

I am with Hugh, this very ordinary task of shopping suddenly becomes something wonderful. I watch how he carefully checks each apple I will be eating before he selects it.

Hugh has to leave at 4:30 for a meeting that evening so we do not have a lot of time together. I know Marnie will think that her plan "saved us from each other." But the opposite happens. Being together like two ordinary people—talking and eating, shopping, sightseeing, walking through Delaware Park—makes me, and I believe Hugh, aware of how completely compatible we are, how comfortable it is for us to be just regular people, how happy it feels. We laugh and kid each other. Under the umbrella of a giant maple tree in the park, we whisper prayers for happiness in my new life and in his life as a priest. We suddenly find ourselves holding hands in the grocery store. To be totally free to be oneself without roles to play, rules to follow, or people to please must be one of God's greatest gifts.

Just before Hugh is ready to leave, he says, "I know presents are off limits, but I have something in the car for you and I hope you will accept it."

He returns with a large dress box tied with ribbons from a fancy store. I open the lovely box to find the most beautiful soft, pink shantung sleeveless dress and matching jacket with sparkling-pink rhinestones on the two buttons. It is something Jackie Kennedy would wear. My first thought is, *When would I ever wear something so beautiful?*

I tell Hugh it is the loveliest dress I have ever seen and ask him how in the world he chose it. He explains that, to thank his sister Dorothy for letting him recuperate at her home, he had gone shopping for a dress for her. While in the store, he felt a strong urge to buy me a dress, too. He did not worry about size. He pointed out a woman shopper to the sales clerk and said, "That size." He was dead on.

Hugh had told Dorothy he'd left the sales slip in her dress box so that she could return the dress if it was not the right size or style. When Dorothy saw two dresses on the sales slip, she asked him where the other dress was. Hesitantly, he told her who would receive it and then told her about us. All of Hugh's sisters idolized him, but Dorothy turned out to be the most romantic one. She had compassion and sorrow for him. In fact, she said she would like to meet me. But, of course, that would not happen.

"I'll understand if you don't keep it," Hugh tells me. "If you want to, just give it away. It just looked like you."

"A farewell gift?" I ask.

"Maybe, my darling. Maybe."

He hugs me gently. I feel so at home, like I was meant to live in his arms. My heart breaks into two complete halves as Hugh drives away to his life as a priest and I stay in mine as a single woman. I keep the dress.

Because my dorm does not house summer school students, I have way too much time in which to pine away and the summer is becoming unbearably long. Eventually, I make friends with some of the other dorm directors, who invite me to join them to go out to bars, a normal way guys and girls meet each other in 1968, especially on Wednesday "pick-up nights" before Friday and Saturday date nights. We had no online dating sites as people do today. Unless you are lucky enough to meet someone at work or school or through friends or blind dates, meeting in bars is the practice of the time.

I have to make an effort to meet men, and I don't enjoy the evenings in the bars. The smell of beer that seems to come up from the floor boards, the smoke-filled rooms and the feeling of being "looked over" make me uncomfortable. I endure the hours until we return to campus. If a guy does approach me, I am uninterested, and he soon picks up my "vibe". The girls I go with almost always meet guys and, when they don't, they express disappointment. They tell me not to worry. I will eventually "click" with someone. They have no clue that I am in love. Who could I ever meet who would be more than Hugh?

Yet, without knowing it, my new friends help me get through the long days, inviting me to drive with them over the Peace Bridge to enjoy the Canadian beaches, to go shopping, or to just hang out in our apartments. Even so, I don't feel like l belong anywhere. My confusion is not only about Hugh. I am not fully comfortable being back in the "secular" world. Everything seems loud and fast and unsettling. My brother is not the only one who doesn't "get" me. I don't "get" me, either.

Chapter 18

CONFESSIONS OF A CELIBATE

"Ecclesiastical celibacy is not from dogma."
—Pope John XXIII

BECAUSE I AM PRETTY much alone most of this summer, the Newman Center offers something I have sought and appreciated all my life: community. Saying hello to friends, identifying with a purpose greater than myself, worshipping with familiar rituals and sharing common values all provide me with the feeling of family, a place to belong to, to hold on to, to give to. I often wonder what happens to people who do not have any group to enclose and embrace them and to make them feel as if they are part of one another and part of a greater life than just one's own. Although I spend most weekdays alone in my apartment, reading bad novels and feeling sorry for myself, on the weekends I am at home at the Center.

Walking also saves me these summer days. I so frequently visit Delaware Park, located across the street from Buffalo State College, that I have names for some of the trees. "Hello, Protector." "Good morning, Grandfather." "Happy day, Elegant Green Lady." I think of Delaware Park Lake, later renamed Hoyt Lake, as the "womb of the park" and "the lungs of the city." Circling around the lake, I gather the water's stillness into myself and know its peaceful energy stays with me long after I leave. I meditate on the bench near the park's stone arch and never cease to be thrilled with the variety and number of roses in the Rose Garden. When I hear little children squeal in delight as they are pushed on the swings behind the garden, it makes me feel plain happy.

I've come to appreciate the gift of Frederick Law Olmsted, whose landscape designs in the late 1800s gave Buffalo "a necklace of parks" so that people could experience the tranquility of the country within the hubbub of city life, something he also achieved in his design of Central Park in New York City. To watch the sunsets over the water, I ride my bike all the way to Olmsted's Front Park where Lake Erie and the Niagara River "marry" on their way to eventually become Niagara Falls. Olmsted said the meeting of these bodies of water was one of the most magnificent sites he had ever seen. When I am invited to go to a beach along Lake Erie, I take advantage of swimming in her water and become part of her as she becomes part of me.

Although I do not know who I am or where I am headed, Buffalo's parks offer me consolation. And her lakes and rivers and creeks continually talk to me as they talk to each other, conversations that lessen the loneliness that envelops me during this summer. Sister Phillip once told me that nature is "God talking".

What keeps lonesomeness most at bay, and keeps alive a hidden hope, are Hugh's phone calls. There are weeks he phones almost every night to see how I am doing, even though sometimes we don't say a word. Just knowing who is on the other end of the line is enough. Hugh's torment over being so sure of his vocation to priesthood on the one hand, and his feeling torn apart because we can't be together on the other, is often a part of the conversation. We are at a stalemate.

Hugh experiences loneliness, too. For the past few years he has been struggling with an alcoholic pastor who at best, he says, is an "absentee father" to him and to the parishioners. A great challenge of celibacy for him and many priests is living an isolated life in a rectory with the lack of companionship. Alcohol can become a priest's companion. Another problem is that priests are sometimes transferred on a whim. "Priests just start to root somewhere," as Hugh puts it, "and suddenly, after adjusting to new people and developing new relationships, they are transferred. It's not that I personally was transferred so much but, when I was, I found it difficult. Like leaving loved ones. When monks enter a monastery, they stay in the same monastery for the rest of their lives. Something in the human heart longs to identify with one group or place. There is a loneliness in the priesthood, but, Ev, my heart is still pulling me to minister to others. There is so much need. Yet something is pulling me to minister just to you, my love."

One night on the phone I ask Hugh if he were ever in love with another woman. He tells me that he has always been attracted to women, was sometimes infatuated, or "maybe felt love" for someone, but has never been *in love*, as he is with me. He explains that he did not develop an emotionally healthy way to relate to women before he met me. Because he had gone into the seminary after the eighth grade, he believes his sexuality was developmentally halted in adolescence. He knows many priests who, like himself, are attracted to women or interested in them, fulfilling the natural need to relate to the opposite sex, but they never learned how to be emotionally authentic with women.

Relating to women, he tells me, was almost like a game for them. "As grown men, we were like immature high school boys, unconscious of how we were acting. Our training provided almost no education or guidance on sexuality. We did not recognize that celibacy involves so much more than physical encounters. It involves the emotions and psyche of a person."

Hugh also tells me that a priest can use celibacy to hide behind when there is a problem in the involvement with a woman. "If things go awry in the relationship, the priest can escape to his 'celibate' life." He explains that celibacy puts the priest in the "driver's seat." Unlike when a man and a woman relate as equals, the woman in a relationship with a priest could be invested in it, but not be seen or be treated as an equal by the priest. He thinks the reason is because people had grown up believing that priests were above the laity and celibacy mades them a rarified species, as if they were not simply human like the rest of us. Many priests actually believe they are somehow a unique breed, although often unsure of what that means. A mystique has grown about celibate Catholic priests, and many of them see themselves as separate and exceptional. Like maybe they don't have to follow the same rules as the rest of us humans. Some priests see themselves as above women. Above the laity in general. "So where does this put the woman?" Hugh asks.

"To be honest," he tells me, "we are caught in a clerical culture that puts priests on the proverbial pedestal, but priests should not be given special license in any relationship. We are supposed to be servants; that is what Jesus calls us to. As far as I am concerned, celibacy can misconstrue how we are seen and, even worse, how we see ourselves and how we relate, especially if we are attracted to the opposite sex or the same sex. The biggest problem is we don't understand ourselves."

Over his years as a priest, Hugh hesitantly explains, different women told him they were in love with him. Sometimes he was very attracted to the woman. But his promise of celibacy kept him from responding with freedom. He felt confused and uncomfortable and at times personally deprived. He lived with guilt. After several years in the priesthood, however, Hugh sought counsel on how to relate with women in a healthy way as a celibate priest.

"Priest or not, I came to recognize that women have the right to be treated as human beings, equals in God's sight," Hugh states with conviction. "I learned I needed to protect not only my celibacy but also the integrity of the woman. I became sensitive when a woman expressed her affection for me. Love is serious business. But what was I to do with urges of my body and pulls of my heart?"

Hugh admits that, when there was a mutual attraction between himself and a woman, he enjoyed the special vibes they sent to each other. He tells me flirting is possible as a celibate, that it is not right, but possible. He doesn't see me smile on the other end of the phone when he says this. He has also come to realize that what causes even more havoc is when a priest has special relationships with more than one woman at the same time.

"Yes, I mean romantic relationships, like when you know a friendship is more than just friendship. That is even worse for the women. Sometimes the women even know each other. Because 'in theory' a celibate does not relate to women as a sexual man, he thinks he can string along whoever he wants, even though there are definitely sexual overtones. It is how we are made! Just another example of imbalance of power, of not accepting our genuine humanness. I know priests and women who are suffering through this."

Recently, and almost fifty years after this conversation, I read the remarkable and poignant correspondence between renowned Jesuit priest Teilhard de Chardin and American sculptor Lucile Swan in the book *Letters of Teilhard de Chardin & Lucile Swan*. Their correspondence is a study of how a deep human, yes romantic, love can evolve and be sustained between a celibate and someone who does not want to be celibate. And, although Hugh and I expressed our love in a different time and totally different environment, I laughed when I read Lucile's words from her 1934 journal: "He is the man I've been dreaming of all my life everything—ex-

178 The Nun and The Priest

cept why did God put in that little joke of making him a priest!" I could have said the same thing. Also, like me, Lucile believed physical consummation was necessary to express the deepest feelings of their special love for each other; on the other hand, Teilhard believed that the denial of sexual energy would be their way to a closer union with God. They lived out their love for each other in the Third Way.

But more surprising to me was discovering that, later in his life, another woman, Rhonda de Terra, became an intimate, though celibate, love companion of the great theologian. This caused angst and heartbreak for Lucile. The lines from the book's introduction are particularly poignant. "Teilhard returned to America for the last time in the autumn of 1954. There in New York he found the ever-faithful Lucile. He died on the evening of Easter Sunday 1955 while talking to other guests who were also visiting the New York home of Rhonda de Terra." This is an example of what Hugh was telling me so long ago about the consequences of more than one woman in a priest's life. I can't imagine how I would feel if I were Lucile and knew the love of my life died in the home of the "other woman" whether they lived the Third Way or not.

Growing up in a female-centered household, Hugh always felt comfortable with women. He and his sisters and mother shared struggles and joys easily. I believe that is how he developed a highly sensitive feminine side. Yet, many women fell under the spell of his charm and often misinterpreted his ease and genuine concern for them as a caring priest to be a romantic invitation. Even if his and my love for each other will be kept from fully blossoming, I never feel threatened when Hugh speaks of these other women; that is how secure I feel about our love.

Hugh believes that, without intending to, he hurt women who showed an interest in him. He says because he knew the pain he could cause, he had spent hours praying to be able to figure out the right thing to do with his feelings. "It is a little bit of a private hell trying to hide what one feels. I did that for almost three years when you were in the convent."

He does not believe that celibacy is an issue for all priests. There are priests who are able to focus on their priestly roles without being distracted by women or men. If they themselves are psychologically healthy, these priests relate to others with a mature and healthy and loving detachment. He thinks celibacy is an amazing state. It frees a person to live out a life of freedom that married people don't have. But he knows this special grace is not given to every priest. Hugh tells me he is friends with so many loving priests who seek wholesome relationships but suffer knowing God has *not* granted them the gift of celibacy. "As a priest, you sometimes just don't know where to put genuine, God-given human emotions," he says.

"Living a pure celibate life when the spirit trumps the physical is a grace, a gift from God. I know celibate men who become giants of scholarship and discipleship and somehow love with purity and detachment. But that was not me. I can tell you most people would be shocked if they knew this."

I, too, am shocked. Shocked with the whole conversation. I had no idea that Hugh struggled with his feelings about women before he met me. He is seen as so holy, so priestly, even to the point that some people, especially the Sisters, believe there is a mystique about him. I thought he was blessed with a pure gift of celibacy. I now understand why I carry so much guilt and feel responsible for his promise of celibacy. The conversation makes it clear to me that he is fully free to make his own choices and to live with the consequences. A burden has been lifted from me. I admit that I have not been given the gift of celibacy. And now he is telling me that he has not, either. I made my choice; I am not responsible for his. It all is clear in my head, at least at this moment. But my heart knows our love is so inclusive, so true, so huge, I do not think I can breathe without him.

Hugh goes on to say that he wonders how many priests are graced with a genuine internal and external experience and expression of celibacy. Celibate in body and soul. He tells me to be celibate is not how God made most of us, is not how humans are biologically wired. He states with authority: "Grace builds on nature" and the human being's essential nature is not to be celibate. "I fought nature all these years, but now I wonder if I can continue. These days I can only believe in love and where God is leading us. Yet I feel called to be a priest in every fiber of my being. Giving up marriage is the price I have to pay to be one. What a high price, what an unnecessary price. What a painful price. But, Ev, I don't want to lose you."

Hugh had never been physically involved with a woman, he adds, but even now in his early forties, he sees himself as an immature celibate. He tells me he wants to be totally honest with me and emotionally open about every aspect of his life and of mine. Even if we made mistakes with physical expression, our relationship has helped him grow in his understanding of what true celibacy means. What love means. He prays he will eventually fully accept what both demand.

In a letter written after the phone call, in August, 1968, Hugh further explains his thinking about celibacy.

> *Right now, I am a celibate, but I do not believe this is my*
> *grace. I have not thought celibate, except neurotically*
> *and with guilt feeling about infatuations and attractions*
> *in the past, thinking them "un-celibate". I certainly have*
> *not acted celibate, "cultivating" friendships, self-seeking*
> *etc.-the adolescent's search for fulfillment, <u>unaware that</u>*
> *<u>he was even searching</u>.* (Hugh's underline)*Today, thanks*
> *to you and to God's speaking through our love, I believe*
> *I know what celibacy is. ... but I do not embrace it. I am*

not an honest celibate no matter how chaste and pure I
may remain."

Celibacy for priests comes out of a Church rule in the Twelfth Century forbidding priests to marry; it was primarily instituted to address the Church's political and economic needs at the time. Eventually celibacy was enshrined in Church Canon Law 277, which imposes an ideal, namely, perfect and perpetual continence as a requirement for presbyteral ordination. The priest witnesses to the eternal oneness with the Divine. Nothing can impinge upon that relationship, not even a loving woman. In 1967, I wrote in my journal: *Why isn't human love good enough for a God who created humans to love?* Furthermore, Church rules on celibacy are not scripturally based. In fact, we know at least one of the apostles was married: St. Peter asked Jesus to cure his mother-in-law. Was St. Peter less worthy to spread Jesus' message because he was not a celibate? Ironically, Peter, a non-celibate, was our first Pope. Would Hugh be less of a disciple, less spiritual if he married? We both believe the Vatican Council will revisit the question of priestly celibacy and open the window for a married clergy to be instituted. It can't come too soon for me. Even Pope John XXIII said, "Ecclesiastical celibacy is not from dogma." He added that his pen could end this rule. I would be glad to give him the ink!

Questions about celibacy fill my journals. The more I reflect on them, the angrier I become about the Church's utter lack of trust in the goodness of human love between a priest and a woman.

July, 1968 journal:

> *The sacraments are our way to God. Why should priests*
> *be kept from the sacramental graces of marriage? Why*
> *should women be kept from the sacramental graces*
> *of ordination? Does God actually see us according to*
> *gender? Why would God give us a natural attraction to*
> *the opposite sex yet want a man to sacrifice this natu-*

ral need if he is called to be a priest? Are we like the
Hindus worshipping Lord Ayyappa, the god of celibacy?
Hugh has told me how my love for him has strength-
ened his priesthood. This church drives me crazy. Does
celibacy make people more spiritual, closer to God?
What about those celibate priests who are much less
spiritual than many married lay people? Those guys
more interested in decorating their rectories and build-
ing up parish empires than living for the poor. Like those
materialistic, overindulgent monks in "The Canterbury
Tales." I am positive what Hugh and I experience is real
love and from God. Why can't we support each other to
build God's kingdom through our human love for each
other?

And, from another journal entry in August, 1968:

Who is he kidding? He knows most priests are not given
the gift of celibacy. Does he really think we can be
around each other and not hold hands or hug or kiss
each other? Aren't the body and soul one? Yet, he loves
his priest life, his servant life and he has a gift to touch
and heal and bring life to so many. How can I take him
from those in need?

Ironically, despite all the freedom in my new life, I somehow feel more imprisoned than ever, as if a feast were set before me that I am not allowed to eat.

Chapter 19

ROLLERCOASTER

Slip slidin' away
Slip slidin' away
You know the nearer your destination
The more you're slip slidin' away.
—Paul Simon

IN LATE AUGUST OF 1968, I buy a car. It isn't Skycar. But I adjust. My first big trip is to pick up my sister Lillis in Rochester; she is returning from three years in Africa as a Peace Corp volunteer. Hugh had told me that he would very much like to join me at the airport. As usual, I thought he was crazy. As usual, I said okay. If there were a contest for weak people, I would have no competition.

I am thrilled to see Lil. She looks thin and tan and happy. As she later told me, when she saw me with Father Brady, she thought to herself, "Oh, boy, did the Church make some big changes since I left the States?" She has no idea, but she acts as if it is perfectly normal for a priest she hardly knows to come to the airport with her sister to welcome her. As Lillis and I are driving to Hornell, she asks me what the heck is going on.

"Nothing, Father and I have become good friends."

"Wow," she responds, "I guess so."

On Saturday, there is a welcome-home party for Lil. It's not that I am not being welcomed home. My mother and family want the party for both of us. But I told everyone that I really wanted a special party to celebrate Lillis' return from her great adventure in Africa and that I will be able to see everyone, too. I think I honestly did not want the focus on me because somehow inside myself I think of leaving the convent as a failure. The old tapes in my head keep playing over and over.

The morning of the party, I take an old bed sheet and paint in large, bright green, red and blue letters: "Welcome Home African Lil." Keith and I hang it across the front porch. We all shop and cook, clean and polish, garden and hose everything spotless. I am feeling the comfort of being back in the rythmn and familiarity of my family home.

Mother invited Hugh to the party, and while he is there, she keeps filling up his drink, even though he has an almost full glass, and often she offers him another plate of food. So proud that a priest has come to her daughter's party, she insists that he meet everyone. She pleads with him to stay afterward, but he says he has another commitment.

After Hugh says his good-byes, I walk him to the front porch. I wish I hadn't. He is suffering; I am suffering. We want to talk but there are no words. When he takes my hand, his fingers feel as soft as blossoms. Then out of the corner of my eye, I happen to see neighbors across the street are waving at us. I start to shake Hugh's hand up and down and loudly say, "Thanks, Father Brady, for coming." He looks at me like I am crazy.

The next morning at Sunday Mass, Hugh's homily is on how God is found in the love we experience in our daily lives. He says love changes everything. He uses examples of how parents with a newborn find themselves forgetting their own needs to devote themselves to the tiny, vulnerable baby; how the love between siblings, who might fight and taunt, creates unwavering friendship when one or the other is in need; how the love between soldiers makes them willing to die for each other.

Then he starts talking about men and women falling in love and how their world changes as a result. I am sitting in the pew twitching with my purse strap, looking down. "The hunter who focuses on finding a deer," he tells the congregation, "suddenly sees violets growing out from under the rock, or for the first time notices the way a shaft of light opens up the patterns of the tree branches. The moon is always sacred for lovers because, no matter how far apart, both see and experience the same light."

He ends by reminding us that love is God's way of talking to us, being with us, affirming us. "Love is God's greatest gift; yet it is really unexplainable. We can only know that love is."

I gasp and drop my purse in my lap. Hugh had told me months earlier that whenever he prayed at the Consecration, the highest point of the Mass, he held me in the sacred words: "Through Him, in Him, with Him in the unity of the Holy Spirit, all glory and honor is yours, Almighty Father, forever and ever. Amen." I am part of the sacrifice he offers to God at this sacred time of worship. When he speaks these words over the Eucharist this morning, I can't think.

I leave St. Ann realizing that I cannot continue to be so much a part of this man's life—this man who even includes me at the Consecration— and yet not be a part of him. At breakfast after Mass, my mother and her friend are talking about how Father Brady understands what it is like to be a layperson and how he values human love between a man and a woman even as a priest. I feel like a hypocrite listening to them. I know Hugh is talking directly to me when he says these things. My mother is being betrayed; pain sears my body..

I am so nervous driving back to the college that my hands are slippery on the steering wheel and make it dangerous to drive. I can't tell if I am angry, feel manipulated, or just done in by it all. My stomach aches the whole way. When I get to the dorm, I call Hugh and ask him if we can meet halfway between Buffalo and Hornell the next Wednesday on his day off. I am so off kilter, I don't even care what the secretary thinks.

"Are you okay? Something happened with your mom?" he asks when he gets on the phone.

"No. Something happened with you. With us. I am emotionally shot. If we don't talk, I will go crazy. I will meet you half way."

Hugh insists on coming to Buffalo. Remembering Marnie's advice, I suggest we meet at Howard Johnson's on Delaware Avenue. I give him the address. He says he won't get lost; he'll look for the orange roof with the weather vane on top. When Wednesday arrives, we sit on the aqua-colored vinyl seats not knowing how to start our conversation. We stare without uttering a word.

The waitress breaks the silence and Hugh orders a vanilla ice cream for me and a black raspberry for him. Despite the seriousness between us, we comment that a selection of twenty-eight flavors is amazing. I'd like to think now that I just let my ice cream melt as we dealt with the huge emotional issues consuming us. But I swear ice cream is the food of the gods. I eat mine slowly, savoring each spoonful as soon as the waitress puts the frozen dish in front of me.

While enjoying the ice cream, I suddenly become lighter. I update Hugh on my decision to go to Buffalo State College instead of State University at Buffalo for my master's degree in English because of the convenience of being right on campus. I also share how excited I am to discover that the distinguished scholar of Irish studies, Dr. Fraser Drew, will be one of my professors. Later, Dr. Drew became my thesis advisor.

"I am glad for you, Ev. But I just drove two hours," he says with a gentleness that could melt steel. "And you could tell me that on the phone. What is this meeting all about?"

"The homily! The homily! That is what," I say a little too loudly.

"It was my way of telling you how I feel," he smiles.

Raising my voice even more, I say outright, "But I can't take how you feel."

Hugh moves uncomfortably in his seat and suggests that I tone it down.

"Okay, but including me even at the Consecration?" I ask in a stage whisper. "I can't do this. I am not strong enough to carry our secret or hope for an impossible resolution or wait for your calls. Can't do it."

Taking a deep breath, Hugh takes my hands away from the cold ice cream dish.

"We can't hold hands here. People will see your collar," I tell him.

"Okay." He lets my hands go and holds on to his empty, frosty dish. "My emotions are frayed, too. What do you think we should do?"

"Let's try to lead our own lives. Give me a chance to find out who I am without you. You know I don't have a chance of finding out with you." With tears welling in my eyes, I plead, "Let me find my life."

"Evie, can we really not see each other? I will try. I hope I can do it." We sit quietly looking down at the table. Then, turning each of my hands over, Hugh traces a small cross like a tiny blessing on the inside tip of each finger. "Put your fingers on your face when I am not around," he says deliberately. "You will feel that I am blessing you, loving you."

"Okay, but I am going to try not to," I whisper. "You leave first."

"I won't be in touch if this is what you want."

"You know it's not what I want; it's what we have to do. Both of us."

"I know, Ev, I know," he says, shaking his head to no one and with tears welling up.

Hugh pulls himself out of the booth and stands and looks at me. I am worried he will lean down and kiss me, but he dries the tears from his eyes with his immaculately white hankerchief. He puts his right hand on his heart and leaves. With a gentle breeze blowing through the window, I drive back to my apartment completely numb.

With the arrival of the new school year, my life opens up to something outside of myself. Students fill the dorms, bringing with them their politics and prejudices, their fun and worries. I deal with calls in the middle of the night, sometimes because students are drunk and have no ride back to the dorm, other times because someone loses her key and is locked out of her room. Some situations are more challenging, such as boyfriends who show up in dorm rooms, roommates who have differing tastes in music or the scent of marijuana and at times alcohol. Some roomate situations can become contentious.

Nonetheless, I feel for the students in my dorm. These young women are trying to deal with not only the normal challenges at this stage of personal development, but also the unrest on campus, which reflects the country's turbulence over racism and the Vietnam War. Protests are happening all over the country. As the dorm residents worry about their personal problems and academic demands, their boyfriends, brothers and, in some cases, fathers are being drafted and shipped off to a country in far-away Southeast Asia.

Although I am busy with students and my own academic work, I know that Hugh and I are connected in such a way that I will never stop thinking of him. I try to ignore the spirit of his presence inside of me. But at the same time, because of the great strength and comfort it brings me, I want to experience it. I continue to ask God to help me ignore these feelings. God needs hearing aids.

At the end of October, Dean Palmieri sends a letter to my coordinator to say I am off probation. She feels I can do the job "competently." With the security of employment and an apartment, I feel as if I am no longer "renting" my life, and I am grateful that the days are demanding. I attend dorm meetings, student forums, protests, and many administrative meet-ings on housing and security. I go to graduate classes and have perpetual assignments of papers to write. Even though I do not have any idea how to sew, I buy a portable White Sewing Machine that feels like it weighs more than a car engine. Nonetheless, it works. With the help of evening classes in a local high school, I learn to make some simple clothes. I become more active with the Newman Center's social justice group and liturgy committee.

I also enjoy Fr. Weimer's gourmet table, where on one occasion I meet his best friend, a saint of Buffalo, Father Joe Bissonette, who so many see as another Christ. An outspoken champion of justice not just for the voiceless in Buffalo but also for those suffering in Third World countries, Joe makes every person he encounters feel totally accepted and loved. Years later, Father Joe is murdered—martyred—by two young men who came to his door asking for food. Buffalo does not have a monument to Father Bissonette. But his spirit remains in our city, bigger than any mon-ument we could build, as do the spirits of other beloved Buffalo "saints" such as Sister Judith Fenyvesi, SSS, a holocaust survivor, and Sister Karen Klimczak, SSJ, who ran a halfway house for former inmates and was murdered by one of those she gave a home to. And so many more. Out of Buffalo's poverty, strong saints appear.

Throughout these days of longing to be with Hugh, the Newman Center continues to offer support and becomes the hub of my social life. I enjoy the dances, the wine tastings, and especially the weekly "coffee hour" after Mass, which Sister Frances calls "the second Eucharist." There, as we break the breakfast bread, we "break each other open" in conver-sation and friendship. Many Catholic churches in the 1960s "opened the door" to welcome people in this very human, simple and hospitable way. And they continue to do so to this day. Church is no longer only a formal liturgy directed by the priest for devout though passive attendees; it is now a vibrant community of engaged believers.

As full as my life has become, however, Hugh is always in my heart and mind. It is around the time I get off probation that Hugh and I weaken and we start phoning again. Before we know it, we begin to talk on the phone several times a week. After Hugh pays for a post office box to protect me from the rectory secretary, and who knows who else, we find letters in our mailboxes from each other. I don't know how it happened that we reconnect; we just do. As the weeks pass, I am hearing in Hugh's voice the anguish he is experiencing over our dilemma. He has always been strong in his conviction that he was born to be a priest. Now it is becoming clearer how conflicted he is and also how much he wants to be with me. He mentions marriage. I daydream about it. I can't imagine my life without him.

The tone of one letter speaks of Hugh's suffering because of our separation.

> *...the peace didn't last. I am being eaten up with feelings*
> *for you. Have to go to the parish dance tonight. Asked*
> *Fr. Sturmer to preach for me tomorrow. I am really not*
> *up to it. Emotionally I am more and more convinced that*
> *we should be married. Can't think clearly at all."*

The "*I am more and more convinced that we should be married*" is familiar. And I know that in his next breath he will speak of his love of priesthood. As much as I long to, this teeter-tottering makes me hesitate to put any trust in the idea of marriage. But I recognize the depth of Hugh's anguish. He is someone who does his duty under almost any circumstances. And to hear that he'd asked another priest to fill in for something that was his responsibility makes me realize the extent of his suffering. The more hurt he experiences, the more pain I hold in my body. Fortunately, other letters come that make me realize he also lives out of his grounded, open self.

One continual theme in his letters is Hugh's great desire to become the best human being possible.

> *...that I fully develop as a person... I want this so very much. It was this that occasioned my first real surrender to God, though the desire simply to please him was probably foremost. But out of the letting go came the drive to improve as a person... I feel so strongly that you are in my life for this very purpose.*

Yet, in the same letter he admits:

> *I have simply not gotten the message that I must leave off active priesthood at this time as a means to my personhood. It may come. I continually pray for the honesty that is so important for us both.*

Teeter-tooter. Rollercoaster. Somersaults. I live them all. And he does, too.

When Hugh shares with me the blessings and challenges of his many ministries, his words about wanting both to marry me and to be true to his priesthood confuse me and leave me feeling as if I am hanging onto a cliff and don't know whether to let go or not. I experience freefall more than once. My life these months reminds me of the game "Red light! Green light!" When someone calls out, "Green light," I run as fast as I can toward Hugh. When someone suddenly says "Red Light," I have to stop. If I try to sneak up to gain distance, I am caught and go back to the beginning of the line to start all over again.

From my journal:

> *Hugh says he is committed to his priesthood. I get that. At the same time, Marnie is right. I will never be emotionally free to meet another man as long as Hugh is in my life. I do not want to be free. I want to have Hugh in whatever way is possible. I want to be married to him.*

My stomach is killing me.

Later that November, I am consumed with the feeling that we are
"playing at" our relationship again. Deciding I have an obligation to myself to meet other men, I start dating. I tell Hugh that I have to be open to
all of life. After all, I say, he is filling the obligation to himself to be a priest
and has a full life. Maybe meeting other men will be glue for my fractured
heart. I have to see about those "other fish in the sea."

He writes,

> *It hurts me to think of you going out with other men.*
> *Emotionally I rebel, intellectually, I understand and*
> *agree. It is part of this ever living in openness. I am*
> *afraid that I shall lose you even as I am afraid that God*
> *is re-directing my life... Fears will not leave until the*
> *truth and reality free me.*

The fishing is poor. Friends "fix me up" and, as hard as I attempt to be
open to some very attractive men, my heart isn't in it. Hugh comes to see
me before Thanksgiving. Knowing in my head our meeting is somehow
wrong, being together for even a short time feels natural, a relief, as if
the world has righted itself. We give each other small Thanksgiving gifts.
I type out a quotation by Rainer Maria Rilke and frame it. "Believe in a
love that is being stored up for you like an inheritance and have faith that
in this love there is a strength and a blessing so large that you can travel
as far as you wish without having to step outside it." I hope the quotation
will give Hugh permission to do what he has to do and still know he will
find love either with me or in the priesthood.

Hugh gives me a small, beautifully wrapped box that contains handmade drop earrings, with a center disc of a carved ivory face of the sun
with delicate metal rays around it. I have them to this day. He also brings
copies of his old *National Catholic Reporter* which he knows I will read

with great anticipation. Because of a Cursillo meeting in Rochester, he does not stay long. But we are grateful for our own holiday of gratitude. We are each other's Thanksgiving. Each other's Eucharist. Before we part, we hold each other as if our embrace will save the world.

In December, I begin to have serious sleeping problems. Concentrating on my graduate work is like Sisyphus pushing the boulder up the hill. And I am short-tempered. Again, as hard as I try not to, I begin to lose weight. I go to the doctor and am told that I have colitis. He gives me an antibiotic and a special diet to follow. Because my brother-in-law Andy is a pharmaceutical representative, I phone him about my condition to ask him what he thinks of the prescribed pills. Although I tell Andy I do not want my family to know about my condition, he tells Marnie. Marnie tells Hugh. Hugh drives to Buffalo the next day. He hadn't called ahead. When he arrives, I am on the couch covered with orange and brown afghans crocheted by my Aunt Marie. I wear them like tinker's shawls when I open the door.

Without enthusiasm, I simply ask, "What are you doing here? I am a mess."

I go right back to the couch. I haven't washed my hair and my purple flannel shirt looks as if I'd slept in it. I probably had. Hugh looks at me and says, "Oh, Evie." He holds me for a long, long time as I nestle into his arms finally feeling some relief. He begins talking with a preternatural calmness.

"I know I am the cause of you getting sick, Ev. How has it come to this?" Hugh looks at me weighted down with sorrow. "I can't do this to you."

"You're not doing this to me. We're doing it. It's just my make-up to get sick."

"Ev, I can't even tell you what I want to say. It will only hurt you more," he whispers.

"I know. I can't tell you, either. You shouldn't have come," I whisper back to him.

"What can I get you?" he asks with such aching tenderness, I begin to feel worse.

"Nothing," I reply. "My friends come to check on me. They bring me food from the cafeteria. Soup."

"How will you get home for Christmas?"

"Mary Anne said she will drive me. Our relationship isn't going anywhere, Hugh. And it shouldn't. I just need to get better and start my life."

"Yes," Hugh replies quietly. Uncharacteristically, he suddenly gets up, puts on his coat and hat, kisses me gently and speaks with a tone so full of compassion that I ache for him. "I will pray constantly for you. I will leave now, my darling. I promise I won't hurt you anymore. I won't see you unless God directs us otherwise. Please, do everything to get better, but know I love you however you feel. Whatever happens. I beg you to get better. This is my selfishness. My fault."

As he walks toward the door, I wait for him to turn and put his hand on his heart or blow me a kiss or to at least bless me. He only opens the door and goes out into an overcast sky with a light snow shower falling. He drove two hours and was not here more than ten minutes. I am feeling too poorly to analyze it. But it just seems strange, as strange as my life.

I am so exhausted that I hardly care. I go home to Hornell for Christmas and do not go to Mass once. My mother insists I see a specialist at Strong Memorial Hospital in Rochester. The doctor tells us that colitis can be the result of different kinds of infections in the colon and that emotional trauma can exacerbate the symptoms. He asks me if I am under any undue stress.

Mother answers. "She left the convent and the adjustment back to secular life is very hard."

He agrees. Fortunately the medicine works, and I eventually feel better and begin to eat small amounts of regular food. I am glad the second semester does not start for several weeks so I can rest and recover at home. Although my family home is only two miles from Hugh, we have no communication. I live on the couch in a kind of a limbo, a no-man's land, an empty vessel that echoes no sound from the crack that is splitting it open. My mouth is always dry. My eyes shed no tears.

One afternoon, home by myself, I watch the TV movie "The Umbrellas of Cherbourg." It's the story of a frail umbrella maker who falls deeply in love with a handsome mechanic who is shipped off to war. They do not think they will ever be together again. In this desperate possibility, they express their undying love through a song: *If it takes forever I will wait for you /For a thousand summers I will wait for you /Till you're back beside me, till I'm holding you /Till I hear you sigh here in my arms.*

Even though I know it's futile, I sing these words to Hugh over and over in my head. I repeat the lyrics with my parched, cracked lips until I am beyond exhausted. The making of a masochist.

Mother could not be kinder to me, making me soup and tea and continually washing and rewashing everything in sight with Murphy Oil Soap, her medicine for any ill. Marnie and the kids come over to visit. Whenever I secretly ask Marnie if she has seen Father, she says that he is okay.

One day as she hugs me, she whispers into my ear, "I know, I know. I can't imagine how painful, but this has to end. It is just as hard on him. You both will move on. You can be happy with someone else, I promise."

I just say, "Okay," and weakly thank her for visiting.

On New Year's Eve, my mother toasts me: "To 1969 to be a year of promise and fulfilled dreams."

I so wish that I could tell Mother what I am experiencing and that my dreams will not be fulfilled. With her traditional Catholic background and her hero worship of priests, especially the town's beloved Father Brady, it is impossible for me to believe she could ever understand. I toast Mother back, but I am not looking forward to the New Year: 1969.

1969 – 1970

THE FOURTH SEASON

Winter passes and one remembers one's perseverance.

Chapter 20

REVELATION

"...everything carries me to you"
—Pablo Neruda

IN MID-JANUARY IN THE new year of 1969, I return to my apartment in Buffalo for the spring semester feeling stronger, at least in body, and I am eating more regularly. Even though in my heart I know my relationship with Hugh is over, I look for a letter every day and wait for a call each night. I often have my hand on the phone to call him. But I worry about the secretary. Or, if I call in the evening, that he might not be there. Or, even if he is there, that he might not accept my call. I don't dial his number.

Everything on campus is frozen, the trees, the walkways, the light poles. And my spirits. But a February thaw comes. Late one afternoon in mid-February, the phone rings. It is Hugh. He wants to visit me, just briefly. Despite his gentle voice, he sounds distant, almost business-like. I come right out and tell him that the visit will only make me sick. He begs me and tells me he absolutely must see me. I am incapable of refusing him, but know I will regret it.

It is now almost two months since we have seen each other. Hugh says he will be at the dorm at 1:00 pm on Wednesday and, because he has an appointment with the Bishop at 4:00 in Rochester, will leave by

2:00. His mentioning the Bishop takes any small joy out of the thought of seeing him. I figure he probably is being promoted to some diocesan position and this will be the "official" break. With pain lodged in my sternum, I breathe my way through the next two days of terrible waiting.

Wearing his heavy black wool overcoat over his perfectly pressed priest suit, Hugh arrives exactly at one o'clock. The outside apartment door does not have a storm door on it so I hurry him in against the snow. It is a grey Buffalo day, but his smile warms and brightens the room.

"Hello, Evie."

"Hello, Father. Come in."

The familiar sound of his voice and the way he moves his tall, strong body make my heart stop. I do not realize how much these things affect me until I am with him again. He removes his gloves and drapes the heavy wet coat over a chair. Still smiling but not saying anything, he turns to me. I don't know what to say to him. Reminiscent of that Sunday night in the convent when he first declared his love, he takes both my hands and holds them as he leads me across the room. We find a place to sit on opposite sides of my small, green Formica kitchen table. I notice we are seated with a barrier between us and I see this as a signal. I immediately put up invisible barriers around me.

He leans forward pressing into my hands and says, "I have something to tell you."

Pulling my hands away and crossing my arms, I look right at him and say, "Go ahead. Say it fast."

"I am leaving the priesthood."

I gasp. I freeze. A hurricane suddenly comes into the room, and I have no place to run.

"No!" I yell out loud.

"Yes, Ev, I am certain."

I get out of my chair and start walking around. I am totally unhinged with this news. Talking like a crazy lady I turn to him, grab his arms and say words that come from the deepest place in me. "No. I beg you not to do this. No. Not this. I will move away. You love being a priest. Why are you suddenly telling me this? I haven't seen you in months. You are crazy right now. You can't make a decision like this so suddenly. I can't be responsible for your leaving the priesthood," I cry, choking out the words.

Then, feeling like the center of my world will fall apart, I say in a voice on the edge of yelling again, "Don't do this. You will regret it. This is impulsive. You're not impulsive."

"It is not impulsive. I am very free about this," he replies trying to talk louder than my shouting.

Feeling desperate, I raise my voice even louder and speak in short, clipped words. "You don't know what you are doing. Your devotion to people. Mother Bride. The Sisters. The Cursillo. You can't leave." I turn on the ball of my foot and with my body leaning forward, I face him. I speak with anger. "I am just beginning to accept that we won't be together and I can never go through this again. And the scandal. My mother. You are mixed up. People need your help. What will happen to them? You are a priest. How can you suddenly come to this and why are you telling me?"

Hugh sits quietly with his hands folded taking in all my explosions. Getting up from the kitchen chair and moving to the uncomfortable olive-green striped couch, he pats the hard seat cushion next to him and asks me to please sit down. Crossing my arms again, I go over to the couch. My face is red; my teeth clenched. Not looking at him, I sit down and lean back on the couch so we won't touch. I stare straight ahead. Without any expression, he turns toward me and gingerly takes my hands. Slowly kissing each of my fingers, still without a word, he remains absolutely peaceful. I catch my breath and finally look at him; we just stare at

202 *The Nun and The Priest*

each other as if we are in a twilight zone. Nothing is real.

Finally, in a very quiet voice, he speaks calmly. "I am absolutely certain about leaving, Ev. I love you with my entire being and I have not stopped loving you for one minute since we last saw each other. I am leaving whether you want me or not."

In a judgmental tone I ask, "Want you to? You are telling me you don't know how I feel about you? Why did you make me think it was over? I don't believe you. How could you hurt me so much? Change so fast? What makes you think I can take a priest from God?"

"You will not take me from God. Nothing could do that." Looking down, Hugh responds so quietly I can barely hear him, "This is my decision. Not yours."

Tears tumble down my burning face. I inch closer and put my arms around him as he grabs me like I am a lifeguard. Floodgates open, releasing months, years of emotions. We weep in each other's arms until we can't breathe.

After dabbing our tears with Hugh's always-ready hankies, I get up to find us something to drink and to look for Kleenex. I sit back down and set the drinks on the steel and glass coffee table. That is when Hugh starts to talk about something I have never heard before. I reach for his hand.

He tells me that when I left the convent last July, he realized that I was free to marry anyone and he did not think he could bear it. "Yet it wasn't only about you," he said, "but about me. What I deeply desire for my life. The chairs on the deck all changed for both of us. I have been in counseling since July."

Knowing that I was now free, he became more aware of feelings that he'd always ignored or put down or run away from. Feelings of not being free. Feelings about his life-long desire to marry and to have children. Feelings about his lonely life in rectories. In the eight months since I left the convent, he was so torn apart and overwhelmed that he could hardly perform his duties as a priest. I find it hard to imagine "Father Brady" not being fully devoted to his people. Over those months, he'd never mentioned to me anything about getting professional help for what he was going through. And I never suspected what he wrestled with during that time.

In late July he'd made an appointment with a psychiatrist the diocese had recommended. He was feeling he would go crazy if he didn't get help. The psychiatrist judged him to be psychologically healthy but told Hugh he had an almost neurotic need for approval and should look at that issue and how it might be affecting the decision he faced. He also suggested that Hugh seek further counseling to work through the choice of marriage or priesthood. Hugh started regular counseling appointments soon after with a minister he trusted, a trained therapist who he described as "a man of God and deep faith and a highly skilled psychologist."

With a sadness I had never seen in him before, he speaks from the center of himself: "I vowed to myself that I would accept whatever I unearthed. Our love was affecting my life in a way that if I did not deal with it head on, I would not be able to function as a person, let alone a priest." Pausing again, he looks down, takes his hand out of mine and closes his eyes. He whispers almost as if he is saying a prayer. "It takes a long time before one reaches a knowledge of his whole being, if ever. I could only lay myself before God and dare to ask for wisdom."

The counselor advised him to wait out his uncertainty, to "live it out", and to be patient for the peace that would eventually come with the right decision. He advised Hugh to face his choices squarely and to be "truthful by the day, by the hour." If one moment he felt he wanted to stay in the priesthood, he should live through that feeling, be with it, and express it, as he often did to me. If the next moment he felt he needed to leave the priesthood to marry, he had to face and live through that possible reality and experience those feelings. They also explored why Hugh had the issue of neurotically seeking approval. This choice had to be his. Only his approval of the final decision was necessary. This life-altering choice could be based on no one else, not even me.

The counselor also told Hugh he had to be truthful with me, whether it was staying or leaving. If we had a relationship of trust as beautiful as Hugh told him it was, I had to be aware of the confusion and contradictions, so that, in the end, I would also understand the result. Hearing all this, I begin to understand why in some letters he would say both that he was committed to his priesthood and that he wanted to marry me.

Because he honored both ways of life, the priesthood and marriage, the counselor explained that Hugh would suffer from contradictory feelings. Giving up either would bring sorrow and grief and even regret. But the counselor also assured Hugh that when the right decision was made, though he did not know how long it would take, the agony would end and peace would come. He warned Hugh that he would be tempted to retreat from the painful feelings, but that he needed to stay with the pain. Staying with his feelings was the only way to come through them. As much as he was encouraged to live with his feelings, Hugh also needed to detach himself from them so that he could grow through them and not be controlled by them.

"He continually encouraged me to 'engage and detach,'" Hugh tells me.

I am trying to absorb his words while adjusting to the fact that he is physically sitting beside me. I can feel the comfort of his kindness vibes travel through my body. *He is here,* I think to myself. *He is telling me he will give up the life he loves and he still loves me.* I close my eyes and think. *This is impossible. Can it be right?* Surreal.

"My job was to face what I felt and surrender," he goes on. "My God, in one day I could be in ten different places. The counselor assured me that God would work within the mystery of my being, in ways I would not know. Those times were difficult. But, my darling, even when I was convinced I would not leave the priesthood, I was certain I would always love you."

Hugh tells me he understood the counselor's emphasis on "engage and detach." For him it was how the Holy Spirit worked. In fact, it was what he had taught me during my Canonical year about making right decisions with the Spirit's guidance.

In one of my Canonical year journals:

> *Be aware of and live with every side of the decision even when it is painful. Stay with what you are feeling and then surrender to the Holy Spirit until the right choice emerges. You will know the right decision because you will be at peace.*

Although he'd often told me about what he was feeling since I'd left the convent, Hugh had never mentioned to me he was in counseling to help him make a final decision. I asked him why. I would have been able to comfort him, support him, be with him through the challenges of unearthing his truth. Then Hugh talks for the remainder of the hour, the longest air time I can ever remember him taking.

"This is my life," he says pointedly. "I did not want you to be involved in my ultimate decision in any way. I wanted to take full responsibility for my decision, just as you took responsibility for leaving religious life. You did what you had to do for yourself. I had to understand what God wanted of me on my own."

With a quake in his voice, he tells me that when I got sick in December, it took everything in his power not to give in and leave the priesthood then. But he had to be "unshakably" certain that this decision to leave the priesthood was about his own heart and not about me.

Knowing his decision was contributing to my illness, he whispers, was as hard for him as making the decision to leave the priesthood. "Your suffering was my worst suffering," he says. Yet he knew I would suffer even more if he changed his mind, went back on his decision, whichever one it might be. "But, Ev, I have lived in dread that you would meet someone else or that something would happen to you," he says, with tears in his eyes.

He then explained that all those days I was in Hornell, he often called Marnie. Or he talked to her after Mass and felt relief when I began to feel better. Marnie thought he ended everything between us and that he simply needed to know about me because the break would be so hard. He did not tell her what was going on with himself. "I told no one. I am telling you first," he says still in a whispered tone.

He prayed that I somehow felt his prayers of healing and the longing in his heart. He tells me he offered up every suffering for me and that his decision had to be from God or he could never live with it. "Marnie suffers for both of us. She's been a lifeline. Always caring and worrying about everyone. Andy, too. Thank God for them."

He also wanted me to know that, even if we do not marry, he will still leave the priesthood. In the deepest recesses of his being, he understands his need to be a husband and father to fulfill his personhood and, for him, his priesthood.

Hugh adjusts himself on the couch so he can look me directly in the eye to say: "Never think you are the cause of my decision. You are the occasion. I thank God that I found you. You have helped me grow and become so much more of a person. It's like something was locked up in me and, when I am with you, new doors open. Like being happy in a way

I could have never imagined. Like God is with me. Like God is with you."

He becomes even more serious and emphasizes again that leaving the priesthood is his truth, not mine. He is sure. He explains that he felt ripped apart for so long when he thought about giving up priesthood. Some days he could hardly function. He could never explain to me how much the decision affected him. But one day, he was so overcome with grief, he threw himself on the altar, begging God to give him a sign. He told God he could not endure the indecision much longer and he would stay a priest if that was His will. "No matter what the cost." He tells me that he was terrified, but "soon a calm came over me." He stayed in church for a long time that day and, during the late afternoon, he came to know he would marry. It was not some great elation. Just peaceful calm. Since then, he has felt no fear, no sorrow, no regret. "Now I will give myself to Christ in a new way," he says, holding my hands tightly again. "I will be baptized into a new life and will feel humbled to live it out. I hope we will be baptized together."

I feel a settling, a peace, pressing down through my body like a gentle snowfall. I sense truth surrounding us and anchoring us to each other. But, having psychologically prepared myself for the opposite reality, I am also in shock. I realize I should say something amazing and profound and supportive. But I simply ask, "How do you leave the priesthood?" He tells me he is on his way to Rochester to tell the Bishop and then his family. This suddenly makes everything very real. I ask when he will leave Hornell.

"That is a problem. I have scheduled retreats and have to attend major meetings with the national and local Cursillo into late March. There are people I want to talk to personally. I don't want to just walk out the door and have people think I don't care about them. I also have lots of threads to tie up with various organizations. I will let people know just before I leave."

He assures me that the first person he will talk to in Hornell is my mother. He will explain how he came to his decision and how he hopes to marry some day—just in case she hears rumors. He doesn't think she will. Telling her himself will help. He will be sure I know when he is going to meet with her. It won't be right away because he doesn't want her to have to carry the burden of this information too long. His plan is to leave St. Ann in early April. "I know God is leading me, Ev. I have not had one moment of doubt. I feel joy grounding me. I will be in touch with Mother Bride. I am sure about this. Sure of this peace. Sure of leaving. Sure of my love for you."

There is one other thing Hugh wants to say. In order to make certain that I will not be implicated in any way in his decision, he thinks it best that he not visit me until he leaves Hornell. He says he will call and write.

"Will you wait for me?" he asks in all seriousness.

"I am already waiting," I say, as I touch his cheek with my trembling fingers.

"I want you to be so much a part of me, but right now I have to do this alone."

"Okay," I whisper, hardly believing this is happening.

Our kiss good-bye is tentative, as if everything were too big to express in a kiss. Or if the kiss might actually be legal. Or if a kiss is appropriate for one leaving his sacred vocation. Just before he opens the door, Hugh takes his finger and traces a cross on my forehead. I trace a cross on his.

Holding me closely and looking into me, he whispers, "Let God bless both of us."

After he leaves, I touch the cross he'd placed on my forehead. It is not Ash Wednesday, but our own Lent will be coming

Chapter 21

FAMILIES

"You are born into your family and your family is born into you."
—*Elizabeth Berg, The Art of Mending*

BECAUSE BISHOP FULTON SHEEN is away, retired Bishop Kearney meets with Hugh in Rochester. Hugh had expected the bishop to challenge him, to accuse him of turning his back on the Church and breaking his vows. But Bishop Kearney says with genuine kindness, "I am sad to see a priest who is so dedicated leave us. You are a good man, Hugh. I will remember you in my prayers." Hugh is humbled and grateful.

After his meeting with the Bishop, Hugh calls his sister Dorothy and asks that she and her husband gather their other four sisters and spouses so that he can talk to them. Never having had a family meeting like this before, they are concerned about what could be so important.

When they meet, Hugh tells his family he has made a big decision, and he wants them to know about it right away. First, he wants to share how God has been present to him throughout his life. He starts with his call to priesthood in the third grade at St. Joseph School in Buffalo, where the family had moved for a few years because of their father's job. He explains that ever since he was a young boy, all he ever wanted was to be a priest. His sisters know this. Over the years, they had watched him grow with a quiet and gentle spirit and a special devotion to Jesus and

Our Lady. They enjoyed peeking into his bedroom as he pretended to say Mass.

Hugh goes on to explain that once he was ordained, even with the inevitable missteps, he devoted every day of his life to being a good priest and servant of God. For him, priesthood is a sacred and unique calling to lead people into the life of Christ, to create community and to celebrate the sacraments and other holy rituals to help people understand and thrive in their personal, spiritual lives. "To bring Christ's love."

With the exception of a clerical culture and the overlay of politics in the Church that makes some priests feel they are superior, separate, and more important than other people, Hugh states what his family always knew: he loves the priesthood. He then shares with them that, during his early years as a high school student and college seminarian, and continuing through his eighteen years as a priest, he did have one constant suffering: a strong but secret desire to marry and have children. He went on to say that, although he had been attracted to women through the years, as any healthy man would be, and despite the fact that he tried to keep focused on his promise of celibacy, he always suffered with longings to marry and share his life with a woman. He would dream about the joy of having his own children.

When he met me, he continues, he tried to ignore the strong attraction he felt. Each time he attempted to walk away, he fell more deeply in love. He explains how we struggled to live out the Third Way, how we failed when deciding to not see each other, and how we earnestly prayed that we would only follow God's will. He adds that he is now at peace with God's will for him. He needs a personal and loving human relationship.

"My yearning to be married is *not* about *not* wanting to be a priest; it is about answering another strong pull to fulfill my true self." He wishes he could live out both. "The married clergy is a possibility with the new

Church. I hope that will be how my life goes."

He then states simply, "I have decided to leave the priesthood."

He stresses that I am not the cause of his decision but the occasion. Even if I chose not to marry him, he would not return to the priesthood— that is how deep his need for personal fulfillment in marriage is. He also says that after the many agonizing months it took to make the decision, he feels freer and more at peace than he ever has before.

By the time he finishes, Hugh's sisters and their husbands are crying and hugging him and telling him that, no matter what he does, he will always be their beautiful brother whom they accept completely. If he has found true love, they are happy for him. When Hugh warns them that they will hear criticism about his leaving the priesthood, they resolve as a family to "hold their heads high." He is more important to them than what anyone says. They assure him he is not doing anything wrong.

Hugh asks his family to keep this news to themselves, even from their children, until he is ready to leave St. Ann's at the end of March or early April. And they do. They later call their brother Jim who lives out of town to tell him the news. Like Hugh, Jim is a very quiet man, but he always knows how to make people feel loved. He, too, supports Hugh uncondi- tionally.

This encounter is typical of Hugh's family. He comes from simple peo- ple, simple in the most profound sense of the word: kind, unassuming, nonjudgmental, humble, and accepting. They were raised in the Depres- sion and value frugality, practicality, and self-discipline. The Catholic faith and the Democratic Party have always been the centerpieces of their world. They work hard, go to church, and live fairly uncomplicated lives. Their parents, who had died by this time, are still their role models.

Anna, their Pennsylvania Dutch mother who'd converted to the faith, was a devout Catholic and was adamant that her children adhere to the Church's rules. She also taught them to cook from scratch, to keep their homes spotless, to raise glorious flowers, and to win at playing cards—as if it were a matter of life and death. Their dad, Hugh, a quiet and gentle Irishman, was a steady provider as a salesman who loved his wife of over forty years and his children. For Anna and Hugh, life was about being good Catholics and ensuring the security and happiness of their family.

I am not counting on the same experience with my family. Thinking about my mother fills me with anguish. After all, she lives in the town where the news will break. Although things are quiet for a few weeks, I live with dread. Hugh's letters come frequently, assuring me how much he is loving me, supporting me, and praying that I continue to feel better. He calls often to check on me. Even with all he is going through, he worries most about me. He reassures me that he is filled with peace and anxious to follow the graces of a new life.

Still, day and night, I worry that my mother will somehow hear the news before Hugh tells her. And, as things turn out, she does. On March 10, at her women's group in the parish, a member asks her if it is true that Father Brady is leaving the priesthood for her daughter. She tells the woman that Father is not leaving the priesthood and that her daughter, of course, would never be involved in anything like that.

Shaken, Mother stops at Marnie's on her way home. When Marnie indicates that what she'd been told is true, Mother looks like she is having a panic attack. She can't breathe. Andy wants to take her to the hospital. But she refuses. She takes sips of water until she can control her breathing and then insists on driving herself home.

"I thought she would be angry," Marnie tells me later. "But her physical response is something I have never seen before. Like she could not comprehend or maybe because she did comprehend."

Marnie calls Hugh to tell him that Mother heard the news of his leaving and that I was involved. The next morning, Hugh goes to our home and, with all the sincerity in his heart, apologizes that Mother had to hear about his leaving before he told her. He assures her that he'd planned to visit her the next week. He also says he naively believed that no one knew. Then he explains how he had come to his decision. Mother is not impressed. She is hurt—irate—and tells him that priests take vows for life and that he is a priest forever according to the order of Melchizedek.

"I have heard that reading all my life," she tells him. "You will always be a priest. Human love is not part of it. You did this behind my back. I even entertained you when Evelyn was home. People know that. Will they think I am a part of this? I would never be. I go to confession to you. Where does this leave me? You have always given me so much attention. It was not because of me. It was because of my daughter. You obviously don't care about me at all. You both should have broken this off as soon as it started. You are only thinking of yourselves. I can't believe this of you. I don't know how I can go to church again."

Hugh quietly tells her that he is not leaving for me, but for himself. He says I might not marry him. He has no guarantee.

"I pray she doesn't marry you. I have been through many battles in my life but none like this. A priest belongs to God and God alone. Aren't priests married to God? How could Evelyn do this? This is wrong. It is a sin."

My mother hates to cry in front of anyone, but she breaks down. She does not want Hugh to comfort her. After he leaves, she phones me and tells me she does not want me to say one word, especially about Father Brady. She is going to talk.

"You have betrayed me, taken advantage of all I have done for you. You are your father's daughter."

The last comment stabs me like a dagger. Maybe I am like him. She states unequivocally that I cannot marry Father under any circumstances.

"It is a sin to marry a priest," she yells over the phone. "A priest belongs only to God."

Mother then tells me not to come home. She has to figure out how she can ever go to church again. How she can walk down the street. I listen and feel the lashes of pain and shame on both of us.

I want to visit her on St. Patrick's Day for her birthday, which we always celebrate with great fanfare. She does not want to see me. Fortunately, my siblings show up in Hornell for "Pat's" birthday and for several weekends after.

Whenever my mother has a problem, she goes crazy with cleaning. And this crisis is no exception. She appreciates having the helping hands of my siblings. But she primarily needs them to accompany her to Mass. At the same time, through it all, they support me. Whatever they think of the situation, and as hard as it is on them, my siblings circle the wagons around me—except for my brother Keith. He is very angry and phones Hugh to say they need to meet immediately. Keith told me later he fully intended to beat up Hugh. They meet at Keith's house in Rochester. Betty has taken the little girls out for the day. When Hugh arrives full of his gentle optimism, Keith looks at him and says, "You son of a bitch! Making a fool of my sister and my family."

Hugh is startled. Keith moves toward Hugh and Hugh realizes that they may have a physical confrontation. He is afraid. Keith raises his arms. Hugh grabs Keith's wrists above his head.

"Please, Keith. What are you doing? What is this about? Tell me."

Hugh releases Keith and he shakes himself off and lights a cigarette. He tells Hugh to sit down.

"What the hell are you involved with my sister for?"

Hugh leans forward and says, "Can we talk about this? I know how much you and everyone else have suffered. I am glad you called me."

That is when Keith hears the full story. The two men drink beer and talk for three hours at the kitchen table. Hugh explains that we did not intend to fall in love and shares how we had fully intended to stay in our vocations. He talks about the counseling, my illness, all our ups and downs. He apologizes for the hurt this has brought upon Keith and our family. Keith heard Hugh that afternoon and Hugh sees that his anger comes from a need to protect me and my family. Once again, Hugh learns that my family is all about protecting each other.

Fortunately, I have experienced this "protection", the constant support of siblings throughout my life. Sometimes the support comes by phone calls or letters, sometimes money, sometimes simply being with me or offering physical help, like with cleaning or cooking or gardening or babysitting. Whatever would ease my burden. I would do the same for them.

In thinking about family dynamics these many years later I remember reading Margaret Mead's writing that growing up in a large family is a natural training ground for people to live in community. Children in large families learn how to adjust and compromise and they bring these skills to their adult lives. Of course, there are also amazing gifts for children reared in small families or as only children. I see this in my own grandchildren. Still, I believe siblings in a large family have a head start on working out the interaction of group dynamics. They have to if they want to survive! Mead also wrote, "Sisters are the most competitive relationships within the family but, once the sisters are grown, their relationships become the strongest relationships." That has been my experience with my sisters. I can trust them to be loyal to me, no matter how off-base or lost I get. They are always there for me, accepting me and supporting and I am equally supportive of them.

Without being conscious of it, I realize now that I bring the same openness and energy I share with my siblings to my friendships. Over a lifetime, friends have become my family. How we relate to friends is sometimes based on how we relate to siblings. At least for me this is true.

I especially needed friendship with siblings and friends during this hard time that many regarded as "scandalous." When the news broke about Hugh, backlash came frequently. A few days after my mother's call, our pastor at St. Ann phoned and accused me of being a "gold digger," of taking a holy priest from the people of Hornell.

"Go to confession," he screams over the phone.

Although I know he is an alcoholic, and can almost smell the liquor coming through the phone lines, I am heartbroken. Soon letters arrive in my Buffalo State College mailbox that are so painful I can hardly hold them in my hands. Only a few people sign their names, but none I recognize. The postmarks on the envelopes are from Rochester, Watkins Glen, Corning and Hornell, all places where Hugh was stationed. Their messages range from civil requests such as, "It is not too late. Let Father Brady return to the priesthood." to "You are another Mary Magdalene. You have tempted a priest to leave the holy Church." One envelope came with one word on the stationery: "Harlot." I cannot catch my breath.

Yet, I am grateful for the comfort one letter brings me from an elderly man in Hornell I never knew. "It seems it is just about time that the Catholic Church realizes that being married as a priest does not take anything away from goodness. I would say after 47 years of marriage that marriage is where I learned goodness. I wish you and Father Brady luck, but I sure will miss his smile."

I am amazed by Hugh's equanimity throughout these days of scandal. He makes it a point to visit many parishioners and friends in Hornell and tells and retells the story of why he is leaving. He explains that he personally needs a married life for fulfillment of his personhood, and, because he loves the priesthood, he hopes that a married clergy will be instituted soon. When asked, he says that he has no specific plans but would like to be married someday.

Hugh is brave to face people, and many are touched that he reaches out to them. A few ask him if he would possibly reconsider. But most parishioners are warm and open and wish him well. Several say they can't understand why the Catholics don't allow married priests.

Devoting the rest of his time to tying up his obligations, Hugh also walks through his days with an underlying fear of the unknown, as well as with the heartbreak of leaving the Catholic priesthood that has been the desire of his life since he was ten years old. In another week he will be forty-two. Yet he also experiences joy and optimism for the future. Optimism is Hugh's middle name.

During this time, there are people in Hornell who continue to gossip behind his back and spread rumors. "Father Brady is already married. He has been living part time in Buffalo with the McLean girl." Unfortunately, my mother's neighbor keeps her abreast of the rumors. I am helpless to protect her and can barely deal with my guilt and heartbreak. I encourage Hugh to return to the priesthood if, after all this, it is what he now wants to do. Fortunately, Hugh's letters of reassurance keep coming.

> *I am writing to set you at ease. I am not worrying. I feel free to do whatever is God's will and have great confidence that life ahead is to be filled without complications. I am not afraid, but look forward to it with enthusiasm. I long with all my heart to marry you. With all the freedom I am experiencing that has not changed. As I take these first steps into the open air, I have no indication that they are leading me toward a return to priesthood.*

You have been everywhere before me these days, in peo-
ple, in chance sayings. ... My love for you deepens day
after day.

Without Hugh's expressions of love, I cannot survive the phone calls
and letters or the unrelenting sorrow that I feel for having put my mother in what for all of us is a new shame. I am a hundred miles away, and I
cannot protect her. In a large family with a single parent, there are unique
family dynamics. For our family, it is an us-against-the-world mentality.

Over the years, Mother took the scraps and remnants of life and, with
an iron will, pieced them together to keep her family whole. Although she
could be far too controlling, she kept us together as a family. Is that not
what all of us are asked to do? Take the life we are given and, despite its
hardships or short-comings, live it as fully as possible? Isn't that Poverty
of Spirit? As strong as she is, however, Mother will not accept or tolerate
having a daughter in love with a priest. I am "shunned." Through it all, I
know that we only get one mother, and I am choosing to continue to love
mine. I doubt that she believes it.

Chapter 22

SONG TO MY MOTHER

"A woman writing thinks back through her mother."
—Virginia Wolff

~What would be the balm for such a bruised and aching spirit?
Who could soothe these hardships?
"I can, I can," I sang each day to my mother,
harmonizing with my siblings.
-Evelyn

MY MOTHER'S EYES ARE corn-flower blue; my father's, blue as the sea. Their blues create a blue rainbow of family, a unique and different blue for each of their children. Except for me. My father and I share the same shade of sea blue. Mother's eyes are the blue that brings you to a place far away, a place in the sky where she holds onto her life. A life of hurt and shame. A place of anger. Life has beaten my mother down. She is determined that her children will bring her to her rightful place in that sky. Some do. Some don't.

My mother's eyes are oceans,
No one knows their depth.

I wait

for her waters

to break over me

like a mother wave,

baptize me into completion.

But her ocean roams the sky,

looks down on me

like sky does

without noticing who is below.

As a little girl, the seventh of eight children, I knew my mother as another adult in the house, maybe like Hattie, the lady who helped cook and clean, or maybe like a friend who came to visit for a while. When I went to bed, I tried not to go right to sleep because, as darkness came, Mother would put neatly folded clothes into our dresser drawers. I wanted to breathe in her gardenia presence. If she knew we were still awake, she would speak to us in words that had the softness of flannel and I would wrap myself inside of them. I would take her words with open hands and place them in my heart. She often checked on my sister Lillis, putting her hand on Lil's forehead to make sure her allergies did not run away with her health. Or she might cover Janice, the baby, and kiss her head. I waited. She knew I was all right.

At six or seven, I would often wake during the night with cries of pain in my legs. When that happened, Mother would run in to check on me and rub my skinny, toothpick limbs. With the polio scare, the doctor would come, even during the night, and each time he told Mother, to her great relief, "More growing pains." I loved my growing pains. Of course, I saw my mother when she cooked, served food, and cleaned. Or when she was reading her pile of novels. Or calling out the door that dinner was ready. I remember her bathing us with military discipline. Water temperature just right. Every part of our little bodies and hair washed thoroughly, rinsed and toweled dry. Next child. She may have spoken sweet and tender words then. If she did, I forgot to open my hands to put them in my heart.

There were no divisions in the layers of Mother's suffering. The crosses she endured in childhood opened their arms wide to hold on to the pain of adulthood. At the age of seven, Mother was taken from her family and the Mother she loved. She was forced to move in with her Aunt Dehlia to help raise Dehlia's children, who'd been left fatherless from the great influenza epidemic. Patricia, my mother, was a child raising children for an aunt who cast her grief on all of them, year after year. Every day Mother cleaned and babysat and even helped with cooking.

When I think of today's parents whose children are often the center of the family universe, my mother's misplacement might seem harsh and even unimaginable. But for many immigrants, survival took precedence over a child's wellbeing. The role of children was to support the parents, not the other way around. When I reflect on what happened to my mother and how little understanding the adults in her family had about children, it helps me to understand her parenting style. And yet my mother developed a resilience that grew out of her hardships and it was her resilience that saved her and all of us.

Despite Mother's feelings of not being wanted by her own family, and the difficulty of caring for three small children as a child herself, my mother Patricia Mescall achieved the highest average in grade eight at School #26. Even today in Buffalo, the eighth-grade student with the highest average in each public school is awarded the prestigious and coveted Jesse Ketchum Award which will soon celebrate its 150th Anniversary of recognizing young Buffalo scholars. In that year, 1918, however, Mother's principal decided a boy with the next highest average would receive the award. This had never happened before.

Mother pleaded with her parents to go to the school and claim her rightful honor. But they did not have the courage to protest. They were immigrants from Ireland shaped and formed by fear of the British and the Catholic Church. They experienced this same fear when they encountered other institutions in their new land. At ninety years old, not long before she died, Mother again told us how she should have had the Jesse Ketchum medal to leave to us. Some childhood experiences are never forgotten, and for Mother, this event profoundly influenced how she saw life. How she trusted life.

Seven years after she was sent to Aunt Dehlia's, now ready for high school, Mother returned to her family home. She continued to be an outstanding scholar at South Park High School and she loved her principal, Dr. Bapst. At their assemblies he introduced the students to classical music and talked about values and the lifelong gift of learning. School was like a church for Mother and Dr. Bapst the high priest. No matter what else was going on, the classrooms and assemblies of South Park High School provided Mother a refuge and the endless world of learning and a way to gain access to a life where she could excel. Every Saturday, to have more books to read, Mother walked three miles or, if lucky enough to have money for carfare, rode the bus to the downtown library. Another sanctuary in her life.

We were often told that she raised us on Dr. Bapst's philosophy and she did: education, a spotlessly clean home, Christian values, especially our obligations to those less well off, and exposure to literature, classical music and the arts. But in her senior year of high school, just as she was advancing toward more recognition for her academic gifts, her father, my grandfather Michael, demanded that Mother quit school. She had to find a job because he drank away his pay check. Mother, the responsible child, was designated to pay the bills. The chance for further education and where it might have led her, ended.

At eighteen, and without a diploma, Mother found a job as a "Larkin Girl" at Buffalo's iconic Larkin Soap Company. In 1922, although society was not ready for young women to travel alone as saleswomen, the bright, attractive Larkin Girls were eager and prepared. Unaccompanied, Mother traveled by train to the North Country, stayed alone in boarding houses, represented Larkin mail order products and telegraphed money from her pay check each week that only her mother could sign for. Her sales skyrocketed; her accounts were meticulous. It took courage. She traveled for the Larkin Company for ten years until she met my Canadian father one snowy afternoon at a bus stop in Buffalo.

In marriage, her needs continued to be dismissed. She married a man whose purpose was to succeed in business. Mother's emotional needs simply did not exist for him. After my father died, my mother's basic distrust of people only exacerbated her insecurities, especially about Hornell. Without my father's financial and social status to give her an identity, Mother felt like a refugee in our small town. She believed that people in Hornell thought if you were not born and reared there, you were simply a guest, maybe a foreigner, maybe an imposter.

In contrast, I wanted to make Hornell my home. I wanted to plant its flowers, organize a community picnic and cheer for the hometown team. To Mother, Hornell was enemy territory and I a traitor ingratiating myself into its culture. She was as mistrustful of me as she was of the town's people. But courage was always her companion.

~What would be the balm for such a bruised and aching spirit?
Who could soothe these hardships?
"I can, I can," I sang each day to my mother,
harmonizing with my siblings.
-Evelyn

Courage is not always one grand gesture. Courage is seen in the endless responsibilities to keep yourself and others going: putting food on the table, paying bills on time, making education a priority for children, keeping a house achingly clean. Doing it without another adult to help or support you. No relative in Hornell. Few acquaintances. Rushing to be on time for a job way below your abilities, coming home to cook something, facing the laundry and the arguments among siblings, weeding the garden. It was a painful life and lonely. It was exhausting.

Out of her suffering, however, a great compassion grew in my mother. If someone needed a few extra dollars, or if a neighbor or one of us was sick, or if someone died, my mother made her soup. We were all part of the ingredients and, like one body, the kindness soup would be offered from all of us to anyone in need.

One crisp Columbus Day, when I was visiting Hornell on my day off from teaching at Painted Post, I decided to collect fallen leaves at Maple City Park. I would iron the colorful leaves between long sheets of wax paper and hang the sheets in my classroom windows. Stained-glass leaf windows for the sun to shine through on autumn days. A man passed, and then walked back to me.

"Hey, aren't you a McLean girl?"

"Yes," I replied, wondering how he knew me.

"How's your mother? I'm Frank Dolan."

"Fine, Mr. Dolan. You know my mother?"

"Yeah, I know her. She works in the Unemployment Office." He looks down and scuffs his feet through the layers of bright red and gold maple leaves that had fallen across the path and then he states: "A saint, that woman." Frank takes the cigarette, that is drooping between his lips, out of his mouth and throws it into the leaves. He grinds the cigarette into the ground with the toe of his shoe to be sure it's out and looks up at me. "A few years back, I was down and out. Drinking a lot. My wife sick. I looked pretty rough and didn't smell too great, either. No one at the Unemployment Office wanted to take my claim.

But your mother always called to me to come to her window. Like I was goddam Ike himself! One time she had to tell me I would be getting five dollars less in my check. She knew about my wife and asked me to wait a minute. When she returned, she gives me the envelope with my unemployment check and three smackers with a note, "For medicine, not drink."

"Sounds like my mother," I smile.

"Tell her I won't never forget her."

"I sure will, Frank. It will make her day."

In May of my senior year of high school, my friend Sally and I went to McBride's, the most expensive store in Hornell, to see the gown that Sally had put on layaway for our senior prom. That was the day I saw the gown of my dreams. As my sister Blanche and I were doing the dishes that night, I described the layers of lilac netting with tiny gold sparkles through the tiers of the full ballerina-length gown, its pleated silk bodice and the tiny braided gold spaghetti straps.

"That sounds beautiful," Mother said as she worked at the kitchen table writing out her bills.

The next morning Mother told me to meet her after work at Mc-Bride's to show her the gown. "Oh, no, we could never afford it," I said. "I was just talking about the material."

"Let's go and see," Mother replied.

For the next six weeks, Mother gave me seven one-dollar bills, carefully counted out, to put down on the lilac gown. My friend Sally told me she was jealous that I would wear that dress. I told her I was jealous of myself.

One other particular memory about my mother has stayed with me. When we were getting ready for Sunday Mass, she always held out a portion from the small amount of money she would otherwise put aside for the collection at Sunday Mass. That portion she gave to the Salvation Army.

"I don't care what structures the Church thinks it needs. The Church builds buildings, but the Salvation Army builds people."

Because of how she lived her life, we all learned to look beyond our needs to the needs of others. Despite her goodness, however, mother's emotional pain wore her down and seeped into my consciousness.

She tried to fit me into that world. She and I both knew it was a losing battle. Even as a child, though neither of us was at fault, I felt the chasm of our differences. I just wasn't the right kind of daughter for her. It is not easy for a mother to birth a child who reminds her of the husband who was so focused on himself that he didn't see who his wife was or take care of her. It is hard for a child to figure out what is wrong with the way she is. It is hard for her to figure out how not to be her father.

~What would be the balm for such a bruised and aching spirit?
Who could soothe these hardships?
"I can, I can," I sang each day to my mother,
harmonizing with my siblings.
-Evelyn

Chapter 23

Poverty of Spirit

You're blessed when you feel you've lost what is dear to you.
Only then can you be embraced by the One most dear to you.
—The Beatitudes: Matthew 5:1-3
The Message

At 5:30 AM on March 30, 1969, in the dark and chilling rain and wearing a black knitted hat and long, black raincoat, Father Brady walks quickly from the rectory and crosses Erie Avenue to St. Ann Church. He carefully carries a box under one arm to keep it from getting wet and does not notice how the bottom of his long black cassock sweeps through the puddles, dragging the hem down around his shoes. At the church, with his free arm, he reaches in his pocket for the familiar key and unlocks the side door. He turns the lights on in the sacristy, the room behind the main altar of the church, and puts the box on a table. He takes off his wet hat and coat, drapes them over the back of a chair, and then opens a closet to select his vestments. He begins to vest for Mass.

First he holds the amice, a white, narrow oblong linen cloth and places it around the back of his neck. He then puts on the alb, the long white cotton robe that goes down to the ankles. A silk, purple stole, which he kisses, is placed around his neck. He ties the white cord called a cincture around his waist and puts his head through the hole of the chasuble, a purple, tunic-type silk vestment trimmed with gold braiding. The purple indicates we are in Lent, the penitential season.

Now vested, Father takes one host from the box of unconsecrated hosts and pours about two tablespoons of red altar wine into one of two cruets. He pours some water in the other cruet and places the corporal, the large, square white cloth, underneath the chalice and the paten on the unlikely altar, a cabinet in the sacristy. He opens *The Bible* to the readings of the day and strikes a wooden match to light a single white candle.

Taking a deep breath, he blesses himself and slowly and reverently genuflects to begin his last Mass without a congregation, without a prepared homily, without anyone but himself. He deliberates over each word of the liturgy, whispering out loud or talking silently in his heart and, as he has always done, gives his full attention to every aspect of the ritual. When Mass is over, he speaks out loud, "Go in peace to love and serve the Lord," and crosses himself. He then walks to the opposite wall and sits down on one of the wooden chairs. He puts his head in his hands and weeps.

After wiping his tears with his hankie, he returns the vestments to their proper place in the closet and carefully puts away each sacramental item except the chalice, which he rinses and wipes dry. He opens the box and, in the original satin lining, he places his chalice, an ordination gift his parents had given him with an inscription on the bottom: "Rev. Hugh Francis Brady. Ordination 1951. Love, Dad and Mom." It is 1969. In a few weeks, Hugh will be celebrating his forty-third birthday. He has been a priest for eighteen years.

Carrying the chalice in the box, Hugh walks back to the rectory in the faint gray light of the early morning and goes directly to his room to finish packing all his earthly possessions: a suitcase of clothes; his grey winter jacket bought in 1951; his leather gloves; his brush and comb from his seminary days in the 1940s; two paper bags filled with "stuff" and six boxes of books and notes. He carries them to his 1965 blue compact Pontiac Tempest parked in the rectory's side lot. No one sees him.

Later, Hugh has lunch with the pastor as well as the new assistant and talks in pleasantries but not about the momentous day this is for him. Since he has spent the two previous days going over information for the new assistant, there is no need to discuss the routines and obligations any further.

Hugh calls me from the rectory after his lunch. He has a question about his chalice. Some priests who leave the priesthood to marry keep their chalices, which are personal property, and have them melted down into wedding rings. He asks me if that is something I would want. I ask him what he wants to do with the chalice.

"I want what you want," he assures me.

"I only want what you want," I respond.

"If you really mean that, I will leave it here at St. Ann, Ev, but if this is something you would like, just tell me. I am okay either way," he states clearly in a low voice.

"It should stay at St. Ann. That way something of you will always be there."

"It has held the body and blood of Christ. I will put it in the sacristy before I leave. I just wanted to check."

"Thank you. I think it is best to leave it," I say with my heart aching for him. "How are you doing?"

"A funny feeling. Sad but totally peaceful. Yes, my love, I am fine but, as you know, leaving isn't easy. I am anxious to be on the road in about an hour."

He had rented an apartment in Wellsville, a town near Alfred University, not far from Hornell. He has been taking a sensitivity course at the university and wants to complete it.

I often daydreamed what it would be like if Hugh and I ever had the chance to freely be together. It wouldn't be "roses and violins" or fireworks or any big celebration. We both knew the enormity of this possible decision. Rather, I pictured us walking in a park holding hands, grateful that the time had finally come when we could be with each other in freedom and without guilt. The reality is, because of the continuing tension over the scandal, we feel estranged from each other and confused. I am afraid to see him for fear we will be "reported on". Always on my mind is what is happening with my mother. Not knowing the direction the Spirit will lead us, we are all experiencing a seismic shift and none of us knows the aftermath.

When he arrives in Wellsville, Hugh calls me again. I feel that I should be more loving and supportive and worried for him, as I know he would have been for me. Instead, I can't get out of my head the suffering I am causing my family and the people in the parish. Somehow, I am angry at Hugh, as if he were responsible for the rumors getting out before he spoke to my mother.

As it turns out, he tells me, he is responsible, though not intentionally. The rumors most likely originated with a young woman in Hornell. She is a friend of a girl in Rochester whose brother is a priest. Apparently at a priests' gathering, Hugh took aside some of his classmates and told them about his decision to leave and asked them to keep his news confidential. However, one of the classmates told his sister that Father Brady was leaving the priesthood for some woman from Hornell. The sister then told her friend in Hornell. For several months Hugh had been counseling this very friend, a nursing student at St. James Hospital.

At his final appointment with the nursing student, without knowing the news had gotten out, Hugh inquired if she had any things that she wanted to ask him because he would be tying up their counseling sessions. Guilt ridden, the student blurted out that her friend from Rochester had told her he was leaving the priesthood to marry someone from Hornell and that she had told her mother. She overheard her mother telling her grandmother. Who knows who told whom next? Nevertheless, she thought she was responsible and was sad that she had hurt him.

Hugh was completely accepting of how this had happened and thanked the young woman for being so brave in letting him know. He told her not to worry at all. "These things always seem to get out in one way or another—and who knew? Maybe it got out through someone else," he consoled her.

When Hugh tells me about it, I do not feel so big-hearted. My family is still suffering, as if they, too, are responsible for our parish losing its beloved priest. Even though Hugh continually tells me that I am not responsible for his leaving, and certainly that my family isn't, it does not feel that way.

Soon after Hugh moves to Wellsville, my brother-in-law Andy visits him in his tiny apartment and calls to tell me that he thinks Hugh is okay. But, because Hugh was boiling peas in a frying pan when Andy was there, Andy worries how he is going to cook for himself. He need not have worried. Hugh turned out to be a fabulous cook, a master chef who learned from his Pennsylvania Dutch mother how to make delicate sauces, a variety of entrees, rich desserts, and all from scratch. He was simply using the only pan in the apartment.

During his first week in Wellsville, Hugh discovers a deeper meaning of the Beatitude, "Blessed are the poor in spirit." He is living in a sparse three-room apartment without his identity as priest, without a job, without a community, without a direction—and without me. He lives in this darkness for eight straight days, going to Mass, praying, trying to read

232 The Nun and The Priest

scripture, attending class twice a week and each day walking for hours without any destination. He tells me he will wait for me to call him if I want to talk. I do not feel up to talking. But his letters of love soothe and support me.

> *Not since January, 1968, have I felt so much love for you. It is as if I discovered you all over again... But I suffer with you, feel your pain, your anguish, your confusion ... I prayed sincerely to know more deeply your suffering. It continues to come to me, yours, your mother's, your family's. What a great price I have brought upon you all. How can any of you love me? How much you bring me again of God, his love for me in your great love! ... I have asked God to give me your suffering and to fill you with peace and calm.*

He signs off,

> *'I love you so much. I believe your suffering will lead only to true happiness and deep union with God. I continue to give you to him.*
>
> *Hugh*

As much as I burn to be with Hugh, or to just hear his sweet, healing voice, something holds me back. It is a twilight time: night does not come nor does the day leave. Guilt grabs me by the throat and keeps me helpless. I ask myself over and over, *How should I relate to Hugh and how can I be free of despair?* I fall behind on my graduate papers, avoid students, and barely go to meetings. I am awake half the night and sleep half the day. Then one day I cannot bear not talking to him.

When I phone to ask Hugh when we can get together, he sounds more broken than I feel. Hesitantly, I ask him how he is doing. He simply says it is difficult. He assures me that God is speaking to him, shaping him, loving him in this wilderness. I remembered what I had written in one of my convent journals: *"God fills us in our emptiness."*

"Poverty of spirit?" I gently ask.

"Yes, just hanging on."

"Me, too."

I then tentatively ask, "Second thoughts?"

"Not a one."

Hugh wants me to know that his love for me is even stronger—which he had not thought was possible—and that he is suffering while waiting to be with me. I tell him my heart is crowded with everything about him.

This phone call releases us from our prisons. Hugh has to give a presentation at his 5:00 PM class the next day, Thursday, and will drive to Buffalo before he goes to Rochester to visit his sisters on Friday. "I know you need to take this slowly. I have the rest of my life," he assures me.

When we are ready to hang up, Hugh tries to make his voice sound hopeful and happy for me. But I can hear it quiver. I wonder if I can wait two more days to be with the one who completes me. I also worry how it will be when we are with each other. Robert Penn Warren's words come into my head, "For what is a poem but a hazardous attempt at self-understanding: it is the deepest part of autobiography." A poem comes to me; I pick up a pen. *"There is nothing left but love./All we had is gone and all we have is now./This moment of sky./This hand to hold./This breath of life./Come then my love./Dance sorrows down the morning./Save grief for another day. ... I am here ... "*

The poem expresses how I am feeling on the most authentic level of myself. At the same time, on another level I am still experiencing almost no feeling and, on yet another level, a labyrinth of confusion and sorrow. I know, even though I have Hugh's love, I have lost my mother's and am the cause of suffering for the rest of my family and the people in my parish.

I also know the poem is who I truly am, "the deepest part of autobiography."

When Hugh arrives that Friday, I sense a huge distance between us. There is an awkwardness with him for the first time since I met him. Dressed in brown slacks and a plaid shirt, he sits down on the couch and invites me to sit next to him. As he puts his arm around me, he takes my chin and turns it toward him and says, "Hi." I move closer to him. He tightens his arm around me. I want to dissolve into him, but the crisis we are living through is wedged between us. We have so much to say and can say nothing. We kiss with an impossible tenderness and weariness.

I ask Hugh if he plans to stay in Wellsville. He tells me he is desperate for employment and envies store clerks and waitresses because their work gives them an identity. He tells me about the organization called Bearings in New York City that helps men who've left the priesthood find jobs. They refer to former priests as "inactive" priests because their organization believes, as we do, that it will be just a matter of time before there will be a married clergy.

When his classes end in another week, he says, he will fly to New York and then return to stay in Rochester with his sister Dorothy and her family. During our visit, we feel drawn to each other like magnets, but we sense a strange distance. Although we are now free to kiss and embrace without fear or guilt, we feel awkward again. At least I do. It's like I have done something wrong and any affection I show is proving it. To adjust to sorrow and joy in the same chambers of the heart takes time.

Hugh phones from New York and tells me about the Bearing's workshops. The men discuss how to integrate the lifestyle of a clergyman with that of a lay person. There are other practical sessions: writing a resume, negotiating a salary, interviewing for a job and paying bills, which many of these former clergymen have never done. One workshop focuses on the importance of sharing feelings, something many priests have not been trained to do. If the inactive priest is with a woman, showing sensitivity to her needs will be paramount as she also will be adjusting to a new way of being in the relationship.

Even though the workshops do not lead to a job, Hugh feels the experience is extremely helpful, especially being with men who are going through the same challenges. When he returns to Rochester, he continues to look for work.

Although I still do not hear from my mother, I call Marnie frequently to ask how Mother is feeling about things. It is never good. I am not only adjusting to Hugh not being a priest, but me not having a mother.

Besides seeing each other on the weekends, Hugh and I continue writing letters to each other. In one, he acknowledges that the transition from priesthood to lay life will take time and has some challenges, but he expresses this in his typical optimistic and deep spirit.

> *I only trust that this Nazareth of my life has meaning*
> *and purpose, and that little things are as redemptive as*
> *the mission of preaching and counseling. Bud* (Hugh's
> brother-in-law and Dorothy's husband) *admitted that*
> *he does not understand the leaving off of the power to*
> *change bread and wine into Christ's body and blood*
> *that—anything could be greater. ... I do not understand*
> *either, unless much more important is the power to*
> *become and to be personally transformed... I was only*
> *reminded of the mystery of it all.*
> *...Maybe it is in exchange for another kind of*
> *consecration.*

Chapter 24

LEARNING LOVE

"When you realize you want to spend the rest of your life with somebody,
you want the rest of your life to start as soon as possible."
—*When Harry Met Sally*

IN EARLY JUNE, A friend tells Hugh that Bill Haupt, a Rochester man who works for General Motors Institute in London, Ontario, is often looking to hire former/inactive priests as trainers for middle managers at the Institute. These men usually make excellent employees: They are well educated, skilled as speakers and writers, disciplined, and possess well-developed organizational skills—all qualities Bill wants to impart to his managers. Also, and significantly, the former priests care about people. Bill is affectionately known as "the bishop".

Hugh applies and is offered a job in London, Ontario. He moves to St. Catherine's, Ontario, about half way between his work place and Buffalo. If the Peace Bridge traffic cooperates, Hugh can be at my apartment in forty-five minutes.

That July, "normal breathing" returns; the crisis is abating. Hugh begins to attend Mass with me at the Buffalo State College Newman Center where Father Jack Weimer and the staff, except for Sister Frances, who is skeptical, welcome him with warmth and acceptance. Sister Frances takes me aside one day to tell me that "It isn't too late. Hugh can still return to priesthood." I am stunned and tell her she should talk to Hugh. She doesn't. But she eventually accepts both of us, and we grow to love her like our Godmother.

During the long-distance courting between the States and Canada, we call each other every night, and we continue to write letters. Now when I reread Hugh's letters from almost fifty years ago, I am more aware of how letter writing was as much a part of our lives as digital communication is now. I sometimes wonder if today's online communications will be saved and cherished the way actual letters can be, passed from generation to generation. To me, letters say so much more about a person than print on a screen. A letter's unique script reveals who the writer is. Is it small and precise writing in almost perfectly straight lines like Hugh's? Or is it a larger with more fluid movement like mine?

When I read Hugh's letters today, I hear his voice and am again moved by the depth of his thinking and the sincerity of his emotions. I become aware of how much time he took to carefully fold the many pages of stationery, how he sealed the envelope with his tongue, how he neatly shaped my name on the envelope. I also recall many of my own feelings during those times of our correspondence and think, *I hold the same paper he touched.* I hope the next generations will know the value of hard-copy letters and cards so that, as years pass, they, too, can hold the messages in their hands and be reconnected with the thoughts and feelings from another era through the intimacy of hand-written letters.

In the summer of 1969, Hugh and I start "courting" in our own way. We have fun with picnics, swimming, bike riding and driving along the Niagara River, always looking for places to stop to sit close to the water. But we also enjoy spending time reading and discussing Scripture. As a pre-Vatican Catholic, I was not raised studying the Old and New Testaments; our elementary religion curriculum focused more on doctrine and prayers. Scripture for the laity was not part of pre-Vatican life.

When I was growing up, if a Bible were in a Catholic home, it would have been unusual to find people reading it. For many years, only the priests were considered educated and "holy" enough to interpret God's Word. Friends told me the focus in their Catholic high school biblical studies was academic and not necessarily to impart lessons related to their lives. Now, the Vatican Council encourages lay people to read the Bible and ponder God's Word in the "context of their own salvation history," as if God is speaking directly to our lives. For me these days, the Bible becomes a sacred braid of holy writings, literature, and life lessons. Interpreting and discussing its passages with Hugh is enriching and, yes, for us, even fun.

We are also excited about the different sections of the Documents of the Second Vatican Council and are filled with hope for a new Church. We pray together and ask God to bring peace to my mother. At the Newman Center, we attend the coffee hours after Mass where we make friends and participate with ministries.

We also have the kinds of fun I am more familiar with. I take Hugh to dances where he stiffly moves his feet and tries to pick up the beat of the music. I laugh and tell him he will eventually just start dancing. "Just like riding a bike! Suddenly you will dance," I say encouragingly. He never does. I often dance around him or by myself or with friends, but for me that doesn't matter. I just want to dance.

I drag Hugh to parties with the dorm directors and he ends up the one who doesn't want to leave. There are plays and concerts at Artpark in Lewiston. It is all new to him and all good. He tells me there was a great gap in his seminary education in terms of the arts and he is "coming alive" in them.

I don't think anyone can be as romantic as Hugh. Each week he fills every room of my apartment with flowers, brings me books and other presents, cooks delicious meals and bakes cookies, cakes and pies from scratch. So that I will have flowers outside my window in the spring, he plants hundreds of daffodil and hyacinth bulbs on the lawn in front of my apartment, even though it is New York State property. He fixes my sewing machine with his careful hands and chips in with cleaning or volunteers with errands. When I have research at the downtown library, I want him to stay at the apartment to be comfortable, but he insists on accompanying me, saying, "I just want to be near you." He asks me what plays people are talking about and surprises me with tickets. We go to the movies if the weekend is rainy.

One Friday evening Hugh calls to say he will be late coming from Canada to my apartment. It is almost 10:00 PM when he arrives. He had told me the night before that we would go on a picnic.

"Are you ready for the picnic?" he asks as he opens the door with a great smile on his face.

"It's too late for a picnic, but we can find something to eat here," I say, gently smiling back at him.

"This is a starlight picnic, Ev. Grab a blanket."

I pull the tattered quilt off my bed and walk to his car complaining that it is too late to go on a picnic. He smiles again and opens the car door for me. We drive across the Skyway and park at an isolated spot on the shoreline of Lake Erie. As we walk along the beach to find a place to "picnic", the almost full moon follows us like a spot light. Hugh carries the shopping bags to a hidden sandy area. I spread out the quilt.

With plates and silverware that he had purchased at the Gold Circle Store on his way to pick me up, he lays the quilt table. He takes two cup-like candle holders, puts a little round white candle in each, lights them, and places them on the quilt. He then reaches into one shopping bag and places a vase filled with yellow roses, my favorites, on the center of the quilt. He pours red wine into cut-crystal wine glasses he had purchased in Canada. Two white, real-linen napkins are set next to the silverware. Then the cheeses. Then the crusty bread. Then the antipasto, followed by peanut butter cookies he had made the night before at his apartment.

After our perfect repast, we pack away the picnic and lie on the quilt staring up at the endless universe. A field of stars shines down on us in the black night as we listen to Lake Erie continually kissing the shore.

"The stars are falling into us, Evie," Hugh whispers. "The sky is in us and we are in the sky."

"Like the universe is the next train stop," I whisper back.

That night on the shores of Lake Erie with my grandmother's quilt now pulled around us, we feel at one with the entire universe and become completely at one with each other.

As the summer weeks pass, we visit local town parks and some weekend nights we drive along the Niagara Parkway on our way to see the colored lights on Niagara Falls. We listen to music on the car radio and sway to its rhythms. We laugh at nothing and everything. On weekends, we visit Hugh's family in Rochester where each of his sisters welcomes me. My siblings are in touch with us, too, and supportive, especially Jan and Joe who live nearby.

I soon realize that what I do for Hugh can never compare to what he does for me. When I worry about it, he always says: "There is no 50-50 in a relationship. No one's keeping score." I do simple things like continually trying to figure out a new way to teach him to dance, the only skill he never mastered. I buy him Bermuda shorts and summer golf shirts. I bring him *The New York Times* on Sundays and cook eggs "over easy" for him like his mother once did. I read him poems which I tell him are prayers in disguise. Hugh's needs always seem so small, and yet my simple gifts are received with so much gratitude that it makes me feel as if they are something spectacular. I also notice how much care he takes with any gift I give.

We become a couple. I feel proud and lucky that this handsome man is always reaching for my hand or has his arm around me at parties or at church. Yet all the happiness of being with others does not surpass being alone in Hugh's peaceful presence. I fall more deeply in love with him each day—and he with me. Sometimes we will be in a room reading or studying and Hugh will look up and say, "Evie, you thrill me." I feel as if the dream I am living is true and no longer believe I will someday wake up to my "real" life. I am in my real life. Being together is almost more than a heart can hold.

As our days of romance continue, one question keeps slipping into my mind. "If we love each other so much, if we are so exclusively 'into each other', what about sharing our good fortune with others? Shouldn't we also be doing at least something for other people this summer? Can love be selfish?" Hugh responds to my concerns in a letter.

> *We have had so many wonderful days together which I would not exchange for anything. They are ours, unknown to anyone, so important, and to me so creative—steps in growing and knowing. Maybe it appears that the ingredient of otherness was missing, too exclusive, inner directed. But not for now. I'd hope, eventually, with you, our love will make us effective to help others ... True lovers expand their love circle. But it is the most natural thing in the world for lovers to want to be together and alone. ... I love you in every discovery of you,*
> > *Hugh*

Hugh reminds me that a sign of a healthy relationship is how open those in the relationship are to each other, and eventually, how open they are to others. "True lovers expand their love circle," he tells me. But that openness will come as the result of first strengthening the bonds of unity between the two people. I begin to accept how important it is that we spend time alone being ourselves, discovering the joy of each other, learning love.

Chapter 25

GROWING

"Here is the truth about self-discovery: it is never without cost."
—*Angela Flournoy*

IN EARLY AUGUST, MARNIE calls to say that Mother wants to visit me and is coming to Buffalo at the end of the summer. I know that she is still reeling from the scandal; it is still breaking my heart that she continues to suffer because of me. But I want to see her. She is my mother.

Every Labor Day weekend, my Aunt Kay and Uncle Clint have a family picnic in their beautiful garden in Clarence, a suburb about a half hour away from the college. When I enter their house, Mother welcomes me with a stiff hug and tells me she has a pot of tea waiting in the kitchen. Sitting by ourselves at the polished maple kitchen table, enjoying Red Rose tea even on a warm day, we try to make things seem normal. I am very happy to be with my mother who is concerned about my health, which, fortunately, is strong. She asks about my graduate studies and what literature I am studying. Then she suddenly says that she hears from Marnie that I am still seeing "Father Brady".

"I am praying you will end this soon," she continues. "You have no idea how isolated I am in Hornell. Even in front of me I hear people say how much they miss Father's sermons. Right in front of me! Well, at least they aren't the ones talking behind my back. Can you imagine what it is like for me to live in that town while you are still carrying on?"

I feel a pain run through me. "I never thought it would happen like this," I respond, my eyes looking down and my voice in a whisper. "I really never thought it would happen, period." I then look at Mother and add, "Hugh would have left the priesthood whether I wanted to marry him or not."

Then, with all the sincerity in the world, Mother asks, "Don't you realize you are committing a sin?"

I bristle. "Celibacy is a man-made rule of the Church written eight centuries ago. It is not in scriptures and not what Jesus teaches."

Mother's voice is so strong, it feels like she is pointing her finger at me. "If a Church rule is eight centuries old, it is a very important rule. You are going against a rule which was put in place to protect priests."

She somehow feels it is also important to say that I was always a difficult child to raise and to remind me of my transgressions, especially how self-centered I have always been.

"I beg you to leave him," Mother pleads. "Meet someone else. This is more than I can bear. There is more than one fish in the sea." Mother stirs her tea and then looks directly at me. "You are enamored by the spiritual aspect of the relationship, which you will discover is totally unrealistic once you know how hard marriage is. Get your head out of the clouds." In a measured voice, she emphatically states, "You know the priest, not the man. You will find out that people will not accept either of you."

As Mother sees it, ending my relationship with Hugh is the only way to remove the shame our family is experiencing—or at least the shame she feels. She tells me Hugh will never be welcome in our home in Hornell.

I cannot respond. Because I love him so much, my mother's threat that Hugh would never be part of our family feels as if it is a complete rejection of me. My anger begins to sink into sadness. Still, I believe I must protect my mother, but I don't know how. I am the reason she is not protected. The old feelings take over. I cannot shake them off. The thought keeps coming to me: *How will I be able to love Hugh and at the same time have a relationship with a mother who stands as a barrier to him?*

When I return to my apartment, the happiness of the summer seems to evaporate before my eyes. I become even more aware of how much I am hurting my mother, and at the same time, how I am allowing her to control me. My feeling that I need to protect her is deep and automatic; I begin to ask myself if I will ever have the courage to separate myself from her. At the age of twenty-eight, I am not proud of the fact that the umbilical cord is still firmly intact.

As I battle guilt and anger because of Mother's visit, I fall into a deep depression. When I talk to Hugh about it, he does not judge my reactions or tell me what I should do. After a couple of weeks, I am emotionally depleted from the physical and psychological pain of depression. I know I need professional help to face this lifelong problem head on. The counseling center on campus recommends a private counselor. The next week, I take the first steps on a journey to try to find myself in a whole new way: as an autonomous human being independent of my mother.

For ten months, I meet each week with a calm and skilled psychotherapist. The counseling opens up layers of issues within me. I delve into my relationship with Hugh and journal about my counseling sessions. *Will I transfer my inordinate need to protect my mother onto Hugh? Where is my independence from him? Am I really the reason he left? Do I know myself well enough to commit to marriage? How can I find my own strength apart from him? How can I build a stronger self-image when I was often told I was just like my father, a hurt that washes over and over me?*

I also explore feelings that I do not think originated within me. *What feelings and inclinations have I inherited? What emotional patterns do I unconsciously carry from previous generations? What's in my genes?* The longer I am in therapy, the more questions I explore. I want to be honest. I want to be open to everything. I want to be free.

The counseling takes extra energy. I need more rest and silence to live with what I am learning—time to process how to accept myself. I experience growth during these months of personal discovery, yet I sometimes get impatient with my progress and want to hurry up the process. I want to get everything "fixed" and move on with my life.

Fortunately, reading "*The Woodcarver*" from the *Tao* helps me look at my life of self-discovery in a new way. This is a meditative story about how a woodcarver finds the correct wood to make a bell stand, which is a sacred piece of furniture that holds the bell the prince uses to summon someone to answer his needs. It is a story that I have kept with my journal and read whenever I need to stop and think about how to get my life back on track.

"The Woodcarver"

Khing, the master carver, made a bell stand

Of precious wood. When it was finished,

All who saw it were astounded. They said it must be

The work of spirits.

The Prince of Lu said to the master carver:

"What is your secret?"

Khing replied, "I am a workman:

I have no secret. There is only this:

When I began to think about the work you commanded

I guarded my spirit, did not expend it on trifles that were not to the point.

I fasted in order to set my heart at rest.

After three days, I had forgotten gain and success.

After five days, I had forgotten praise or criticism.

After seven days, I had forgotten my body with all its limbs.

By this time all thought of your Highness

and the court had faded away.

All that might distract me from the work had vanished.

I was collected in the single thought of the bell stand.

Then I went to the forest to see the trees in their own natural state.

When the right tree appeared,

The bell stand also appeared in it, clearly, beyond doubt.

All I had to do was to put forth my hand and begin.

If I had not met this particular tree

there would have been no bell stand at all.

What happened?

My own collected thought encountered the hidden potential in the wood;

From this live encounter came the work

Which you ascribe to the spirits.

Like the woodcarver, I feel internal pressures to meet expectations from many external influences. Unlike the woodcarver, I look for my particular bell stand, my truth, in the tree before I prepare myself. The woodcarver shows me another way. Instead of being driven by expectations or wanting to get results as quickly as possible, the woodcarver stood apart from his assignment and patiently fasted and meditated until the forces that would influence his work were released from him. He and the task eventually became one. It was only then that the bell stand appeared within the tree. The woodcarver also teaches me a new kind of patience. I begin to learn not to impose the way I or anyone else thinks things should turn out and instead to wait for life to reveal itself—on its own terms. I start to fast. Not from food, but from others' expectations, even from Hugh's, as well as from my own.

Discovering the bell stand in the tree means accepting the reality of who I am rather than who I think I should be, want to be, or try to be. My growth and transformation is in acceptance of what is, something Hugh had told me years before.

From my convent journal in the spring of 1968:

Father keeps stressing how acceptance is a core message of the Beatitude "Poverty of Spirit". When we embrace the reality of our lives, be it good or painful, that genuine acceptance allows transformation in the deepest part of ourselves. Acceptance is not capitulation. It is comparable to Gandhi saying non-violence is not passive, but an active force. This accepting of what happens to us teaches us, transforms us. Father thinks Alcoholics Anonymous has it right. "Accept the things you cannot change." He says acceptance is central to his own spiritual practice. He tries to accept each person just as they are without judgment, including himself. When I ask him how he does it, he says he laughs a lot. I get it; he laughs at himself a lot. When I respond that this practice seems counterintuitive to me, he says it is the central mystery of Christianity, a mystery Jesus modeled for all of us in the final acceptance of his own death. Out of that acceptance comes resurrection, new life, a chance to try again. And it frees us to put our energy where we need it for our own lives. He said most of us expend endless energy trying to change things that will most likely work out in their own way and we are left depleted and angry. Wouldn't it

be amazing if I could accept every fiber of my being so I
could accept everyone else with the same magnanimity?
I have so far to go accepting so much about me ... let
alone about others. Like Mother Edward!

As I have throughout my life, I recently opened the worn folder to take out the wrinkled, yellow sheet of paper to meditate on the woodcarver's words. Some lessons never stop teaching us.

Although growing in self-knowledge with counseling and the woodcarver and other opportunities, I am still confused and feel shaky. I am seriously questioning whether marrying Hugh is right for either of us. Nothing seems to make sense, and I certainly cannot make sense of myself. Although Hugh is also afraid we might not end up together, he continues to absorb my every emotion and thought. He absorbs me. His letters come like loving angels, holding me up, and telling me a different story about myself. They are therapy, too. Every gesture of love heals.

From St. Catherine's, Ontario, Hugh writes:

About our future, I want you to know one thing ...   I
want only what is for your happiness. ... though it
means risking not marrying you. ... May God deliver
you from all the forces that pressure you to marry me!
May he also free you from the forces that <u>obligate</u> you
not to marry me. ... I must ... surrender to the mystery
in you. ...   I love you Evie! xxxxxxxooooooooo, Hugh

Although so much is going on inside me, to other people in our lives we appear pretty normal. Hugh and I are involved with the social justice committee at the Newman Center and fully participate in its many activities. While I am barely surviving emotionally, society is in crisis as well. Sometimes I can hardly figure out what I am responding to. With the war, racism, escalating poverty in Buffalo, an education system in crisis, nothing is holding together. Yeats' "the center cannot hold" from "The Second Coming" runs through my mind.

Yet, in late autumn, I begin to realize more clearly that life is not black and white and that, sometimes, if you move on what is in your heart, doors you thought were locked will open. One day out of the blue, I decide to call my mother. She sounds happy to hear from me. Soon I am calling every week just to say hello.

It may be difficult for others to believe that I would want to be in in touch with my mother. But that is how strong my emotional connection to her is. There is also the comfort of just hearing her voice, knowing what is new in Hornell and sharing family news. She never asks me about Hugh. A little before Christmas our weekly phone visits are severely tested. Every year, my family gathers for Christmas in Hornell. When Mother and I talk about it, I tell her that I want to spend Christmas with Hugh and I understand that he cannot go with me to Hornell. Mother asks me to come home alone. I tell her it will be the first time Hugh and I can celebrate Christmas together. She tells me I have a choice. I make it.

Hugh and I go to Christmas Mass in Buffalo and then drive to his sister Catherine's home for dinner and a wonderful family gathering. Although it is very hard for me not to be with my own family, I am surprised at how happy I am that day with Hugh's. Mother says I am selfish, only thinking about myself. Maybe I am. But it is a healthy step in my commitment to being myself, not only my mother's daughter.

With the new year, 1970, comes my determination to continue to look for "the bell stand" in myself. During these months, life on campus is rife with protests over the war. And, like campuses across the country, Buffalo State College experiences serious racial strife. The unrest spills into the dorms. Somehow, I keep myself afloat in a world that seems to be imploding on all fronts. Knowing that I will be with Hugh on weekends is like balm on an open wound. No matter what we are going through, how exiled we may feel, we find a home in each other. We cannot imagine life without each other. We are best friends. We are lovers.

Yet I am not the only one who is trying to cope with life. Hugh also has struggles he is dealing with. He is forty-four and thirty-one of those forty-four years have been spent in and shaped by a clerical culture. He'd entered the seminary after grade eight and has adjustments to make in becoming a lay person, which I think he does seamlessly. He seems so at home in his own skin. But he misses his life as a priest. As we walk around the frozen lake at Delaware Park one January afternoon, he talks about his feelings of loss.

"Feelings aren't facts, Evie, but flotsam and jetsam are floating up these days. The ocean is deep, sweetheart, and its depth is where my truth lies, but I miss the priesthood. I miss sharing in so many people's lives, saying Mass, working on renewal, anointing the dying and encouraging the ill. And baptizing babies. So many need to be ministered to. I miss the role that awaited me each morning."

He stops for a moment, puts his arm around me, pulls me closer to his heavy brown jacket and says, "But I have never felt so much myself as I am now. I am happy. Honest. I just start missing the gifts priesthood brought me. Feeling a little down thinking how fulfilled I was. Just unsettled these days. Maybe it's the weight of winter."

I look up at the snowflakes twirling around us and tell him to think of the snowflakes as little notes, messages that will dissolve into him and encourage him to accept what he is experiencing. To embrace the poverty of himself. To know God waits there. I say to him just what he would have said to me.

"Eskimos have thirty-six words for snow," I tell him. "The snow falling today is the snow of mystery."

"Yes, my love. Or maybe the snow of confusion," Hugh responds, smiling.

I know what he means. Much of my own life these days is lived in a state of confusion. As I continue with counseling through February and March, nothing is linear or logical or rational. I go through more periods of upheaval. When I explore my deepest feelings, I sometimes feel as if I am drowning. In March, my spirits are as low as I can ever remember. Even with all the love Hugh showers on me, I again believe I cannot marry him. I do not feel I have anything to offer him. I tell him that he should return to the priesthood or that he should look beyond me for his future. I feel as if I am incapable of having a relationship with anyone. The diaspora of my fragile spirit is depleted. These days are the nadir of my counseling. I tell Hugh repeatedly that I am sure I have nothing to give him. He is devastated. I am, too.

Hugh writes referring to his agony, his hope, his faith:

> *I have always related with hope, with a view to the future, with desire. It is this that seemed to be shattered. … Once again I find myself without a frame of reference and life without direction. I thank God for faith that tells me that my future will be happy and a loving Father is making all things work together for good—your good and mine. Still there is no happiness now in the thought that my future may be without you—that you think it will be without you. … I pray for wisdom for you, that you may know your own heart and follow it.*
>
> *I know I have no calling to return to priesthood. I can only go on into an unknown future and wonder the mystery of my leaving at all.*
>
> *I desire with all my heart that you come to your full*

maturity which frees you from all obstacles, however
deeply they have been built in by parents and circum-
stances. I will do anything which is clearly God's will for
me to do in your becoming—and in so doing I know that
I too shall become. My darling Evie, I love you.

Willing to walk these uncertain detours and rock-strewn roads with me, to accept my sufferings without trying to "fix" them and to know how the ramifications can affect both of our lives, Hugh is a faithful angel. Unfortunately, however, I am so into myself that I do not realize how profoundly difficult all this is on him. Through it all, and despite my irrational doubts, we both continue to live our very busy lives and some-how experience a healing balm whenever we are together. Paradoxically, underneath our very real concerns about not ending up together, we want our lives to be united more than anything else and to share whatever life presents, even my emotional rags. I think Hugh is right. The name for the snow is "confusion".

Chapter 26

THE QUESTION OF LAICIZATION

"Once a priest always a priest, according to the order of Melchizedek."
—Hebrews 7:17

THROUGHOUT THESE MONTHS OF searching and growing, Hugh and I find comfort in the womb of our love, but, like everyone else, we have to address circumstances specific to our everyday lives. In our case "laicization" is a question that hangs over us. It is something we have discussed on and off for almost two years. Laicization is the process by which the Church offers a priest the means to leave the priesthood: for marriage; for disagreeing with and often rejecting particular Church teachings; or, in some cases, for having committed a serious transgression.

If a priest is laicized, he forfeits all rights to priestly life and he is considered a layman. In fact, although he can remain a member in good standing in the Catholic Church, the Church regards the laicized priest as never having been a priest. Some of Hugh's inactive/former priest friends at General Motors who plan to marry *refuse* to request laicization from the Vatican. They see themselves as inactive priests and do not believe a church rule can remove the gift of the Sacrament of Ordination nor can they ignore Scripture's' teaching: "Once a priest always a priest, according to the order of Melchizedek." (Hebrews 7:17) They definitely will not admit to "never having been a priest."

During our era of the 1960s and 1970s, when these men left the priesthood and chose not to be laicized, they were excommunicated and lost their standing as members of the Catholic Church. This punishment was eventually changed and reduced the former/inactive priests' excommunication to "being censured or denounced." Priests who leave are no longer expelled from membership in the Church.

Catholic Churches are filled with former priests, both laicized and not, who participate and contribute as parishioners in meaningful and important ways to the life of thousands of parishes. Even though the hierarchy forbids them from participating in any formal priestly role, in our diocese of Buffalo these men are often found in leadership on parish councils, on committees, especially spiritual life and social justice groups, and they perform corporal works of mercy in many ways. They also participate in planning liturgies, retreats and, in some cases, are sought out for counseling. Being welcomed by a pastor and the parish staff makes a singular difference in the life of an inactive/former priest who may want to continue to be a part of the Church to which he had given his life.

Father Jack Weimer at Buffalo State Newman Center is one of those hospitable pastors. He and his team welcome Hugh and recognize in him a spiritual depth and a dedication to supporting our Christian community. Soon Hugh is working on retreats and leading several initiatives promoting spirituality and justice. One Sunday, from the podium, Father Weimer announces to the parishioners: "If you are seeking spiritual direction, I can't think of anyone better than Hugh Brady. You can contact him through our office. I am the liturgical leader here and my brother Hugh is the spiritual leader." People respond to Hugh; he becomes central to the community. In some ways, he fulfills his role as priest, as servant.

Father Weimer is magnimous to say this, especially since so many pastors see their parishes as a personal "fiefdom" that they and, to some extent, their parish councils control. Not Jack. His parish is collegial. He lives out Vatican II's invitation to the laity to participate in the life of the Church. He is open to the gifts of his parishioners. Hugh thrives in it. I do, too.

Eventually, in the quiet of his heart, Hugh chooses to be laicized and tells me why he has decided this. Like many former/inactive priests, he feels a rule cannot remove the sacrament of Holy Orders or determine that he has never been a priest. He also knows that, for both himself and his future family, he wants to participate as a member in good standing in the Catholic Church, the church to which he has dedicated his life, even if he has a continual "lovers quarrel" with it. He believes his heart is sealed with the words from his ordination, *Tu es sacerdos in aeternum.* "You are a priest forever." Still, he is convinced that being laicized is best for us. To him, the Church's laicization rule is an external, legal act, a way to cope with the numbers of priests leaving. In his heart, he knows the Church has declared him a priest forever and that is how he sees himself.

Hugh is one of the over 100,000 priests worldwide who have left the Catholic priesthood in the past fifty years. However, unlike some of our inactive/former priest friends who are laicized or chose not to be, when family members or others ask Hugh if he will marry someone or baptize a baby, he refuses. Even though he accepts and supports those men who comply with such requests, he says he made a choice and cannot straddle two worlds. He tells me he will live as a layman. "Our children would be confused not knowing whether their father is a priest or not. You and I would be torn with a double identity as well. What life style would we have? I can only live in both worlds when they become one," he explains to me. "We'll keep praying for a married clergy to come soon."

Although Hugh chooses to live as a layman, his priest heart is intact and he continues to serve in every way he can or is allowed to. He does not know how not to. People who do not know his background will sometimes say, "That man brings me so much peace, like he is a priest."

In April, Hugh submits a petition for laicization to Bishop Gerald Emmet Carter, Bishop of London, Ontario, as that is the diocese where Hugh resides in Canada. Once again, Hugh finds a bishop who is kind and respectful. Bishop Carter tells Hugh his application will be sent within the week. As it turns out, Bishop Carter's brother, also a priest and assigned to the Vatican, is in charge of laicization petitions for North America and is expediting the requests that come to him. Hugh receives his laicization exactly six months later, in September of 1970.

We know many priests who wait two years or longer for their laicization papers. They question if the delay is a means of punishment by their local bishops. As a result, several of these men who sincerely want to be members of the Church in good standing give up on waiting for laicization and marry outside of the church. Some are bitter and leave the faith and sometimes go to other denominations so they can continue to be religious leaders. Others ignore the Church's rule and participate fully in the life of parishes. We are lucky they do.

Even though the Church's interpretation of laicization is written in terms of the priests being "regularized", "reduced", or "dispensed", Hugh sees it as something he must follow to be in good standing in the Church. He never feels "regularized or reduced." He never experiences being "dispensed." He knows he is not changed simply because he no longer wears a Roman collar. He is God's man no matter what the Church says.

Meanwhile, I continue to be committed to sorting myself out through counseling. I tell Hugh it is my time of purification. He tells me that I am already pure but that he hopes I will receive this "holy guidance" for as long as I feel I need and want it. He believes that exploring one's motivations and behaviors with the help of a professionally trained therapist is among the most sacred journeys a person can take on the spiritual path. Hugh reminds me that he could not have addressed the truth in himself about his need to be married without his openness to the Holy Spirit and the steady and skilled help of a therapist. He calls counseling "spiritual excavation" and me an archeologist of the Spirit. He believes that spirituality is an essential companion to psychotherapy and prays that, through it all, I will open myself to the Spirit. And I do.

By May, the therapist assures me I am ready to end my sessions. He reminds me that self-discovery is a lifelong journey and that I should never hesitate to work to make conscious what is hidden from me in my subconscious. I take his advice seriously. On and off throughout my life I "give myself over" to discovering the deeper and sometimes painful mystery of myself, especially when problems seem intractable or when hurt will not leave or when depression creeps into my life. I am grateful for the golden road of counseling, which leads me back to the goldmine of my true self, the self that God created me to be. The goldmine where love lives. I remember Mother Bride's words: "Everything is about love." For me, the ultimate purpose of self-discovery is just that: to become more loving to myself and others.

In Buffalo, the spring of 1970 arrives in early May, and I feel like Persephone returning from the netherworld. After the long, hard winter, the flowering spring gardens within me and outside of me are reminders of what I already know: I am the luckiest girl in the world. Some lines from a poem I wrote in my journal that May: ... *the branches of myself open like morning sunlight. /Eyes deepen /into purple irises /and around my legs /trumpet vines wind their way /to my hips, already a field of azaleas. / My body, a spring garden /His, the morning rain.*

I am coming alive again and growing in my understanding of life. A consolation throughout this hard year and the following years is hearing

Jack (Father Weimer) continually preach that we are *all* "wounded" and that openness to the Spirit brings healing. Jack's reminders help me recognize that I am not the only one who is incomplete or somehow damaged in one way or another. Hugh assures me that God loves us in our "un-mended" spirits. In fact, he says, that is where God waits for us. Hugh and I share our lives so openly and intimately throughout this year that we grow closer than we ever realized was possible. I ask him one day if he thinks our dreams talk to each other. He smiles and says, "Of course!"

One thing that Hugh finds increasingly difficult, however, is my obligations as a dorm director. We talk about getting married all the time now. Because there is so little privacy, he is not comfortable with the idea of living in a dorm apartment when we get married, which I had just assumed we would do to save money.

I had often thought of returning to teaching, so I call my friend Mary Anne, who got me the dorm director's job, to ask if she knows of a teaching position in the fall. She tells me there just happens to be an opening for a teacher of English where she teaches at the Buffalo State College Campus School, a lab school for the placement of student teachers and a setting for experimental pedagogy. I tell Mary Anne she is my personal employment counselor.

Fortunately, I secure the position for September and start to look for an apartment. One summer afternoon, driving down Richmond Avenue, I see the street sign for Anderson Place. I feel drawn to turn onto the one-way, tree-lined street. A "For Rent" sign catches my eye. Within an hour, I rent a turn-of-the-century first-floor apartment for $120.00 a month, including heat. It has bay windows in the large living room, hardwood floors, a good-sized dining room, two bedrooms, a large old-fashioned kitchen, a lovely yard and a unique, tiny room, like a large closet, with a bench in it for two very thin people. It is called a "courting room", a reminder of a custom observed in this house over a hundred years before. I fall in love with my new apartment, courting room and all.

Hugh is making changes, too. Although successful with General Motors, he does not feel comfortable in the corporate culture. When he is promoted and then invited to executive meetings and expensive meals, the men often ask him where he plays golf or docks his boat. These are good men, "the finest", Hugh calls them, but their aspirations are different from his. He applies to State University of New York at Buffalo and is accepted for the following fall into a master's degree program in Rehabilitation Counseling. After he quits General Motors, he finds a little upstairs apartment on Suffolk Street in Buffalo near the University. We are ten minutes apart. 1970 might turn out better than I expected. And, I am grateful that the laicization question is resolved.

Chapter 27

UNEXPECTED TURNS

I don't know that love changes. ... Circumstances change.
—*Nicholas Sparks*

THE FOURTH OF JULY, my birthday, is hot. Late that morning, Hugh arrives at my apartment to take me to his family's picnic in Rochester. I have the drapes closed to keep out the harsh sun so at first I do not see the small boxes tied with tiny red, white and blue ribbons in the basket he is holding.

"Something for my firecracker," he announces as he puts the basket on the coffee table.

"I can't wait, my darling," I say with excitement as I hurry to give him a glass of water and sit next to him on the couch.

There are little presents in each box. In one is the ring. I take it out and become very quiet. I give Hugh a simple kiss. He puts the ring on my finger.

"I love you, Ev. Will you marry me?"

Cold shivers run across my skin. I feel panic take over my body. Words I don't even know are in me spill out. "Thank you. But, my darling, if I accept, I know I will lose my mother. Do you understand this?"

I do not expect this overwhelming feeling of loss and guilt to emerge at such a special time for us. I have spent ten months with a therapist dealing with these emotions and think I have rid myself of them. The feelings quickly become threatening and stabbing. I've already caused my mother too much suffering throughout my life and most especially because of the scandal. Accepting the ring somehow means that I don't care about her. Our engagement will bring devastating pain to her. The beast of my guilt is still here, holding me down and telling me that my first obligation is to my mother. I cannot respond in any other way.

Looking at me with shock and hurt, Hugh says, "I have been secretly planning to surprise my family with our engagement. What the hell are you saying?"

I smile at him and quickly say, "The ring is beautiful." I hug him, but he does not hug me back. I still do not accept the proposal. Since he knows me so well, he senses what I am experiencing. He asks me what is wrong.

But I interrupt. "Please, Hugh, I might never see my mother again. She will shun me. But I will wear the ring at the picnic."

That day, for the first and last time in our life together, Hugh becomes extremely angry at me. Livid. Irate. He raises his voice and says in a loud, shaking voice, "I do not want you to go to Rochester. I do not want to be with you. Give me the ring."

Stunned, I take the diamond off my finger and hand it to him.

With slow, staccato tones, Hugh states, "I do not give a damn about your mother. Or your family. Or you. I will make up some excuse for my family. I am embarrassed to tell them the truth. Do not phone me. Do not write. Do not."

He gets up, puts the ring in his wallet and, before he slams the door, turns, looks at me and yells, "I do not care about any of you!"

I stand looking at the door. I have never seen Hugh like this. Every ounce of life drains out of me. Am I crazy? What have I done? Why can't

I simply walk away from my mother? It comes to me to run after him. By the time I get to the parking lot totally out of breath, I see the rear of his car disappearing on the road leading off the campus. For the rest of the day, I can hardly move. I feel sick in my stomach with something worse than the flu. I experience feelings of loss, feelings close to what death must be like. I am still that little girl who has to protect her mother.

Stone cold on this eighty-seven-degree day, I lie for hours on the couch in a fetal position and shiver. Cold and numb. When darkness comes in the evening, I drag myself to my car and drive to watch the fireworks. I have never before missed the fireworks on my birthday, always thrilled with the sound of a whistle rising to the sky and then the booms of colorful, sparkling umbrellas lighting up the night. But on this Fourth of July, the harsh clashing colors clang, cut me like knives, pull pain across my eyes and fill my mouth with dust. I do not stay. My stomach heaves as I drive home to a desolate campus. I hardly have the energy to unlock the door to my apartment. From my journal, July 4, 1970.

> *My world changed today/Doors locked/Color leaked out*
> *of flowers/Stars turned their heads./I walk on an empty*
> *moonscape,/a bone caught in my throat./The problem?/*
> *Me.*

Over these following days, I am bereft. Hugh is all I think about. I can hardly eat and I do not know how to relate to what I know is his justified anger. I look around at the unwashed dishes in the sink and papers strewn across the apartment. I wear wrinkled clothes and have no interest in food. My body moves in sheets of freezing pain. I feel like I am the only person on the planet.

A few days later, with frayed emotions, I return to my counselor. I have long realized that counseling is not about getting answers from anyone else. It is instead about the right questions. I search for the questions but find none. I can only make lists in my journal. Lists of regrets. Again I attempt to be aware of the mystery of subconscious feelings that determine my choices. I agonize over whether I will ever be free of my mother's power over me. I pray constantly.

At my first appointment, even though I know that it will not work, I want to beg the therapist to tell me what to do. I become very angry at him. While admitting that something is seriously wrong with me, I tell him that I have learned nothing through the previous year of counseling. I actually ask him if he knows what he is doing. He simply listens to me vent. I explain that when Hugh gave me the engagement ring, I became paralyzed; I was in a vise and completely incapable of hurting my mother, which I believed our engagement would do. I could not abandon her. I could not bear the thought of losing her. The old emotions were still controlling me. My mother was still controlling me.

"I thought I had resolved these feelings," I cry.

My counselor looks at me with genuine sorrow in his eyes. I know that he hears me and that his heart is breaking, too. Gently and quietly, he tells me that my reaction does not diminish my love for Hugh in any way, which I know but don't think Hugh believes. I appreciate the counselor saying what is so true in me. He points out that it is often a major life event like an engagement that brings up subconscious feelings we thought we had finished dealing with. Granting that it is an imperfect metaphor, he uses a garden image to illustrate what sometimes happens in therapy.

A gardener plants bulbs in a particular spot and flowers bloom. The next fall he removes the bulbs from that spot. But when the following spring comes, the gardener sees that flowers are growing in the area he thought he had cleared. Some bulbs lay buried so deep in the ground that the gardener does not know they are there. So, too, can deep subconscious feelings and beliefs be raised up, recognized and explored in counseling, but there may be deeper, hidden "bulbs" not known until a crisis or life situation causes them to emerge.

"What more can I say to you?" I ask.

"Whatever you want," he replies. "Let's start with Hugh."

That is just where I want to start. I want to start with Hugh, be with Hugh and live the rest of my life with Hugh. I have to rid myself of hidden bulbs or they will plague me all my life in whatever relationship I might have. And I am terrified of the real possibility that my relationship with Hugh could be, or is already, over. I become a gardener.

On July 10, I call Hugh. I can tell things are not the same between us. He sounds defeated and tells me that he is now ambivalent about whether we should marry. Even though he says he knows he loves me with a love so "fierce" it will not change no matter what happens with our relationship, he also realizes that, because of my attachment to my mother's needs, he has to decide if I am the right person to marry. He knows my love for him. I can hardly carry it.

Considering the real love we have for each other, none of this makes sense. Hugh understands that I am valiantly trying to grapple with the huge barrier in my psyche. But he doesn't know if it will or ever could be removed. Neither do I. I live in constant fear that Hugh will leave me, even though we still have a palpable, underlying connection to each other. We communicate in a strained way for almost two months. I go to counseling every week, fill my journals with reflections and questions and pray my heart out. A new loneliness accompanies me everywhere and, even though Hugh is peripherally in my life, I believe I have lost him. I know I have lost myself.

Chapter 28

GRACE

"It is at the bottom where we find grace; for like water, grace seeks the lowest place and from there it pools up."
—Richard Rohr

IN THE WANING DAYS of late August, I wake up one morning feeling unexpectedly calm, refreshed, and light. I am rested. In that moment, I know that, no matter what my mother suffers, I will choose Hugh. I am not expecting such a peaceful revelation. But it is crystal clear. The fear in my body is gone. This is different from the feelings I'd had after my earlier counseling sessions during the school year. I call Mother later in the morning.

"Mother, I know this is very hard for you but I am going to be married."

"When?" she asks in an abrupt tone.

"I am not sure, but I wanted you to know first." I tell her about not accepting the engagement ring on my birthday because I did not want to hurt her anymore.

"I am not to blame. I haven't taken a priest from God," she says.

Calmly, I interrupt, "I am not taking Hugh from God. God is very much in Hugh. He did not leave the priesthood only because of me but because of who he is. I just happen to be the lucky one he wants to marry.

I am going to marry Hugh and I hope you will be happy for me."

She responds, saying with hurt in her voice, "You have put me in a terrible position."

I again express my sorrow for her suffering and admit to the pain the scandal has caused her. I tell her again that she did not deserve this. I say, "I love you."

I also share that I have been in counseling for almost a year and am confident in my decision. She wants to hear about the counseling and thinks I have probably made her the villain.

Gently, I try to explain that the counseling is about me. She can barely get out, "I wish you and Father Brady well." I ask her to please call him Hugh. The conversation hurts, but in some mysterious way, my truth is the beginning of setting both of us free.

That afternoon I call my counselor and tell him about the phone conversation with my mother.

"I am positive. I have chosen Hugh," I say deliberately.

"No," he says, "you have chosen yourself."

Just because I've come to a final clarity, however, does not mean that Hugh is in the same place. Wounded in a way he never thought would be possible, he says, "I need time. I need some distance from you."

His response is like a sword splitting me in two. But I completely understand the seriousness of what I have done. When I did not accept the ring, I rejected Hugh. We had been ecstatic that we'd finally be engaged to be married. Then, without any warning, I'd changed my mind. Who wouldn't be upset or worse? Hugh has the ring. I wait in the desert of myself to see what he will do.

As September days pass, we slowly turn back toward each other. Although Hugh is a busy student and I am challenged by teaching in an urban classroom for the first time and coping with the burden of completing my thesis, the need to be with each other is as strong as ever.

Hugh recognizes my new freedom, my confidence, the soft joy of my spirit, yet he tells me with great tenderness that his illusion of me has been broken. He now lives with a new reality. I understand. But I also know that reality is the only soil where true love will flourish. I ask him to accept me. I ask him to open himself to my love. Even though I have hurt him so terribly, I tell him my love for him never changes and only grows.

In some ways, we fall in love all over again. The urgency to be with each other as often as possible intensifies. We call each other every night and, when possible, during the day. Sometimes I call in the morning before I leave for school to tell him my love will accompany him during his day. When we are together, we constantly hold each other's hand, even when just sitting in the living room. It is as if we are afraid of losing each other. We have long discussions about everything, never letting go of the other's hand.

We fall back into the enjoyment of simply being ourselves. I proof-read Hugh's graduate papers with their nearly perfect grammar and punctuation. He scrapes together enough money out of his small graduate stipend to keep my apartment in flowers again. He teaches me how to make delicious soups and casseroles that we share with friends. But, as before, nothing is better than just the two of us being together, just living life together as a couple. I move through those weeks with an unchanging feeling of calm and joy. Hugh is the same as he's always been, living out of the deep peace within himself that everyone experiences in his presence, especially me. Often, before he goes, Hugh leaves me messages on the kitchen table or taped on a cupboard or sometimes on my pillow. The notes are always filled with reminders of God's presence in our lives. I still have these notes in dozens of boxes.

9/22/70

Evie,

*Thank you for our being together, always in each
other's presence unknown to each of us how God's
presence dwells in us, loving us for each of us, knowing
our love is never yet enough—the reason God is always
touching us with Divine Love. So often I experience that
touch of God showing itself in you and through you. ...*

These messages reassure me. Still, Hugh never mentions the engagement ring. Then on October 18, he arrives with a huge autumn bouquet of mums, dahlias, bittersweet and sunflowers tied in a bright orange and brown ribbon—and a safety deposit envelope that contains the engagement ring. When he puts the oval diamond on my finger, there are no bells and whistles, no tiny boxes wrapped in ribbons, no champagne. Only a profound knowing that nothing will ever again stop me from marrying this gentle, wise, generous, and inordinately patient man.

We want to get married immediately, but our academic obligations make us question when and how. I am teaching and finishing my thesis and Hugh has papers due before the semester ends in mid-December, only two months away. Winter is our season; we decide that Christmas will be the perfect time for a wedding. Because Christmas falls on a Friday this year, we decide on Saturday, December 26, 1970. Everyone will be in a festive mood and the altar will be decorated. We won't have to pay for flowers!

When we meet with Jack, he says he will be happy to marry us. He explains that the Chancery, the diocesan office that handles official business of the Bishop, will not allow any "public" weddings for former priests; we will have to be married privately without any guests in our local parish which is the New Cathedral, just around the corner from Anderson Place.

But, he then invites us to have a Eucharistic Celebration, "a nuptial Mass" and reception, with our family and friends at the Newman Center after the private ceremony. His dad had owned a catering business for forty years, he tells us, and promises that our guests will eat the most tender roast beef on "weck" (a Buffalo favorite) anyone has ever tasted.

In late October, Hugh and I ask Sister Eric, a Rochester Sister of Mercy who is also a fine arts jeweler, if she would be able to create rings in time for a Christmas wedding. She says she will make the time. We each talk to her privately about what we want for each other. I know Hugh loves birds and remember John Donne's metaphysical wedding poem, "An Epithalamion," in which birds, including doves, celebrate married love. I decide on a dove for Hugh's ring. Sister Eric designs a stylized dove carved deep into the heavy white gold ring to represent nature's celebration of marriage but primarily to symbolize the Holy Spirit, whose presence is the source and companion of our love. I do not know what Hugh requests.

Because Hugh's laicization papers had arrived, he is now considered a layman and we are permitted to be married in the Church. Hugh phones Marnie to ask if she and Andy will give a witness talk on married life, like an instruction, a wedding custom in early Christian communities. They agree. When I call my mother to let her know that Hugh is laicized, she is greatly relieved to hear that Hugh is no longer seen as a priest in the eyes of the Church and is in good standing as a lay person. She tells me that she'd decided to come to our wedding under any circumstances, which I feel is magnanimous of her. At times like this I know she loves me. Later, she says she'd be "happy" to have her name on the invitation.

The next two months are a blur of activity. Hugh's sisters give me an elegant shower. My mother and sisters drive to Rochester and the Bradys treat us, and especially Mom, with warmth and love. We invite the Bradys to a shower my aunts give me at Aunt Kay's. Friends arrange an engagement dinner for us. I shop for a wedding dress and order invitations. I finish my thesis.

In early December, the Church's liturgical season of Advent arrives with its cloak of expectation, with its circle of an evergreen wreath holding three purple and one rose candle, one to be lighted each of the four Sundays before Christmas. Out of darkness comes Light. The Church is preparing for the birth of the Light of the World. And we are preparing for a wedding that for us is the light at the end of a long journey. We do not separate the two celebrations. Hope fills the air. Whether it's the quiet of the snow or the beauty of the readings, I've always treasured the holy rituals of preparation and expectation that make Advent my favorite season of the Church's liturgical year. Hugh and I participate in the days of Advent as if we are on a retreat. We reflect on coming from isolation to communion, from despair to promise, from exile to home. Isaiah's familiar words that I always hear in Advent bring special meaning for me.

> *'Comfort, comfort my people,'*
> *says your God.*
> *'Speak tenderly to Jerusalem.*
> *Tell her that her sad days are gone*
> *and her sins are pardoned.'*

Yet even with the beauty of scripture and the sacredness of this liturgical time, however, we still live in the real world with its wedding plans and professional and academic deadlines. Just weeks before the wedding, the real world presents us with a "wardrobe" glitch—shopping for Hugh's wedding suit. And it makes me crazy. A requirement for one of his rehab counseling courses is to "take on" a disability of someone who has to deal with the challenges of living. Hugh decides he will take on blindness and buy his wedding suit as a blind man. Now is there anything more ridiculous? But he is determined.

On a Saturday night we go to the mall. Of course, I drive. I am to take notes on everything that happens without anyone seeing me. Carrying a cane and wearing dark sunglasses over closed eyes, Hugh hangs onto my arm as we walk into the men's section of a department store. No one comes to help us.

I approach a sales clerk and ask if he can assist us in picking out a wedding suit. I explain that the customer is blind. Hugh tells the clerk his size and specifics. Wide lapels and pin stripes are in style so he says he would like a dark pinstripe suit. (My fashion instructions.) When the sales clerk brings some suits, Hugh touches the materials and I begrudgingly describe them to him. Because we are pressed for time, I do not want to do this. Whenever Hugh thinks he might like one of the suits, he goes into the dressing room and tries it on. (Only I know he is looking in the mirror!)

After visiting three stores with Hugh's closed eyes behind dark glasses and his cane pointed to avoid running into anything or anyone in the busy pre-Christmas crowds, we drive home without a suit. It is three weeks before the wedding. Hugh says not to worry. He will find something. The next week he tells a fellow student, a young African-American man, about his suit dilemma. The young man knows exactly where Hugh can find a suit. They go downtown to some kind of a zoot-suit clothing store and, sure enough, Hugh purchases a dark suit with small white and red pin stripes. I do not say a thing.

Christmas arrives. I give Hugh Pedro Neruda's *One Hundred Love Sonnets* and e.e. cumming's *One Hundred Selected Poems* and a pair of cufflinks. Hugh gives me one pearl on a gold chain.

"A pearl of great price?" I ask him.

"When he had found one pearl of great price, he went out and sold all that he had, and bought it," Hugh recites. "Yes, my beloved, I've sold all I had for this pearl, for you but also for me. It's Christmas for both of us."

Every Christmas thereafter, for our anniversary, another pearl is added to the necklace. Its chain today holds forty-three anniversary pearls.

Chapter 29

THE GIFT OF CHRISTMAS

"Love alone is capable of uniting living beings ...
for it alone ... joins them by what is deepest in themselves."
—*Teilhard de Chardin*

THE NEXT MORNING, MY wedding day, I open the drapes to find the world covered in bridal white. I can almost hear tinkling sounds as the snow flakes, with glints of diamonds, fall.

My reverie is interrupted when Hugh calls me. He has been feeling bad that his family cannot be present at our private wedding, which will be held in St. Joseph New Cathedral before our Newman Center celebration. I am feeling the same way.

"Let's just have our families with us, Ev."

"But what if we get caught?"

"Maybe we will have already said our vows! What can they do?"

"I don't want Jack to get in trouble. But I really want my family there, too."

To avoid putting Jack in a compromised position, Hugh thinks we should simply not tell him our plan to include our families. We know the Chancery said we could have only two witnesses, my sister Lillis as my maid of honor and Dan DePalma, a dear friend of Hugh's from the Cursillo, as his best man. I tell Hugh that Jack has put his trust in us and that we absolutely have to inform him about what we are thinking.

When Hugh calls him, all Jack says is, "Well, I told you only two people. If others happen to show up, what could I do? But why do you and Ev have such big families!"

That evening at 6:00 PM, we gather at the New Cathedral at the corner of West Utica and Delaware Avenue. Our families fill the first pews. The cathedral lighting is very dim. But soft lights, positioned as if spot lights, shine down in front of the altar where Hugh and I stand facing Jack. After he welcomes us—but not the family members sitting in the pews—he begins to talk about the Holy Season of Christmas as the time the Church celebrates "the marriage of heaven and earth. In his infinite wisdom and love, God has brought both of you to this moment."

Then he prays over us, blesses us, and asks us to share our vows as part of the ring exchange. Jack invites me to recite my vows first. I have written a poem.

> One time when the snow fell,
> a man and a woman found love
> and their love knew many seasons.
>
> Each season brought change, pain, and wonder.
> Each season pruned and tested the love
> until no test did the love need.
>
> One time, again, the snow falls.
> A man and a woman are
> Love
> And their love exchanges rings for
> Every season.

I take Hugh's left hand, slip the Holy Spirit ring on his finger and recite what I had memorized: "I vow to you, Hugh Francis, that nothing, not even death, will separate me from you. I will cherish every gift of your heart, every breath of your spirit, every atom of your body. I will take care of you in every season of life where our love will be lived out in the light of God's grace and mercy. I did not know one human being could hold this much love for another, but my love for you fills the universe, including the stars that fell into us on a summer night."

Hugh speaks his vows spontaneously, saying he will dedicate his entire life to me, that he will be faithful in all the large and small events of our lives, that nothing will take precedence over our relationship and the children he hopes God will bless us with. "I vow to God and you, Evelyn Faith, that our lives will be rooted in the Spirit's divine, ongoing and creative love. I will be faithful in the good and bad times, in sickness and health all the days of my life."

Hugh turns to our families and says that, in coming to know me, he entered the world of poetry, a new world to him. Then he reads e.e. cummings' "somewhere i have travelled gladly," which ends with:

> *(i do not know what it is about you that closes*
> *and opens; only something in me understands*
> *the voice of your eyes is deeper than all roses)*
> *nobody, not even the rain, has such small hands*

As he puts a simple white gold band on my finger, he says, "My love for you is God's love for you and God's love for you is my love for you. Your love for me is God's love for me and God's love for me is your love for me. In love, there is no separation." Then, surprising me, he takes out a second ring identical to the first. "And this ring is to remind you to always be yourself." Two wedding bands.

Father Jack pronounces us husband and wife. And we kiss. In the cavernous marble cathedral, the clapping of our families reverberates off the white walls and columns, echoing and re-echoing our happiness. Twenty-seven family members witness our marriage. After our ceremony,

Hugh's sister and brother-in-law tell us that they saw a priest standing in the shadows of the side aisle throughout the whole wedding. Thankfully, Father Jack was never called into the Chancery.

As we drive to the Newman Center, I touch my two wedding rings and think that nothing ever has or ever could surpass the celebration that has just occurred. But I am wrong. At the Newman Center, elation is in the air. The words from "Morning Has Broken" sung by Rochester Mercy Sister Phyllis Contestable fill the chapel with anticipation as Hugh and I, glowing, walk hand in hand to the altar for our nuptial Mass. The fragrance of the chapel's blue spruce Christmas tree decorated with tiny white lights, the brilliant red poinsettias, and the dazzling candles on the altar create a world of holy celebration.

Our guests hang on to every word of Father Jack's homily. He says the season of Christmas is the communication of God Himself to us, his people on earth. "God is with us: Emmanuel." He points out that Jesus, who loves each of us in our personal history, came to us in poverty and was open to whatever God would ask of Him. Father explains that we, too, share in the mystery of what God has in store for us. We are called to birth Christ in our hearts and lives each day. We are to be open so we can receive Him. We are to be Christmas, Christ bearers, all year long.

"Christians celebrate Christmas and Easter every day. Each moment we love, we birth Christ on earth. Each moment we hope, we live Easter. Christians do not make a distinction between the two holy seasons.

"Two people marry but three share in the wedding vows: the Holy Spirit and the bride and groom. Ev and Hugh, you will never have to go it alone. The Holy Spirit will be as 'present as you are open.'" Jack encourages us to not "hide your love under a bushel basket," but to let it "shine like a city on a hill" for all to experience, the lovable as well as the *unlovable*.

"Your marriage will share in divine charity," he tells us. "Bring the ideals and gifts of religious life and priesthood that you have loved and lived to your new life as a married couple. Bring those gifts to our broken world."

He cautions us not to be exclusive with each other, but to be two candles that share one light for all to see and share in. "When a candle shares its light, its flame is not diminished; it is increased," he adds.

Father admonishes us to "create your own unique married life." Others may look happy, or appear to know what a marriage should be, but we are to create our own partnership, not what anyone else thinks or expects. If we are true to ourselves, our lives will reflect this truth in love. Our marriage will be a daily Epiphany and we will bring sacred gifts to each other and to the world.

"Furthermore, even as a married couple, you are to find your own individual paths in life, to develop your own unique strengths and talents." But we are "never to leave home without a map to find each other." He quotes Kahlil Gibran's famous words: "Let there be spaces in your togetherness. And stand together, yet not too near together: For the pillars of the temple stand apart. And the oak tree and the cypress grow not in each other's shadow."

At the end of the sermon, in the humblest of voices, he says, "It is Christmas, the birth of love. Live in Christ. Be Christmas love for each other and for all of us. Emmanuel. God is with us."

Marnie and Andy decided beforehand to give their witness talk in the format of "The Prayers of the Faithful." I treasure their words not only because of their meaning, but because five years later, we lost our beloved sister Marnie. She had been an anchor of love for all of us, especially for her young family of now six children; her siblings, especially our sister Blanche, who was her best friend; and my mother, who relied on her and loved her. And me. Marnie knew how to throw me lifelines.

On this Christmas, even with Santa's presents to buy and wrap, with decorating her home and the traditional food they prepare, Marnie, with Andy, found the time to put their hearts in these prayers:

A PRAYER ON THE WEDDING DAY OF
EVELYN AND HUGH BRADY

As our attention turns on this joyous and Holy Season to the birth of Christ and the Holy Family we are here to celebrate the creation, the birth, of another family: the family of Evelyn and Hugh Brady. For this new family, we pray tonight.

We pray that ... Evelyn and Hugh

> *... know Love is not a blindfold. It is an eye opener. You begin to love each other when you begin to make something of each other.*
> *... remember Dag Hammarskjold's words, "Never for the sake of peace and quiet deny your own experience or convictions."*
> *... remember marriage, like faith, keeps our gaze fixed on each other. Like faith, is attacked by the same enemy: routine.*

And Finally,

> *... celebrate that the purpose of marriage is to enable you to live all the love of which you are capable--a love which is so vast, so creative, so full of wonder and joy that it may take you a whole lifetime to understand it. (Full text: Addendum 1)*

When Mass ends, Hugh asks people to look at the paintings on the opposite walls of the chapel. On one wall, creation is depicted in its chaotic beauty; on the opposite wall, the chaos is ordered with clear images and patterns that bring meaning and a new kind of beauty. Hugh says the two walls represent the journey we'd taken to our marriage and would always be a symbol of how God brings us new life out of suffering and confusion.

By then, we hear the band playing, calling us to go upstairs to the community room to continue the celebration. Along with Mother Bride, Sister Marietta, Father Valente, the loving Mercy Order's chaplain, my dear friend Sister Carol, who later becomes our first child's Godmother, several other Sisters and priests, and our family members and friends— we dance! We dance in a line. We dance in a large circle. We dance by ourselves. We dance as couples. Hugh invites my mother to dance. She is in her glory. They see me clapping for them on the sidelines and they open their arms. We dance as a threesome. The first steps of walking with Jesus' words: "See I make all things new." Even though Hugh does not feel comfortable dancing, especially when no one else is on the dance floor, he and I dance to "I remember you/You're the one who made my dreams come true." We do not notice our feet moving.

We all enjoy a Buffalo fare of Mr. Weimer's delicious roast beef on weck rolls. Beer and wine and champagne flow. Hugh and I cut a cake with two little angels on top that represent us as bride and groom; those angels are placed on the top of our family Christmas tree each year thereafter. Everyone is so happy for us and enjoying each other so much that we are all surprised when midnight comes. It is time for Hugh and me to begin our married life, a life committed to giving all the love we have to each other and to sharing our love with God's people.

Outside the snow is falling.

1970-2014

THE FIFTH SEASON

Epilogue

Chapter 30

EPILOGUE

When we deepen our presence to each other, we participate...in the
transformative power of love.
—Hugh F. Brady, D. Min.
A Spirituality of Being Human

A strong July sun breaking
through the jeweled stained-glass windows
fell like colored snowflakes
on the white robes of the many priests
celebrating the life of their brother Hugh,
ordained a priest like them,
but who chose to live priesthood in another way.
As I watched the funeral concelebrants,
my life passed before me, as if I were drowning,
and I remembered how seasons
of marriage taught me
Love is presence.

In the first three years three babies,
Eric Hugh, Matthew McLean, Marnie Faith,
baptized us in wonder and thanksgiving.
Family became sacrament,
the ground where we would learn
 Love is presence.

From Hugh's former parishioner,
an unexpected inheritance,
 a down payment on a house.
Our home: a gift of priesthood,
where doors opened for children
to let the world in,
for groups to gather,
for friends and family to celebrate
or hold each other in sorrow.
A respite for refugees awaiting entry to Canada,
a kitchen to make soup and share bread,
rugs that rolled themselves up for dancing,
a garden with so many colors
it looked like a constant party,
and a sandbox to dig all the way to China.
A home to discover
Love is presence.

And a second home:
The Buffalo State Newman Center
where Jesus' words of justice exploded,

where Eucharist was offered
in a hundred different ways.
Where coffee hours and parties,
discussion groups and workshops
created a community of belonging.
And Hugh's leadership alive
through retreats and prayer groups,
social justice and spiritual life meetings.
He ministered to every person he met
for he did not know how not to.
And I participated in it all
with our children, growing in
Love's presence.

I flowed between family life and ministry,
loving children at home and adolescents in urban schools,
attending soccer games and meetings for justice,
birthday parties and protests.
And an unexpected journey,
Mother's move from Hornell to Anderson Place.
Finally, without responsibility or worries
at 78 years, Mother blossomed into herself,
savored the last and happiest 12 years of her life,
cherished by her children and grandchildren.
The Paschal Mystery of my family, a reminder
Love is presence.

Through it all, Hugh placed me like the sun
in the middle of our universe,

brought me flowers every week for 43 years,
absorbed my body, revered my spirit,
sealed his heart to mine,
listened to me the way you know
Love is presence.

Still our love had arid seasons:
Words and feelings could turn dry and parched.
He could be stubborn; I could be unreasonable.
We'd eventually nudge each other,
unfold our maps to find our way.
Still, even with our mistakes
neither ever criticized the other.
We accepted the poverty of ourselves,
found the beauty of our fragility where
Love is presence.

We grew in new understandings of Church.
Yet today, as I sit in the pews of my youth,
I hold the Jesus who weeps
over the Church's grave sins,
its horrific crime of
protecting its image rather than
its own vulnerable and innocent people.
I struggle with what faith means to me,
wonder where it leads me.
I am only sure of one thing:
Love is Presence.

At our Fortieth Anniversary, I wrote Hugh a poem, a poem which ends my story, a poem that celebrates the mystery of human love, human love that cannot be separated from God's love.

Forty Years of Loving

We found love in winter
a thousand layers of snow and ice
melted into springs of new beginnings.
Summers of children
and each other blossomed
before autumn brought a new kind of loving.

For forty years we shared the softness of the first snowfall,
the startled shock of cold on skin,
traces of breath on the glass pane,
the first scent of cut pine
and the sound of ice cracking.

Each new winter froze us into
who we thought we were
until the melting and new seasons
taught us to turn with the sun,
be who we are in each moment,
know we're ever the same and ever changed
by each other
and the way snow falls.

(December -2010)

Hugh Francis Brady   Evelyn Faith McLean

Living it up the night before the convent.

Entrance Day on steps of Motherhouse

Father Brady & Sister Mary Emily at
reception after
receiving the veil as Canonical Novice

Mother and third year novice.

Mother Bride Claire, RSM

Fr. Brady at party to
welcome Lillis home

Hugh at our first Christmas together

Dorm director at Buffalo State College

Hugh and I at General Motors Christmas Party

Dancing to "I remember you, you're the one who made my dreams come true."

Singing at our wedding at the Newman Center

Our home, a gift of priesthood

Matthew, Marnie and Eric on
Matthew's rocking horse

Thirty-fifth anniversary.
Wearing anniversary pearls.

Summer 2006: Eric, Jackie, Matthew's wife, Jenn, Eric's wife holding son Greyson, Benjamin, Hugh, Evelyn, Madeline, Carlos, Marnie's husband holding son Ramon & Marnie
Front: Matthew

Summer 2013: Back row: Carlos, Jenn, Eric, Evelyn, Madeline, Benjamin, Jackie, Matthew
Front row: Greyson, Marnie holding Maeve, Ramon, Hugh

Acknowledgments

As I was writing this memoir, many people carried lamps to illuminate my path. Keith Elkins and Patricia Wille accompanied me from the very beginning. They held their the lights high and for long periods. Pat Wille, friend and technical editor, kept the material organized with her magical technology skills. But equally important to me was how approachable Pat was, how endlessly kind and professional. Not once did she let go of my hand.

Editor and friend, Keith Elkins, held my other hand. Each time I thought the book was finished but then started again, Keith re-read and re-edited every word. He always made me feel I was doing just the right thing. His heart is a gold mine; his eye is a laser. If you meet either of these people, you will notice their wings, or perhaps halos.

As in anything I undertake, it is the support and love of my beautiful children, Eric Hugh, Matthew McLean and Marnie Faith that sustains and encourages me. They always point me to the brightest paths and accompany me on my journeys. Benjamin Matthew, Madeline Frances, Ramon Hugh Brady, Greyson Eric and Maeve Lillis, my grandchildren, are simply a constant source of light wherever I am.

Throughout the writing, I asked friends and family if they would give me feedback on the manuscript. A sincere thank you to Fr. Fred Leising and Denis Woods and Eileen Dooley for steering me through the channels of church and clergy information. My friends Pat Nightengale, Kathy Shoemaker, Linda Drajem, Dianne Riordan, Sara Reis, Mary O'Herron, Mary Herbst, Patricia McClain and Rev. Patricia Gulino, and most especially Julie Ricci offered insights and helpful feedback on the first draft, as did my sister Marnie's daughter, Mary Hope Benedict. Their input became invaluable to subsequent drafts and their friendship always goes beyond what anyone could ever expect.

Karen Brady Borland was the first person to encourage me to publish. I am deeply grateful for her professional suggestions and never-ending kindnesses. I thank Paula Voell for her very helpful feedback and interest. Em, Elaine Martynkiewicz, friend and artist, always leads me to deeper meaning, as she did designing the cover of this book

The Sisters of Social Service: Sisters Anne, Angela, Maria, and Teresina, my informal but true spiritual directors, continually encouraged me during this project. I am simply thankful for their lives.

I hold special gratitude for those involved with the review and editing of the final manuscript: Audrey Mang, Mary Dee Martoche, Esq., and Lisa Murray Roselli. Each of these women generously gave time and very careful attention to the details of the writing, as if it were their own.

A sincere thanks to other members of my poetry groups: Barb Faust, Esther Roblins, Kath Betsko, Sally Johnson, Margaret Cusack, Carol Pasiecznik, Ginger Cunningham, Marj Norris, and Linda Murphy, who support me as a writer and graciously understood when I needed a "time out" from our group to follow this new, unexpected journey.

I save my most heartfelt thank you for my surviving siblings: Blanche Mary Buono, Lillis Catherine McLean and Janice Frances Hinson. For the past seven decades at unexpected turns and through foggy byways, they have held and relit many lanterns for me. When I asked if they wanted me to remove any information from this memoir, they responded: "Don't change a thing. This is your story," a story they are so much a part of.

For anyone I have failed to mention, my apologies and sincerest thanks for supporting this work. I publicly announce loudly my love and appreciation for each and all of you whose bright lanterns helped me share a story of how human love triumphed and grew even with the Church's law on celibacy.

Addendum

Addendum #1

A PRAYER ON THE WEDDING DAY OF
EVELYN AND HUGH BRADY

As our attention turns on this joyous and Holy season to the birth of
Christ and the Holy family we are here to celebrate the creation, the birth,
of another family; the family of Evelyn and Hugh Brady.

For this new family, we pray tonight.

We pray that . . . Evelyn and Hugh never forget the joy and love they
enjoy tonight, and that love means putting your trust in someone and in
doing so you surrender a part of yourself forever.

We pray that . . . Evelyn and Hugh accept fully that when two people
really love each other, they help each other to stay alive and to grow. They
come to know each other as no one has ever known them before. Love is
not a blindfold, it is an eyeopener. You begin to love each other when you
begin to make something of each other.

We pray that . . . Evelyn and Hugh accept their marriage as a history to be written by the two of them. Marriage is a web of memories, of
hopes, of anxieties and of sufferings that are shared jointly. It is a bond
between two people, it is a happy, joyous, glorious thing and it is also
a source of suffering. Nothing ties two people together so much as the
things they have known and suffered together.

We pray that . . . Evelyn and Hugh recognize that marriage is a tight
rope between two cliffs: unreasonable demands and total resignation.
And with this thought in mind we recall that Dag Hammarskjold wrote in
1952 – "Never for the sake of peace and quiet deny your own experience

or convictions."

We pray that . . . Evelyn and Hugh recognize that the worst sin of all is the sin of omission and neglect. A marriage is not destroyed by quarrels, by unforeseen difficulties, by financial difficulties, or even by infidelity. What destroys a marriage is the rut of a routine, when, without realizing it, you stop looking at each other, or, stop wanting each other. Then, the marriage is in danger.

Marriage, like faith, puts us in a living relationship with one another, it keeps our gaze fixed to that other person. Marriage, like faith, is attacked by the same enemy: routine. Marriage, like faith, is nourished and kept alive by attention and hopeful expectation.

And Finally,

We pray that . . . Evelyn and Hugh grow in the knowledge that the prime purpose of marriage is to enable you to live all the love of which you are capable – a love which is so vast, so creative, so full of wonder and joy that it may take you a whole lifetime to understand it.

And, in this knowledge, to quote again from Dag Hammarskjold,

"You dare your YES – and experience a meaning

You repeat your Yes – and all things acquire a meaning,

When everything has a meaning – how can you live anything but YES?"

December 26, 1970

Addendum # 2

To purchase **A *Spirituality of Being* Human** by Hugh F. Brady, D. Min.
please visit Amazon.com
For more information please visit evelynmcleanbrady.com.

Author, editor, and poet, Evelyn Faith McLean Brady taught high school English in the Buffalo Public School System and retired as the co-director of the Buffalo Teacher Center. Evelyn lives in Buffalo, New York, where she has been a life-long participant in peace and justice movements. She is the mother of two sons and a daughter and is the grandmother of five.

Evelyn served as editor for *A Journey of Light in the Darkness* by Sister Judith Fenyvesi, *PEACEPRINTS: Sister Karen's Paths to Nonviolence*, *The Lost Son* by Peter McNeela, M.D. and *A Spirituality of Being Human* by Hugh F. Brady, D. Min.

Made in the USA
Middletown, DE
25 August 2019